Stephen King
The Second Decade,
Danse Macabre to *The Dark Half*

Twayne's United States Authors Series

Warren French, Editor
University College of Swansea, Wales

TUSAS 599

Photo © Tabitha King

Stephen King
The Second Decade,
Danse Macabre to
The Dark Half

By Tony Magistrale

University of Vermont

Twayne Publishers • New York
Maxwell Macmillan Canada • Toronto
Maxwell Macmillan International • New York Oxford Singapore Sydney

Stephen King: The Second Decade, Danse Macabre to The Dark Half
Tony Magistrale

Twayne Publishers   Maxwell Macmillan Canada, Inc.
Macmillan Publishing Company   1200 Eglinton Avenue East
866 Third Avenue   Suite 200
New York, New York 10022   Don Mills, Ontario M3C 3N1

Macmillan Publishing Company is part of the Maxwell Communications Group of
Companies.

10 9 8 7 6 5 4 3 2 1

The paper used in this publication meets the minimum requirements of American
National Standard for Information Sciences—Permanence of Paper for Printed
Library Materials, ANSI Z39.48-1984. ∞™

Printed and bound in the United States of America.

Library of Congress Cataloging-in-Publication Data

Magistrale, Tony.
    Stephen King : the second decade, Danse macabre to The dark half /
by Tony Magistrale.
        p.   cm. — (Twayne's United States author's series ; TWAS 599)
    Includes bibliographical references (p.   ) and index.
    ISBN 0-8057-3957-2
    1. King, Stephen, 1947-   —Criticism and interpretation.
    2. Horror tales, American—History and criticism.   I. Title.
    II. Series.
    PS3561.I483Z78   1992
    813'54—dc20   91-44424
                                                            CIP

For the Boys in Buffalo:

Daniel
Christopher
Sam
Norman
Mauri
John
Mort
& Ken

Contents

Preface

In 1988 Joseph Reino published *Stephen King: The First Decade, Carrie to Pet Sematary*, a book that restricted its critical focus to studying Stephen King's fiction published between 1974 and 1983. If King were a less prolific writer, another Twayne volume considering work outside of Reino's purview might not be necessary for a couple more years, if at all. But Stephen King's canon continues to grow at a truly remarkable rate of speed. The chronology that follows this preface attests to King's staggering output; on average, he has published better than a book a year for the last decade and a half. While the fan in me is delighted with such frequent opportunities to read original fiction written by the master of the macabre, the scholar in me wishes that King would be less prolific and more focused in his efforts. As I will discuss at greater length elsewhere in this volume, Stephen King's literary talents have made him not only one of the most popular writers in America today but also one of the best. It is time that his formidable abilities were recognized. On the other hand, even his most impressive efforts are sometimes severely hampered by his tendency to overwrite or, worse, to push the reader's willing suspension of disbelief beyond the realm of acceptability (as in *The Dark Half*).

What is perhaps more impressive than the number of book titles King has published in a little over two decades of writing (or even the volume of dollars he has generated in paperback and hardcover sales) is the range of literary genres and traditions he has incorporated into his inimitable art. His canon belies the easy reductive characteristics condescending academics often ascribe to horror and popular fiction. King invokes classical tragic patterns in *The Shining* and *Pet Sematary*; science fiction themes and hardware in *The Tommyknockers*; epic and mythic paradigms in *The Stand, It,* and *The Talisman*; vampire legend and folklore in *'Salem's Lot*; the genres of the fairy tale and the American western in *Eyes of the Dragon* and *The Dark Tower,* respectively; the tradition of nineteenth-century naturalism in the Bachman books and *Cujo;* the political-historical novel in *The Dead Zone* and *Apt Pupil;* and an innovative variation on the romance genre in *Misery.* King's work has been shaped by low and high culture alike, as well as by his astute awareness

of fundamental American myths and archetypes. His art is the very embodiment of a postmodernist aesthetic.

   This book was conceived in light of Joseph Reino's first Twayne volume
on King. Its scope includes both the literature published after *Pet Sematary,*
constituting King's "second decade," and salient texts excluded from
Reino's study (e.g., the Bachman novels and *Danse Macabre*). To avoid du-
plication of much of the biographical information supplied in *Stephen King:
The First Decade,* this volume does not include the standard biographical
first chapter; readers are encouraged to refer to that in Reino's volume. The
first chapter of this book consists of an interview I conducted with Stephen
King exclusively for publication here. Subsequent chapters were strongly influenced by information gleaned from this interview. King has seldom been
more lucid or effusive about his own work, and I am grateful to him for his
candor and generosity.

   I am also indebted to many other people and institutions who helped to
make *Stephen King: The Second Decade* a reality. The University of Vermont provided me with a sabbatical leave in 1990, thus permitting me to
compose a large portion of this book. Norman and Katherine Tederous,
Michael Stanton, Arthur Biddle, Mary Jane Dickerson, Laurie Berken-
kamp, Greg Weller, Mary Pharr, Len Mustazza, Michael Morrison,
Elizabeth Paley, and especially Samuel Magistrale were instrumental in
helping me to shape and rewrite chapters. Without their guidance, en-
couragement, and critical expertise, this volume would have fewer virtues
and greater flaws. Students at the University of Vermont also provided me
with a critical forum—in English courses analyzing King's fiction, as well
as in several public on-campus lectures—for presenting many of the ideas
found in this book. One of the best and brightest of these undergraduates,
Elizabeth Clark, prepared the map of Derry presented in chapter 6. I am
grateful also to Carl B. Yoke and the *Journal of the Fantastic in the Arts,*
which he edits, for first publishing a version of the last half of chapter 2.[1] I
wish likewise to thank my editors at Twayne, Liz Traynor Fowler, Warren
French, Carol Leach, and Jacob Conrad, for markedly influencing the
contents of this book—from its fundamental concepts and design to the
specific language employed. Last, but always most important, my wife,
Jennifer, remains my most ardent supporter and source of inspiration; in
this particular case she also provided sufficient childcare for me to complete this project and still maintain my sanity.

Chronology

1947   Stephen Edwin King born 21 September in Portland, Maine, second son to Donald and Nellie Ruth Pillsbury King.

1949   Donald King, Stephen's father, leaves house on trip to store and never returns.

1954   Begins writing short fiction modeled after science-fiction and adventure stories and movies.

1962–1966   Attends high school in Lisbon Falls, Maine. Plays tight end on varsity football team. Begins writing *Getting It On* (*Rage*).

1966–1970   Undergraduate years as English major at University of Maine, Orono (UMO). Writes column "King's Garbage Truck" for weekly school newspaper; reflects his changing political identity (from Nixon apologist in 1968 to political activist calling for student strike in 1969). As a sophomore, enrolls in Burton Hatlen's course in modern American literature; introduced to naturalists Steinbeck, Hemingway, Faulkner. Completes first novel, *The Long Walk,* in 1967. Meets Tabitha Spruce, also a UMO undergraduate. Works as laborer in industrial laundry.

1971–1973   Marries Tabitha. Begins teaching English at Hampden Academy, Hampden, Maine; lives in mobile home. Publishes several short stories; sells *Carrie* to Doubleday. Begins writing *Second Coming* (*'Salem's Lot*). Completes *The Running Man* (rejected by Doubleday). Mother dies of cancer.

1974   *Carrie.* Writes first draft of *The Shining;* begins work on *The House on Value Street* (*The Stand*). Moves with wife and daughter to Boulder, Colorado.

1975   *'Salem's Lot.* Completes first draft of *The Stand.* Returns to Maine and purchases home in Bridgton. University of Maine, Orono, establishes special depository for Stephen King collection, which has since expanded to include bulk of his manuscripts, galleys, and working drafts.

1976 Film version of *Carrie,* directed by Brian De Palma.

1977 *The Shining* and *Rage* (first novel to appear under Bachman pseudonym). Completes first drafts of *The Dead Zone* and *Firestarter.* Introduced to Peter Straub during three-month trip to England.

1978 *The Stand* and *Night Shift.* Writer in residence, University of Maine, Orono. Teaches classes in creative writing and Gothic fiction. Uses latter course to launch theories on Gothic genre that inform his study *Danse Macabre* and several nonfiction essays (e.g., introductions to *Night Shift* and to recent editions of Shelley's *Frankenstein* and Stevenson's *Doctor Jekyll and Mr. Hyde*).

1979 *The Dead Zone* and Bachman's *The Long Walk.* Completes first drafts of *Christine, Pet Sematary,* and *Danse Macabre.* Concludes teaching duties at UMO.

1980 *Firestarter,* "The Mist," and "The Monkey." Completes first draft of *It.* Buys current residence, Victorian mansion on West Broadway in Bangor, Maine. Release of Stanley Kubrick's film adaptation of *The Shining.*

1981 *Cujo, Danse Macabre,* and third Bachman title, *Roadwork.* Receives Career Alumni Award from University of Maine.

1982 *Different Seasons,* "The Raft," and fourth Bachman book, *The Running Man.* Begins writing *The Talisman* with Peter Straub. Wins World Fantasy Award for "Do the Dead Sing?" ("The Reach") and Hugo Award for *Danse Macabre.* Active role as both script writer and actor in film *Creepshow,* directed by George Romero.

1983 *Christine* and *Pet Sematary.* Completes first drafts of *The Talisman, The Tommyknockers,* and *Eyes of the Dragon.* Film versions of *Cujo,* directed by Lewis Teague, *The Dead Zone,* directed by David Cronenberg, and *Christine,* directed by John Carpenter.

1984 *The Talisman* and fifth Bachman novel, *Thinner. Eyes of the Dragon* and *The Dark Tower: The Gunslinger* released in limited editions. Film adaptations of *Firestarter,* directed by Mark Lester, and *Children of the Corn,* directed by Fritz Kiersch. Guest of honor at International Conference for the Fantastic in the Arts, Boca Raton, Florida.

1985   *Skeleton Crew.* Reveals "Richard Bachman" pseudonym. New American Library assembles collection of four Bachman novels, *The Bachman Books.* Film version of *Silver Bullet,* directed by Daniel Attias.

1986   *It.* Underwood and Miller release single-volume collection of King interviews, *Bare Bones: Conversations on Terror.* King's directorial debut in *Maximum Overdrive,* (adaptation of short story "Trucks"). Lloyd H. Elliott Lecturer, University of Maine.

1987   *Misery* (originally intended as a Bachman book), *Eyes of the Dragon, Silver Bullet, The Tommyknockers,* and *The Dark Tower: The Drawing of the Three.* Release of films *Stand By Me,* Rob Reiner's adaptation of *The Body,* and *The Running Man,* directed by George Pan Cosmatos. Delivers commencement address, University of Maine, Orono.

1989   *The Dark Half* (1.5 million copies in hardcover—largest first-edition printing in publishing history) and *The Dark Tower: The Drawing of the Three.* Film release of *Pet Sematary,* directed by Mary Lambert.

1990   Revised and unexpurgated edition of *The Stand;* four novellas under title *Four Past Midnight.* Film releases of "The Cat From Hell," King's contribution to *Tales from the Dark Side,* and "Graveyard Shift." Film adaptation of *Misery,* directed by Rob Reiner. *It* televised in two-part, six-hour miniseries on ABC.

1991–1992   Scheduled release of *Dolores Claiborne, Needful Things,* and third volume of *The Dark Tower: The Waste Lands.*

Chapter One
The Writer Defines Himself: An Interview with Stephen King

4:10 P.M. 2 November 1989. We have been traveling due east on U.S. Route 2 for the past six hours. The sun has already begun its descent in my rearview mirror. Huddled in the seat next to me, my wife finds no inspiration to remove her black leather gloves; the temperature has struggled to remain above 30 degrees. We are 45 miles from Bangor, Maine, and the wind has begun to howl.

We pass a landscape of white churches, dilapidated houses and trailers, porches and front lawns strewn haphazardly with the internal organs of various machines. The scene recalls Faulkner's South more than upscale New England. But what ends up distinguishing this corner of Maine from Mississippi backwaters is winter's certainty, the awareness that in this country the season arrives early and lingers late.

There is another difference. This terrain is sparse, arid, sexless. The Southern mind, accustomed to fecund smells, sounds, and colors, would feel totally out of place here. I am reminded of how few of Stephen King's characters qualify as truly sensual, much less sexual, beings; there are no Blanche Duboises in his canon. Indeed, the interrelationship between the physical textures of northern New England and a Puritan consciousness is almost palpable—and this union is as much a presence in King's fiction as it was in Hawthorne's a century ago. Although there are no mountains on the horizon, my wife reminds me of Wendy Torrance's sobering observation, uttered high in the Rockies early in *The Shining:* this is a place that would not forgive many mistakes. Twenty miles from Bangor, Maine, this is Stephen King country, and I am on vampire watch.

Midway down Florida Avenue, one of the most industrial-looking streets in Bangor, between a sky-blue General Electric plant and an airline-food preparation company, is the office of a writer who made $22 million last year. It is not what one might expect. The outside, painted a dull green, resembles a small, one-floor Army barracks. The inside is neither large nor furnished extravagantly. The largest office in the five-room building in which Stephen King and his secretary, Shirley Sonderegger, conduct the business of America's most popular storyteller is as unpretentious as the writer himself. King feels most comfortable dressed in old jeans and purple high-top sneakers, and his office space has a similarly relaxed ambiance: a yellow plaid couch, a desk with a computer terminal, several tables piled high with hardcover Stephen King titles sent from all over the world to be autographed by the author, bare walls punctuated only by several framed posters advertising films that have been adapted from his fiction. Within this anything-but-macabre setting I conducted the following two-hour interview with Stephen King, beginning with an appropriate seasonal reference.

Magistrale: Halloween was less than a week ago. Does the day hold special significance for you, and how did you end up spending it?

King: Yeah, it means get out of town. I've become the Great Pumpkin as the years have gone by. And I'm very tired of it. I hate it. If we're home—if we have the house open to trick-or-treaters—hundreds, sometimes thousands of people show up. It is ridiculous, and the streets get clogged. I owed Viking one piece of publicity on one of the morning shows for my new book, *The Dark Half,* and I told them, "I will do it, but I won't do it on Halloween." You know, that's when they wanted me. If they can't have Freddy Krueger, they want Stephen King. But I refused to do it on Halloween, so they nailed me for November first. Now, guess who they had on Halloween? Of course: Freddy Krueger, nails and all. Robert Englund was in town performing double duty this year as Freddy and the Phantom of the Opera.

Basically, Halloween means get out of town. This year Tabby[1] and the kids stayed, but the house was closed down. It's to the point where you have to put somebody in front of the house on that one particular night because people come from all over.

TM: How much of your own experience tends to find its way into your fiction?

SK: Well, probably all the significant experience shows up in the fiction. What I mean is, I'm like anybody else: 99 percent of what I do on any given day would not qualify for a novel. But sometimes the backgrounds of the novels lend themselves to my daily field of reference, and I draw on that stuff. A lot of people have said I'm the guru of the ordinary, and I am, in the sense that someone like Charles Beaumont was.[2] I think that figures in a landscape show up brighter if the landscape is drab.

I gave someone an interview a while ago, and I mentioned something about a trip I took to a shopping mall. I watched one of those machines that you plug a quarter into and this thing goes around and around. It's a flying-saucer ride made for kids. And I thought, Suppose the kid disappeared. Just disappeared in front of his mother and the people walking around. What would that be like? Now, that interested me very much. That's the sort of fiction that I make. But on the other hand, if you take a situation from John Updike or Saul Bellow, things would be different. You would begin by casting a character as a teacher at a university. This professor would come home early one afternoon to find his wife having it off with the gas man. How would that make this character feel? To tell you the truth, I couldn't give a shit. This kind of situation doesn't interest me at all. So, what I see and what I experience in everyday life become a kind of background . . . to the occasional rare incident.

TM: Do your character names have much significance? I am impressed by the chutzpah you showed in naming the protagonist of *The Dead Zone* John Smith. Are other names in your fiction meaningful?

SK: Sure. Here and there they appear like jokes. The kid in *Apt Pupil,* his name is Tod, which is German for *death.* It seems appropriate, given that he falls in with this Nazi. The guy in *The Drawing of the Three* who likes to push things on the heads of people is named Jack Mort. They are little dark jokes. A forthcoming novel [of mine is titled] *Dolores Claiborne,* and Dolores means *sadness* or *sorrow,* and that's appropriate to the kind of life that she's led. I've used names as a tag since I was a writer in college. I don't always do it, but John Smith was certainly the most obvious case, and I chose [that name] for a purpose.

TM: Has your work been influenced to any extent by mythic theories—for instance, those of Frazer, Campbell, Freud, Jung?

SK: Campbell. I was introduced to Joseph Campbell by Peter Straub several years ago, and I was particularly taken by the book *Hero with a Thousand Faces.* It is a wonderful book, and it definitely had some effect on me. But I suppose I've been most influenced, as a writer, by the Bible and *King Arthur's Tales*—things I read during my formative years.

TM: Perhaps the other theorists—Frazer, Jung, Freud—have found their way into your fictional lexicon through other sources.

SK: Right. The trickle-down effect is absolutely there. A writer would have to come in very late on the movie of the twentieth century and not have his work influenced in some way by Freud. And for a guy who does what I do for a living, that's very rich territory to mine. If I had to come down on one side or the other, I'd definitely be a Jungian rather than a Freudian. Jung's sense of myth and symbol is very provocative, very rich. But Freud's world is so accessible for a writer, and it's so malleable to what a writer does. You can use his theories to advance the importance of dreams. You can use them to advance the plot. As a Freudian, I'm a real opportunist. I'm more apt to use the theories to advance my ideas rather than to use my ideas to explore further the theories.

TM: Fairy-tale references appear throughout your canon. Why are you so fond of fairy tales, and how do they function in the context of your art?

SK: They are the scariest stories that we have. I think that the stories for children form a kind of conduit leading to what adults call horror stories. To my mind, the stories that I write are nothing more than fairy tales for grown ups. And one way to get a grown up is to open up that conduit to the child he was. The stories themselves are not just scary in and of themselves; they provide access to a whole time in our lives when we were scared of a lot more things, when we were more vulnerable than we are now as adults.

A hypnotist is capable of rehypnotizing a subject with just a couple of passes or by using a special word, and I think many fairy stories perform a similar feat; they have a way of regressing us instantaneously to childhood. In the writing I am working on right now, I've been able to play off two— "Little Red Riding Hood" and "Goldilocks and the Three Bears"—in my mind, two of the scariest fairy tales ever written.

TM: Where does your great love for, and understanding of, children come from? Does the fact that there are no children in the Bachman books say something about the general darkness of those novels?

SK: Well, Bachman killed his children before they were out of infancy. I've noticed that in the work I am doing now, if there are any children, they tend to be older, with a couple of exceptions. The exceptions are in a book entitled *Needful Things,* which is the third book of a trilogy that includes *The Dark Half* and a short novel called *The Sun Dog.* There are some kids in that last book who play a pivotal role in the action, but otherwise the kids in my fiction have gotten older, and all these things seem to be keeping sort of a rough progress with my own life.

I have always been fascinated with my own childhood. I was fascinated as an adult with the period when my own children were growing up. And I'm interested in the mythic power that childhood holds over our imagination and, in particular, the point at which the adult is able to link up with his or her own childhood past and the powers therein.

TM: This fascination is everywhere in your work, especially in *It.*

SK: *It* was like a final exam covering this subject. It was a very difficult imaginative feat: not thinking up monsters, because they are easy enough to produce, but . . . reenter[ing] the world of childhood. It had to be a very gradual process to open the time and mindset of my own childhood. The more I worked at it, the more this frame of reference became accessible.

TM: In an interview with *Playboy* you acknowledged a certain dissatisfaction with the women characters in your work and with Mother Abagail and Hallorann as representative blacks. Why are you dissatisfied with these characters? And do you feel that anything you have written since that interview has changed or modified your own self-criticism?

SK: It has changed a little bit in the sense that I've written a novel called *Dolores Claiborne* that I think is a good, strong piece of work . . . not only is the protagonist a woman, she's also an older woman who is *the* major character. There are other characters in the story, but they are always in her shadow; she dominates this particular landscape. And I feel that I did a good job with her and that readers are going to be pleased with the woman they find there.

A lot of my efforts in writing about women were made because I wanted to understand women and try to escape the stereotyping that goes on in so much male fiction. I read Leslie Fiedler's book *Love and Death in the American Novel.* He's great at making outrageous overstatements in order to force the reader to cope with them. His goal is to elicit a response, and before people—writers and students alike—can [respond,] they must first think and look carefully at what they have been reading and writing. Fiedler argues that in American fiction all women are either bitches or zeroes. And I decided I want to do better than that. This was a motivating force behind the writing of *Carrie.*

TM: But it is not only women that Fiedler examines. For example, in *Freaks* and *The Stranger in Shakespeare* he's interested in analyzing those social forces that create outsiders in any given culture. For Shakespeare, it was the Jew in *The Merchant of Venice,* the New-World savage in *The Tempest,* and the Black in *Othello.* These figures are all foreign to the respective communities in which Shakespeare placed them, and they are never able to overcome their status as outsiders. How about the outsiders in your own fiction, especially blacks? What can we learn from them?

SK: My black characters are okay. But there is this unfortunate tendency I have to replicate in Mother Abagail another face of Butterfly McQueen in *Gone with the Wind.* She is the comforting presence that says, "Everythang goin' to be awright, chile." And Halloran is the same way. He's a male face of Butterfly. I look back on those characters and I say, Well, you tried to escape the stereotype, and in some ways you did. But on the other hand, all you did was take the stereotype and give it more delicate shadings and tones and make it seem even more real. In a way, this is an even greater sin than creating a caricature; I've created a stereotype that will make people say Yeah, that's just the way that it is. But all you can do is read what you wrote and make up your mind to recognize where you made mistakes and try again. And so you try again.

TM: Speaking of female characters in your fiction, Beverly Marsh is really the only female protagonist in *It.* How did you envision her role in the novel—and is it significant that she and It are essentially the only females in the book?

SK: They represent good and evil. One of the passages I like the most in that book is where Richie Tozier is thinking about how Beverly is just one of the guys, except he doesn't wonder what color underpants the guys are wearing. Beverly becomes the symbolic conduit between adulthood and childhood for the boys in the Losers' Club. It is a role that women have played again and again in the lives of boys: the symbolic advent of manhood through the act of sex.

TM: This was my next question: How do you envision her as exemplifying that symbolic conduit?

SK: The job of an earth mother is to bring forth adults. Wordsworth reminds us again and again in so many of his poems that "the child is father to the man." The job of the earth mother is twofold: not just to bear children and be a partner in the sex act, but also to raise the children that she has borne into decent human adults—and that means adults who have not lost touch with the essential qualities of childhood.

TM: In many of your nonfictional writings you argue that there is a symbolic subtext at work in horror fiction that speaks to certain social and political anxieties relevant to the time. How conscious are you of this subtext when framing your own fiction?

SK: Not at all. Let me qualify that by saying the reason a second draft is so crucial is that a lot of times a writer is unaware of what he's really writing until after he is done. It's like drawing pictures in a dark room, and then a sudden illumination shows you what you've been drawing. This seems to me to be a very Jungian concept. It is saying, Never mind making theme. Let's not make theme. Let's let theme make its own story. And when a writer is finally done, sometimes it is possible to look at a story and say, What I really wanted to talk about here, what I was really afraid of, only shows up in the second half of this book; the first half is all story that skirts around the edge of the real meaning. I sometimes think that with a really good tale or novel, the theme is there before you recognize it, before you create it. Before you write it down, the story exists, but it takes the actual writing to recognize it. That's a Jungian idea, too.

It's like digging something out of the ground. You dig it up, and maybe you knock some of the dirt off of it, and you look it over and say, This is what it is. But look, this is broken over here. We can put something new on it to make it work again. Because it is mine; I was the one who dug it up and dusted the idea off. It might look to me as if I dug a steam engine up out of the earth, but to someone else that steam engine could look like a car. They might put rubber wheels on theirs, while I might put grooved wheels on mine. It is a question of what does it look like to you. So if part A doesn't necessarily fit into part B, that's okay because this is the way it came out after I wrote it.

If I write a book like *Christine* and decide after it is done that what I am really writing about is the link between cars and girls, and that there is a symbolic representation of masculinity and power going on, especially in the second half of the text, then maybe I will go back and rewrite some of the first part so that these concerns will also be reflected there as well. The point is, I am never certain exactly what it is I am really trying to say in a novel until I actually sit down and write it out. Only afterwards will I begin to understand it, . . . be in a position to reshape it.

TM: In terms of what you just said about sexuality, masculinity, and automobiles in *Christine:* There is a scene early in the novel in which the car won't start, and Arnie must push it. You make a clear allusion to sexual arousal and even sexual orgasm as Arnie pushes Christine steadily—his pulse rises, he begins to sweat, etc.

SK: Right. . . . In the first draft [of *Christine*] he tries to get it to run, and when it won't he calls the car a bitch. In the second draft, after I'd seen the connection the novel made between Christine and Arnie's identity—particularly his sexual identity—I thought, That's right, *bitch* is the right word. You can say that now. It has gained in meaning.

TM: In *Danse Macabre* you note, I think correctly, that the horror genre is obsessed not only with images of death and dying but with transcendence as well. What kind of specific transcendence do you have in mind, and do the transcendent elements found in horror differ from those in other types of literature?

SK: I don't think so. Transcendence is the same, no matter where or how it occurs. It is always accompanied by a real sense of ecstasy, a widening of vision.

TM: So it is something more than mere survival, something greater?

SK: Yes, I think so. And it creates physical behavior that we associate with joy even when it's commingled with terror. You may even laugh. There's this scene in *Creepshow* where the professor starts to laugh at this crate underneath the stairs.[3] He can't control himself anymore. To me this is a moment of transcendence—he's made up his mind to push his wife under the stairs so that the thing can eat her up. All of *Creepshow* is a good-natured takeoff on *Tales of the Crypt* comics, nothing more than that—until this point. At the moment I've mentioned, the tale transcends its genre because he actually begins to laugh. He thinks this act of murder is actually funny. He even asks the viewer to laugh along with him.

TM: But I was thinking in terms of the kind of transcendence that occurs in characters who have managed to endure a great suffering, to rise above supernatural obstacles, to pass through experiences in which they have lost children or parents.

SK: Louis Creed, at the end of *Pet Sematary,* is in such a state of transcendence. He takes his wife—her weight doesn't matter—up to the Micmac burial grounds. He is happy for the first time in over a hundred pages. He thinks, Everything's okay, this time it is going to work. He's beyond such mundane things as sanity at that point. He's in a space that many of us will never attain, and a lot of us would not want to attain. Whether it's heaven or hell, Louis occupies a state of expanded consciousness.

TM: So does this version of transcendence often require a break from what most of us call sanity?

SK: It may. In most horror fiction it often does. Transcendence is a quality that frequently shines through the work of horror. It is a feeling that manages to communicate itself to the reader, and it is not necessarily apparent to the characters in the fiction. I think this is one of the major reasons that we continue to read those stories by Nathaniel Hawthorne, and that they have as much potency as they still do. "The Minister's Black Veil" is still capable of working its magic today. The story's premise has remained viable. That is, there is something beneath that veil that would cause this act of transcendence to take place. That's what the veil is about.

TM: Yes, and so many of Hawthorne's characters take journeys into themselves and end up discovering things—often, things that are not pleasing or self-encouraging—about society, history, themselves. Look at Goodman Brown, Robin in "My Kinsman, Major Molineux," Ethan Brand. But it's interesting that you should mention Hawthorne, not only because he is a writer who works frequently with issues of transcendence but also because I think his work shares a number of other similarities with your fiction.

SK: I am aware of that. You did a piece on Hawthorne and me that I remember reading a couple of years ago.[4] I'm going to send you a Ph.D. dissertation this scholar from Harvard wrote recently about my work and the importance of place in it. I did an interview with her about these very issues, and I can't hope to replicate it here. She's got pictures of the real places—Lisbon Falls, Albion, and other landmarks—faced off against descriptions I use in the books. She talks a lot about the transition from Maine's original rural status to an urban and suburban environment, and the breakdown in communication and community that is a consequence of this change. It is pretty good work; she did well by it.

For me, it has always been a case of being here, living in Maine all my life. The settings are here. . . . Sometimes I'll deliberately move out, but if I do decide . . . that I don't want to be in Maine for a story, my mind always seems to take me back here. If I am in Iowa or Nebraska, it is a place that is flat and empty. A place where I can still recognize a similarity to Maine. So place comes through, and place casts its own weight over whatever you are writing. For me the importance of region has to do with disconnection between people. I am very attracted now, and I don't know exactly how I am going to work it, to the idea of writing a piece set on an island off the coast of Maine. *Dolores Claiborne* is set on an island, but this novel is not a horror story. I want to put a horror story on an island. I want that separation.

TM: There are a variety of scrapbooks and photo albums throughout your canon. They feature prominently in *The Shining, Misery,* and *It.* Do these records of the past serve a common purpose in those three books?

SK: It's a device. Pure and simple. To probe history in a manner that allows me to disclose the past so that it can possess immediate importance for the present. A lot of the fiction that I write follows the Gothic tradition wherein the past has this unbreakable hold on the present. This obsession with the past throughout Gothic literature, up to and including my own work, is an unpleasant thing. It is a twisted influence that restricts and even changes the present. Generally, . . . in the scrapbooks are things that people find unpleasant; they are not good memories.

TM: And this is true in Hawthorne, too. In novels such as *The Scarlet Letter* and especially *House of the Seven Gables,* the past has a tendency to shape events and behavior in the present.

SK: Absolutely. I've never solved a problem in a book with the aid of a scrapbook. I've just used [scrapbooks] to create more problems. And diaries operate in the same way for me. [They are] always devices for deepening the darkness, for helping someone to get in a little bit further over his head. And if you think some more about it, these scrapbooks operate as mirrors to the past; the images they reflect, however, are always cast in the present.

TM: I notice that the protagonists of your last few books have been novelists and that the importance of their being novelists is increasing in successive books. Could you identify your interest or purpose in writing about writers?

SK: I've written so much myself that writing has become a vital part of my life. It is the biggest figure in my landscape, the analogue of the statue of the Bourka Bee goddess in *Misery*. My writing is at the center of my life. Wherever you go in my little part of the landscape, the writer is always there, looking back at the reader. So what I have written about writers and writing in the last five years or so has been a real effort on my part to understand what I am doing, what it means, what it is doing to me, what it is doing for me. Some of it has been out of an effort to try and understand the ramifications of being a so-called famous person, or celebrity. What does it mean when somebody who is a novelist is invited to appear on "Hollywood Squares"? I am trying to understand these things. I have one more story about writers and writing in a novella called *Secret Window, Secret Garden* in *Four Past Midnight,* and then I think I'll try and close the book on this subject.

TM: But it also seems to me that in the many books that feature writers and writing, you have endowed these characters with certain powers. They appear to possess certain imaginative capacities that somehow serve them— even insulate them—in their battles against madness and evil.

SK: Well, we do have powers. The guy in *The Dark Half* says that writers, actors, and actresses are the only recognized mediums of our society. Our job, basically, is to create the possibility of making people believe the unbelievable—the suspension of disbelief. Even someone who does not write fantasy fiction, who writes so-called mainstream fiction, wants to create a bifurcation in the reader's mind: one part of that mind says this is all make-believe, words on a page; the other half is living that life, the fiction becoming more and more real. That is a power. And a lot of what I've written is an effort to understand how that happens, why it happens, and what it does to both the person writing it and the person reading it.

TM: At the end of *Misery* you suggest that Paul Sheldon could write a nonfictional account of his ordeal with Annie Wilkes, "but to do so would be tantamount to admitting to himself that he would never write another novel." Why is this?

SK: I don't know. If he had written such an account, I think he would have lost something even more important to him than those body parts Annie decides to amputate. When the real world becomes so bad that a writer gives up the ability to make fiction, he gives up his soul. The ability to create fiction, to tap into the imagination, is a writer's escape hatch. It's my escape hatch and Paul Sheldon's as well. It's where I belong. I don't belong writing about myself or about things that have happened to me.

I've written nonfiction, but I've never written nonfiction specifically about myself. I've written about everything from book censorship[5] to my son's championship Little League season.[6] That's fine. But to write specifically about my own life, even then I find myself fictionalizing. If I do touch on some personal experience, I find myself making things up. Because when the door of the fictional imagination is closed to you, when you can no longer work out your problem on paper, then the problem has overwhelmed you, taken your control and freedom away.

Sometimes for a writer the idea of explaining his own pain is harder than telling a story. So he turns to the act of storytelling, and this may touch on his pain and talk about it in a way that's more real to you and to me. A lot of the material in *Pet Sematary* is true; my son did run for the road. And I could sit down and say, I want to tell you about how I felt when I thought my son was going to die. But that would require me to tell you exactly the way that the occurrence actually happened because I can no longer take these elements and make them into fictions that I can control. Fiction is in my hands, and that means I can control it. But if it's real life, you can't mold things or change events—all you can do is lie.

TM: I'd like to return to *It* for a moment in order to ask you about the role of the turtle. Does it represent a mythological or religious archetype?

SK: I never wanted to deal with this—at least not publicly. I read an Indian story once, and it struck a cord in me because I remembered the myth of Atlas holding the world on his shoulder. In the Indian tale someone asks the tribal medicine man, "How does the world stay up? Why doesn't it fall? At night the sky gets dark and looks empty, so why don't we just fall down into the emptiness?" The medicine man responds, "Because a man—a big man—holds it up." That makes everything okay for a little while. Then somebody asks the obvious question: "What holds up the man?" The answer to this is, "There is a turtle that holds up the man. The man stands on the turtle's shell and the man holds up the world." Then, one more question from some officious brave or squaw: "Well, what holds up the turtle?" And the answer to this question is, "Don't ask any more questions."

I decided to make use of that turtle. Now, I'm talking to you about this issue, and I'm not going to talk about this to anyone else ever again, because this sounds as pretentious as hell. But in my own mind, when I wrote this down, I knew I was using the turtle as a symbol. I decided that if I was going to cast them (the Losers' Club) out there into the void, then I needed to create a symbol that stands for everything that is stable in the universe, everything that is solid in the universe, everything that holds up our lives and makes it possible for us to get on an airplane and trust to physics to hold us up, or to cross the street and trust to our senses that the way is clear and there really is no car in front of us. I needed a symbol that embodied sanity in a world where we don't know where we came from or where we are going. In a world where we are all falling, the turtle represents stability. A turtle is great; it is slow, and it doesn't move very much, but the animal is strong, and it lives a long time. So, I recreated the Indian turtle myth, brought it to life, and gave it a voice that sounded to me like Walter Brennan's.

TM: Right. Slow and monotonous. But how about the importance of the turtle's death? I feel a little like that Indian brave or squaw you just mentioned in pursuing this, but isn't it significant that the turtle is unavailable to aid the losers the second time around, when they are adults?

SK: The turtle dies, and in his death a strong force of good also dies. For the adults the turtle may be dead, but for the children his spirit may be more vital. And don't forget that in this novel these adults are trying to get back to their childhood selves. Beyond that, the whole subject of the turtle makes me feel uncomfortable, and whenever I get letters about him, I don't answer them. I got a postcard from this guy in New Zealand, and the whole message was, "Read *It*, Steve—loved it. Who was that turtle?"

TM: Some of America's most talented film directors—DePalma, Kubrick, Cronenberg, Carpenter—have done adaptations of your fiction. Do you think these directors are drawn to your work because they find something particularly American about it?

SK: They may. That may explain their later attraction, as each project progressed. I think initially, however, they were drawn out of a desire to make a lot of money. That wasn't the case with Kubrick. He saw a myth, which he took and molded. I'm not real satisfied with the job that he did. I think Carpenter was attracted to *Christine* because he saw an all-American horror story. He saw the chance to use the car in a new way that would be terrifying.

TM: You make me think, to continue this line of reasoning, of Brian DePalma's treatment of the American high-school experience in *Carrie*. Do you think DePalma was attracted to the novel as a chance to reveal some kind of truth about this institution?

SK: Perhaps so. But I think he was just having fun. He was hired to direct *Carrie* because he was available and the price was right. But I wanted him to do it from the start because I'd seen that sense of humor at work. There is another side to DePalma's vision, on the other hand, and this connects to what you were asking about the high school as institution. DePalma has a tendency to embrace darkness. Look at *Scarface*. He is attracted to whatever is blackest and nastiest in society. It isn't that he likes these elements for themselves; he's saying, I want to show this. And he exposes the darkness with a high-powered flashlight. You see this again in *Casualties of War*. There is a cold impulse in DePalma—the impulse of a little boy who wants to turn over a rock and see what's crawling underneath.

Some of this tendency is in Cronenberg, too. But it has served to humanize his work. *The Dead Zone* is Cronenberg's only really "human" movie, I think, and it is very warm and very loving. *The Dead Zone* was a perfect marriage, like two flavors that shouldn't mix but did.

TM: Yes. The entire film is shot with a white background. It's almost as if his use of snow and winter cold deepens and highlights, by way of contrast, the self-sacrificing love of Johnny Smith.

SK: And the interiors are also interesting. They are like the paintings of Norman Rockwell: pastel colors and ceilings with patterns.

TM: *The Dead Zone* may well be my favorite adaptation of any King novel.

SK: I like that one a lot. What continues to stick in my mind about it is the credit sequence at the opening of the film. The letters that make up the film's title come slowly into focus; they almost creep up on you.

TM: That impressed me as well. So much of what happens to John Smith through the course of *The Dead Zone* is a slow apprehension of reality—a new reality by virtue of his changed, postcomatose perspective. The emerging credit sequence seems to parallel nicely the main protagonist's struggle with a new set of personal and moral responsibilities.

SK: Good point. I think that's right.

TM: How well do you feel your work has been understood by professional reviewers and scholars? What is your attitude toward their interpretations of your fiction? What have they done right, and what areas are in need of further attention?

SK: I think I could have been treated a lot worse. And I could have been ignored completely. I've had to face, increasingly in the past six or seven years, reviews of contracts instead of reviews of books.

There has been a good deal more scholarship—or critical work—in the past six or seven years, and some of it has been both more favorable and more intelligent than I ever would have believed or expected. And I think the reason for this critical interest comes from the fact that I've managed to create an integrated world from what I've written—not just geographically . . . but in terms of an overall view about the way in which things in life happen and why they happen. The work underlines again and again that I am not merely dealing with the surreal and the fantastic but, more important, using the surreal and the fantastic to examine the motivations of people and the society and institutions they create.

In this sense, the world's situation has cooperated with me and my artistic endeavors. After eight years of a movie actor as president and the dark events of the Middle East, South America, and the slow collapse of American society itself, it has become more and more important for people to examine the inexplicable. We need to look around and recognize that we are really not solving any problems. We are simply turning lights on in more and more rooms and seeing more and more strange things. Everything from holes in the ozone, to the intolerable number of homeless wandering American streets, to this huge hurricane on the planet Neptune which apparently zips around the planet at 175 miles per hour. It's easy to say, What the fuck do I care about a hurricane on Neptune? Well, it makes you think. After all, it exists in the same universe that we inhabit, so how alien is that hurricane? Should it make us reevaluate the way that we look at the sky, at the natural physical world around us?

To return to your question, I think I am receiving my fair share of critical attention saying enough serious things about my work. I don't think that these critics are always clear in what they say, and one thing that most reviewers and scholars have missed so far is that I have tried to have some fun in these novels and that I've tried to poke some fun along the way. I guess that if people have missed one glaring point, it is that fantasy and horror can be wonderful tools of satire. Look at the great success Harlan Ellison has had in employing these features.

I don't know if you have had a chance to read *The Dark Half* yet, but Thad Beaumont has been interpreted by several early reviewers as an autobiographical character. You will not see Beaumont as an autobiographical reflection of me. You just won't.

TM: I noticed some delightful comic touches in *It*, especially when I read the book a second time. The scenes with Bill Denbrough and that oversized bicycle are a lot of fun. You often manage to capture the most awkward and embarrassing moments from adolescence. And not only are these moments readily identifiable for most American readers; they are also frequently invested with a large measure of sympathy.

SK: Growing up has never been easy. But in spite of the pressures and adjustments, childhood is also a silly time. There's nothing wrong with encouraging a kid to act silly.

TM: Speaking again of *It*, I'm especially fond of Mike Hanlon's role in that novel. I think you should be pleased with him—he's a black character whom you've invested with some genuinely human qualities. And I think what appeals to me the most about that character is his link to his father. Their relationship is one of the few positive parent-child associations in your entire canon.

SK: I was deliberate in making their relationship the only positive (parent-child union) in the novel. I've always been very taken with the way the "Peanuts" cartoons on television deal with the problem of adults. The voices of adults are never clearly articulated but instead are the muffled groans of a trombone or something that sounds like that. There is never any indication in *It,* up to about page 400, that Mike is black. I kept that offstage. And like you, I'm pretty satisfied with how he turned out.

TM: Where do you see your fiction headed in the next several years, and where do you see it in relation to what you have already written?

SK: Castle Rock is almost done. The three stories—*The Dark Half, Sun Dog,* and *Needful Things*—will close off that fictional microcosm. My children-protagonists are just about finished because I'm getting too old, my own children are getting too old, and at this point it would be easy to start making mistakes. I don't want to retrace territory that I've already covered. It is time to be done with Castle Rock because it is too easy to keep coming back to it. Too easy to rehash all the things which have occurred there over the years—the rabid dog, the crazy cop, those kids who ended a summer in search of a dead body along some railroad tracks.

If I have one real interest in the next 10 or 15 years of my life, it is not to lose my courage as a writer. I want to try new projects and big, challenging projects. And to try some little projects, too. I want to stay away from any urge to write a best-seller. I don't need to, financially. A stronger draw than the money is the knowledge that people are coming to my books for one specific thing—to get scared, to learn something about their childhoods or the world they live in, whatever—and when they pick up a new book maybe they will discover that this book isn't the same as any of the others, isn't what they expected. There is a great siren's song to keep giving them whatever it is they want. And I could probably do that, but it wouldn't nec-essarily be giving myself what I want or what I need in order to grow as a writer. I want to continue to grow, but I don't think anybody knows how to do that.

TM: Steve, so many of your characters, especially those who have endeared themselves to your American readership—Jack Sawyer, Frannie Goldsmith, Beverly Marsh, Ben Hanscom, Jack Torrance—have headed west. The westward journey is evident in so much of your fiction. Any reflections on this tendency?

SK: I guess the American myth that I grew up with requires the journey westward. Moving west meant growth, change, a break with the past. I think a lot of this has to do with me being an American writer who is aware of a specific history and tradition. As a kid I was very taken with the phrase "go west, young man," and finally I asked my mother, who happened to be south on that particular day, "What does it mean when they say somebody went west?" She said, "It means somebody has died; it was a euphemism from World War I." My characters head west because Americans have always headed west, and that's where the mystery is.

TM: I've just finished editing the page proofs for a Starmont House book entitled *The Shining Reader.* It is a collection of fifteen interpretive essays on your novel and Kubrick's film adaptation of it. Several authors view the book and film, but especially the novel, as parodies of the American dream. They argue that Jack Torrance is a negative portrait of the American success story, that he wants to write himself into fame and fortune at any cost. The Overlook itself is symbolic of the corporate organization that asks Jack to sacrifice everything, including his family and soul, for the advancement of his career. Does this line of reasoning make sense to you?

SK: Not entirely. I see Jack as a dysfunctional personality. He is clearly alcoholic, but his problems go on to include a negative family history and a fractured personality. And dysfunctional people often do what psychologists call a geographical change, meaning that they will look at the littered landscape, where everything is broken because of their destructive passions, and they'll say, I can never put this right. So they pick everybody up and go someplace else to start all over again. What I was trying to say in that novel is that wherever you go, the same asshole gets off the plane. If you act like an asshole in Vermont, when you go to Colorado you'll be an asshole there.

Jack has one period where he is presented the opportunity to choose a different door and not be an asshole. But the form of this novel, modeled after a Shakespearean tragedy, limits his behavior. Torrance is out of control of his own behavior and fate. Whatever is going to happen to him, in a way, has already been decided. Therefore, when he moves, he carries his doom with him.

There is an organization at work at the Overlook, but I see it primarily as a supernatural recreation of the problems Jack had before. Whatever is going on in the Overlook, on the other hand, is connected to a kind of capitalism run mad. It is the American dream run amok. You can rise in the hotel hierarchy; you just have to be willing to tread on enough dead bodies. The hotel's whole history is evidence of this.

TM: You mentioned the connection between Jack and the Shakespearean tragic tradition, that he "carries his doom with him." I see how this is true, but aren't there also moments in *The Shining* in which Jack, again like a Shakespearean tragic hero, makes deliberate and conscious choices that contribute to his own self-destruction?

SK: Yes. Particularly in the second part of the book. He's brought face-to-face several times with the fact that things are wrong. The basic decision he has to make is one that illustrates free will: to articulate what is wrong at the Overlook and get the hell out, or to cover [it] up, turn his back, and turn away. . . . He's like Hamlet, who reaches a certain point, and then all at once he gets pulled into the machinery. He's lost his autonomy.

TM: I was thinking also of Othello. There are many occasions, from act 2 to nearly the end of the play, when Othello could simply go to Desdemona and ask her to tell him the truth about her sexual fidelity. But he elects not to.

SK: Right. He should have asked her to join him in therapy. And I suppose the same holds true for Jack Torrance: the tragedy of *The Shining* might have been averted if somewhere along the line Jack had taken Wendy by the hand and said, "Dear, I think I need counseling."

Chapter Two

Tracing the Gothic Inheritance: *Danse Macabre* and a Context for Terror

This is the fuming, volcanic country of the Dark Lord, and if the critics who have seen it first hand are few, the cartographers are fewer.[1]

Danse Macabre is King's 1981 nonfictional analysis of the horror genre in literature, film, and television. Many critics have cited this text, but usually only to support interpretations of King's fiction. *Danse* deserves appraisal on its own merits as a critical study worthy of comment and as a sourcebook for better understanding King's philosophy of composition. It offers the author's trenchant reflections on art, aesthetics, politics, folklore, mythology, and modern American society.

In spite of the fact that *Danse* is one of the few examples of nonfictional prose in King's canon, it shares the inimitable writing style of his fiction. On the positive side, the author's voice remains accessible and personal throughout. King's interpretations are rendered in thoughtful and unpretentious language that draws the reader directly into the material under discussion. Although his tone suggests a late-evening dialogue with the reader, his relaxed and often humorous persona is somewhat undercut by the seriousness of the book's pursuit. For *Danse* attempts to trace the modern evolution of an American Gothic tradition, from its origins in the nineteenth century to the present. It is clear that King has drunk deeply from this wellspring; he is certainly on intimate terms with a wide range of Gothic films and literature, and generally treats these texts as legitimate artistic enterprises.

Less positively, *Danse* suffers from several of the stylistic liabilities that have plagued King's fictional work. Too often the critical focus of the book is blunted by careless language, a convoluted and unorganized structure, the repetitive raising of issues, and thoughts randomly brought together without significant concern for the sequential development of speculations or theses. *Danse* was conceived and partly written during King's tenure as a writer in residence at the University of Maine (1978–79). The book shows the influence of the classroom environment, but while ideas are often raised with passion and freshness, they are seldom rigorously pursued or revised. King appears to justify the stylistic looseness of *Danse* in his strong antiacademic denunciations, acknowledging that "literary criticism and rhetoric aren't forms I'm comfortable with" (*DM,* 386). His contention that scholars and literary critics tend to overanalyze art (*DM,* 268) is certainly well taken, but King might have performed a greater service for both the reader and the material under consideration had he mastered a more disciplined and scholarly approach. One longs at times for the intervention of a steely, old-fashioned editor who would pitilessly red-pencil the run-on sentences, the awkward metaphors, and the careless prose. Thus improved, *Danse* would be a dense but magnificent undertaking—a tribute to the underrated, untidy, and overlooked material it seeks to capture.

Interviews and published conversations with King indicate that he is aware of the disturbing tendencies in his prose style, but generally he chooses either to blunt the criticism by interpreting it as a personal affront or to view it as an issue of authorial prerogative: "Those avatars of high culture hold it almost as an article of religious faith that plot and story must be subordinated to style, whereas my deeply held conviction is that story must be paramount, because it defines the entire work of fiction. All other considerations are secondary—theme, mood, even characterizations and language."[2] This is a troublesome remark, for it suggests that it is somehow possible—even preferable—to separate content from the manner in which it is presented. And while this is hardly justification for dismissing King as a writer of serious literature, as so many of "those avatars of high culture" have done with great alacrity, it does underscore a principal liability in King's canon. In his insistence that the "story must be paramount," King sometimes appears to be swept away by the events he is narrating, and the story is weakened by his failure to maintain sufficient control over it.

Steps in the Danse

Part of King's motivation for writing *Danse* was to posit several explanations for the popularity and importance of the modern horror genre. Such speculations occur and reoccur at various points throughout his analysis of

American film, literature, and television. These ruminations may be summarized as follows (in order of increasing degree of aesthetic complexity):

(1) *It allows us to prove our bravery:* that we are not afraid of fear itself.

(2) *It enables us to reestablish feelings of normality:* that nothing we do
and no way we look can be as ghastly as what we read or view on the screen.

(3) *It confirms our good feelings about the status quo:* by showing us extravagant visions of what the alternatives might be, horror makes us see that
our personal lives and society may not be so bad after all. (Thus King's assertion that the horror genre "appeals to the conservative Republican in a
three-piece suit who resides within all of us" [*DM*, 39].)

(4) *It lets us feel we are part of the larger whole:* we identify with the puny
human forces seeking to regain control over the malevolent powers of the irrational and the supernatural.

(5) *It provides an opportunity to penetrate the mystery of death:* we are
drawn to the horror story because we wish to explore a forbidden realm, to
learn more about the "only truly universal rite of passage, the only one for
which we have no psychological or sociological input to explain what
changes we may expect as a result of having passed through" (*DM, 194*).
The tale of terror scrapes the cosmetic mask off the face of death, forcing
us to consider the Reaper's handiwork from a myriad of perspectives. The
horror genre explodes the civilized lies we use to insulate ourselves from
death. Horror serves as the ultimate deterrent to hubris, reminding Western man in particular that his ability to conquer nature's barriers extends
only so far. As Emily Dickinson, one of the greatest voices ever to speak on
the aesthetics of terror, was often to concede, human life is a fragile and
tenuous state of being, and in spite of our conscious efforts at denial we
only truly begin to apprehend existence in the appreciation of its loss:

> It's coming—the postponeless Creature—
> It gains the Block—and now—it gains the Door—
> Chooses its latch, from all the other fastenings—
> Enters—with a "You know Me—Sir"?
> Simple Salute—and certain Recognition—
> Bold—were it Enemy—Brief—were it friend—
> Dresses each House in Crape, and Icicle—
> And carries one—out to God—[3]

While King believes that horror provides readers with a variety of opportunities to witness vicariously the "great irreducible x-factor of our lives,
faceless father of a hundred religions, so seamless and ungraspable that it

usually isn't even discussed at cocktail parties" (*DM*, 194), the genre's treatment of death also provides assurance that there is indeed something beyond the mortal coil. Whether it be in the form of Dracula's restless sleep or the immortality of a benevolent spirit that participates in the struggles of humankind, the horror story relies on the existence of an afterlife featuring rewards and punishments directly related to the lives we have fashioned out of flesh and blood. This last point provides further explanation for the popularity of this fiction: the genre has helped fill the modern spiritual vacuum created in the absence of religious belief.

(6) *It permits us to indulge our darkest collective cultural and social anxieties:* the subtext of horror, which will be considered in greater detail later in this chapter, allows us to confront symbolically the weakening or collapse of social values and the consequences of economic instability.

(7) *It lets us return to childhood:* putting away our civilized and adult penchants for dismissal and disbelief, we become children again, seeing the world through clear definitions of good and evil. This point has two conflicting corollaries. First, the horror genre frequently capitalizes on repressed phobias that have been with us since childhood (e.g., fear of enclosed spaces, the dark, isolation, the unknown). Second, in the horror genre, children possess elements of endurance and innate goodness, which qualify them for hero status; they fill in for parents who have capitulated to the evil their offspring must now eradicate (*DM*, 42). The concept of the hero-child has held King's fascination for decades. This is amply evident in his characters, beginning with Sue Snell in *Carrie* and culminating with the members of the Losers' Club in *It*. "The job of the fantasy-horror writer," King writes, "is to make you, for a little while, a child again" (*DM*, 407). Children may eventually grow up to become adults, but before this process is completed, King implies (in theory reminiscent of Wordsworth), they gain insight into a set of intuitive ethics that adults eventually forfeit. Thus the importance of the child as the being most susceptible to the horror monster yet also the one most capable of destroying the creature. King develops this issue throughout the body of his fiction as well as in *Danse*.

(8) *It enables us to transcend the world of darkness and negation:* the horror story and film paradigmatically end with some sort of reconciliation that renders the powers of destruction manageable once more. Since this thesis (which King illustrates through a plethora of examples) represents a notable break from the stereotypical perception of the horror genre as a domain of bedlam and destruction exclusively, it is worthy of further commentary.

King's premise that the tale of horror is a survival exercise presupposes that the audience is provided with the opportunity to gain deep insights into its fears and, by extension, to acquire an array of coping skills. Like an audience witnessing a dramatic tragedy, we are often pained by the loss of human life in the horror story and, if the story has been aesthetically successful, stunned by how swiftly and ruthlessly the gods affect the human world. Moreover, the horror story, like classical tragedy, frequently educates us morally, suggesting vicarious methods for avoiding a correspondingly tragic fall in our own lives while inspiring a feeling of relief that we have been spared the actual experience. King appears to be critically aware that both horror and tragedy rely upon phenomena that Aristotle recognized— that pity and fear must serve as inspiration for the audience, and that in the production of these emotions the possibility for reintegration, or catharsis, is born:

> Here is the final truth of horror movies: They do not love death, as some have suggested; they love life. They do not celebrate deformity but by dwelling on deformity, they sing of health and energy. By showing us the miseries of the damned, they help us to rediscover the smaller (but never petty) joys of our own lives. They are the barber's leeches of the psyche, drawing not bad blood but anxiety. . . . Because in the final sense, the horror movie is the celebration of those who feel they can examine death because it does not yet live in their own hearts. (*DM,* 198–99)

King's evaluation of the modern American horror film echoes the overall perspective that animates his own fiction and surely represents a partial explanation of why that fiction is so popular. The citation above illustrates King's commitment not to the forces of negation (as claimed by those who have thought insufficiently about his work and its genre[4]) but to the powers of self-knowledge and moral development—the inheritance bestowed on men and women who experience personal tragedy but refuse to be overwhelmed by it.

King's sense that the horror genre embodies songs of "health and energy," even as it does so by means of perversity and fear, is best represented by the Apollonian/Dionysian mythological paradigm to which he frequently alludes. Throughout *Danse* King refers to this Greek construction as a metaphor for defining the mechanics of modern horror. By necessity the order and light associated with an Apollonian world-view come under assault by the Dionysian forces of destruction and chaos. For a period the Dionysian elements thwart the rational inclinations of society and self.

When these forces are in control, the supernatural inflicts its fury on the human world in the form of either mass disorder (e.g., a whole community under siege) or a highly personal assault upon the protagonist's psyche. Thus, argues King, the human world finds itself at the mercy of forces larger than itself. Nonetheless, if the Apollonian urge toward survival and reintegration is strong enough, or the Dionysian powers weak enough, the horror story concludes in a manner reminiscent of classical tragedy. Although diminished as a consequence of what it has lost in this struggle, the human world retains its capability for reasserting priorities and values. "The melodies of the horror tale," King explains, "are simple and repetitive, and they are melodies of disestablishment and disintegration . . . but another paradox is that the ritual outletting of these emotions seems to bring things back to a more stable and constructive state again" (*DM,* 13). The Apollonian impulse, which King affiliates with "the hearts and minds of men and women of good will" (*DM,* 402), eventually overcomes the powers of negation. King thus appears to share Robin Wood's assessment of horror as "the most important of all American genres and perhaps the most progressive, even in its overt nihilism—in a period of extreme cultural crisis and disintegration, [it] alone offers the possibility of radical change and rebuilding."[5]

This optimistic and affirmative defense of a genre that has long been attacked by conservatives and liberals alike for its perceived abdication of moral and artistic responsibilities is the single most eloquent contribution of *Danse.* King understands that horror is frequently condemned—usually by readers who view themselves as too sophisticated to read it—because it emphasizes themes that are fundamental and uncomplicated: pain, loss of control, death. But it is the honesty of this pursuit that so impresses King; this is an art that refuses to conform itself to the conventions of the "acceptable." And because of its stubborn independence, horror has forced us to face the great monsters of our times—monsters that are new, like nuclear war, and those that have been around for quite some time, like death. But for King the great truth of horror is not that we must always be devoured by these monsters or that we must face them alone. Instead, as evidenced by the last third of *Danse* and by novels as diverse as *The Shining, The Dead Zone, The Stand, It,* and *Misery,* King sees the horror tale as an essentially visionary experience. Within the eternal perimeters of death and decay, from which neither *Danse* nor the horror tale tend very far to stray, the possibilities for transformation remain limitless: "It's not a dance of death at all, not really. There is a third level here, as well. It is, at bottom, a dance of dreams. It's a way of awakening the child inside, who never dies but only sleeps ever more deeply. If the horror story is our rehersal for death, then its strict moralities make it also a reaffirmation of life and good will and simple imagination—just one more pipeline to the infinite" (*DM*, 409). For King, the horror genre's *danse macabre* is not about meaningless pain and suffering in an absurdist's universe. The true aesthetic of terror, in his analysis, emphasizes not destruction and violence but reintegration and moral evolution. King stresses throughout *Danse* that the role of the fiction writer is that of moral guardian (*DM*, 402–3). He appreciates that the writer's struggles are tied directly to the search for truth and that this search is perhaps as close as mortals get to moral perfection. The horror narrative may be only a small, underrated subgenre of mainstream art for many cultural historians and critics, but it is still art, and all the attributes of an artistic text are therefore present: conflict and crisis, tension and resolution, violence and death, love and life, ethical choices and their consequences. Perhaps the greatest service King affords the Gothic tradition in this book is to convey his belief that the genre is worthy of serious examination and that the real issues at work in these films and narratives have less to do with grotesque perversions of reality than with reality itself.

Subtexts of Terror

At the end of *Danse* King provides an appendix listing the books and films that he believes "have contributed something of value to the genre" (*DM*, 415). What initially strikes the reader as curious about his selections is that a number of them are not about supernatural occurrences, nor do they provide any evidence of such events. King's list is an interesting reflection of his own belief that "if horror movies have redeeming social merit, it is because of that ability to form liaisons between the real and the unreal—to provide subtexts. And because of their mass appeal, these subtexts are often culture-wide. . . . When the horror movies wear their various sociopolitical hats—the B-picture as tabloid editorial—they often serve as an extraordinarily accurate barometer of those things which trouble the night-thoughts of a whole society" (*DM*, 130–31).

Throughout *Danse* King insists that for the horror genre to operate most effectively there must be a careful blending of reality and surreality: "The audience is propelled . . . by the feeling that, under the right set of circumstances, this could happen" (*DM*, 182). The audience watching horror must be made to feel that what is occurring on the screen or in the text is taking place in their world or in a realm that is at least recognizable. Following Poe,

King acknowledges that the best horror texts possess a "pleasing allegorical feel" (*DM*, 31). And while the specifically allegorical nature of such texts is never given a definitive exegesis, King appears to use allegory as "a symbolic way" of saying "things that we would be afraid to say out straight," a way for the audience to "exercise emotions which society demands we keep closely in hand" (*DM*, 31). Thus, in King's analysis horror is a method for measuring the spirit of a historical time; under the surface of the text is a commentary about the political, social, and economic anxieties of the moment. King begins with the assumption that literature and film are two of many elements participating in a culture's representation of itself—helping to form its discourse on the family, the state, the individual, helping to make the world intelligible, although not necessarily representing this condition obviously or even precisely. Popular culture, like a thermometer that jiggles atop a pressure cooker, measures tensions in the society it addresses, and the horror tale has always revealed the darkest impulses of social man. As Bernard G. Gallagher concludes in his study of King's allegorical mode of composition, "the work of horror provides a vehicle for the metaphoric expression of terror at some everyday event which normally masks its horribleness behind a mundane face."[6] Through such symbolism (or subtext) the audience is provided the opportunity to confront its personal and collective anxieties while still maintaining a safe enough distance from them. In other words, the cultural nightmares represented by the horror tale allow us to vent the subconscious phobias we repress (and vent them we must because their strength and power constitute a serious threat) with the conscious knowledge that horror stories are not to be taken seriously.

Of all the texts treated in *Danse,* perhaps the most astutely explicated is Ira Levin's novel *Rosemary's Baby* (1967). King believes that the subtext of this novel reflects the deeply modern aspects of a world in which trust has evaporated in the anomie of the big city. The novel is symbolic of the dark side of American life that was manifested, several years after its publication, in the erosion of national purpose and optimism after Vietnam and the Watergate scandal. *Rosemary's Baby* signals the breakdown of faith in society's future (the book "deals with urban paranoia" [*DM*, 300]), faith in human relationships (Rosemary is betrayed by her husband, friends, and doctor), and faith in a universe divinely arranged ("the weakening of religious conviction is an opening wedge for the devil" [*DM*, 300]). In his examination of *Rosemary's Baby* King is virtually uninterested in the plot, which concerns the birth of Satan's child—a premise that captivated a generation of readers, as well as viewers of Polanski's film adaptation. King's fascination is with the social and religious implications of the work's subtext.

The subtextual qualities of modern horror intrigue King throughout *Danse*, and this interest has clearly shaped his own fiction.[7] But the presence of sociopolitical elements in the horror tale is not a modern occurrence. And King's paramount thesis in *Danse*, that the horror story is a barometer of an era's repressed psychology, has been applicable to the Gothic tradition since its inception. King makes few references to the birth of the genre in the last half of the eighteenth century, when its early authors—Horace Walpole, Matthew Lewis, Ann Radcliffe—were writing in reaction to the spirit of scientific enlightenment that dominated the eighteenth century.

Few scholars are willing to concede to Gothicism its importance as a harbinger of romanticism. Several years before William Wordsworth was to praise the French Revolution as the event signaling the demise of the safe and orderly deistic universe, Gothic writers were preparing the way for the romantic urge to displace reason and authority by surrendering one's rational will to the powers of sublime dread. The Age of Reason revealed that by proper use of the intellect, humans could overcome the urge to commit acts of evil against themselves and others. As Henry Fielding noted, the noble aspirations of the age described "not men, but manners; not an individual, but a species." In contrast, Gothic tales provided characters who asserted their identities in the face of reason and manners. The conflict between societal repression and the inner drives of men bubbled to the surface in the Gothic text and culminated in the horrid actions of the Gothic hero/villain.

The generation of eighteenth-century Gothic authors, with their tormented skepticism regarding the universality of reason and natural law, lay the foundations for the antivisions of Keats, Byron, and the other dark romantics. The typical ruins of the Gothic castle symbolize the destruction of order and society. As Michael Sadleir argues in his study of Jane Austen's *Northanger Abbey* and its relationship to the Gothic period, "the [Gothic] movement was, in origin at least, a movement toward freedom and away from the controls of discipline."[8] The castle of the Gothic novel, long considered a bastion of social order and moral safety, dissolves in the wake of the novel's attack on social sensibilities, political arrangements, and ethical codes of conduct: "Morally the gothic romance marked a shift from faith in a simple dualism to a fascination with the more complex interrelatedness of good and evil. Politically it embodied the new sense of freedom that characterized the revolutionary age. Psychologically it signalled a turn from the portrayal of manners in an integrated society to the analysis of lonely, guilt-ridden outsiders."[9]

The Gothic family tree (see page 30) owes its very lineage to a long history of cross-cultural fertilization and diversification. From texts as obscure as William Godwin's *Caleb Williams* to the mainstream literary traditions of European and American romanticism, Gothicism has undergone a series of variations and refinements. In his essay on Walpole's *Castle of Otranto* as Gothic prototype, Frederick S. Frank believes that the Gothic tradition embodies an ancestry of anguish, manifesting itself in the actions of the Gothic hero, which symbolize defiance and outrage rather than suffering. This "cry of anguish" can be heard from the character Ambrosio in Lewis's *The Monk* to the characters invented by Mary Shelley, Ernst Hoffmann, Edgar Allan Poe, Fyodor Dostoyevski, Hawthorne, Mark Twain, and Henry James.[10] Gothic iconography and ideology went on to shape the work of twentieth-century writers as diverse as Flannery O'Connor and Stephen King.

From early eighteenth-century texts to the works of contemporary Gothic authors, the tradition has always maintained an allegorical base. The psychosexual conflicts at the center of the Gothic tradition highlight the improbability of ever resolving the struggle between id and superego on both the personal and societal levels. In keeping with this focus on the Gothic tale as allegory, King argues in *Danse* that there are three essential archetypes from the Gothic past upon which subsequent myths of horror have been based. The legends of Frankenstein, Dracula, and Dr. Jekyll / Mr. Hyde are recurring avatars in the evolution of the Gothic canon. These three figures, posits King, have dominated the fictional landscape of the Gothic, eventually straying from the printed text and into the iconography of popular culture:

(1) *The Frankenstein monster.* In the past century and a half, Mary Shelley's monster has been transformed into a cultural icon. For King, the monster is a representation of our own flawed humanity, embodying the conflicting urges to share our love with other living creatures and to reject what is different from us. As Robin Wood has noted in thoughts paralleling King's, "Few horror films have totally unsympathetic Monsters; in many (notably the *Frankenstein* films) the Monster is clearly the emotional center, and much more human than the cardboard representations of normality" (Wood, 27). It remains King's belief that the Frankenstein monster is the prototype for King Kong and a whole variety of mutant creatures that have elicited ambivalent emotions from their popular audiences. But King also sees in Dr. Frankenstein's creation of his monster an illustration of what he terms "psychological horror," wherein evil is created from the refusal to take personal responsibility for one's actions because of pride: "The stories of

THE GOTHIC FAMILY TREE

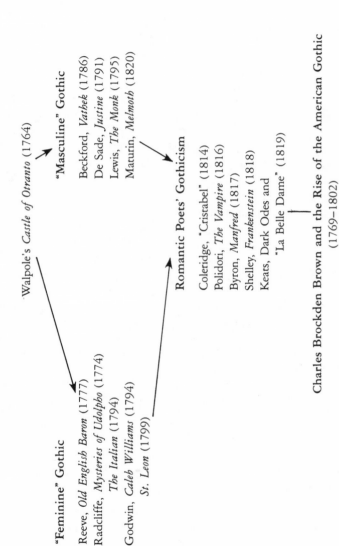

Walpole's *Castle of Otranto* (1764)

"Feminine" Gothic

Reeve, *Old English Baron* (1777)
Radcliffe, *Mysteries of Udolpho* (1774)
    The Italian (1794)
Godwin, *Caleb Williams* (1794)
    St. Leon (1799)

"Masculine" Gothic

Beckford, *Vathek* (1786)
De Sade, *Justine* (1791)
Lewis, *The Monk* (1795)
Maturin, *Melmoth* (1820)

Romantic Poets' Gothicism

Coleridge, "Cristabel" (1814)
Polidori, *The Vampire* (1816)
Byron, *Manfred* (1817)
Shelley, *Frankenstein* (1818)
Keats, Dark Odes and
    "La Belle Dame" (1819)

Charles Brockden Brown and the Rise of the American Gothic
(1769–1802)

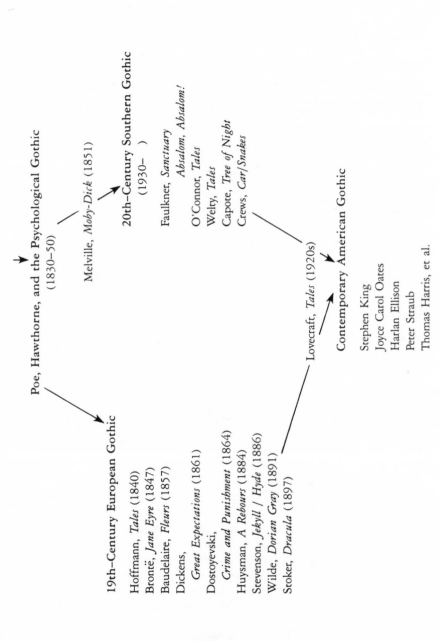

Poe, Hawthorne, and the Psychological Gothic
(1830–50)

Melville, *Moby-Dick* (1851)

20th-Century Southern Gothic
(1930–   )

Faulkner, *Sanctuary*
            Absalom, Absalom!
O'Connor, *Tales*
Welty, *Tales*
Capote, *Tree of Night*
Crews, *Car/Snakes*

19th-Century European Gothic

Hoffmann, *Tales* (1840)
Brontë, *Jane Eyre* (1847)
Baudelaire, *Fleurs* (1857)
Dickens,
    Great Expectations (1861)
Dostoyevski,
    Crime and Punishment (1864)
Huysman, *A Rebours* (1884)
Stevenson, *Jekyll / Hyde* (1886)
Wilde, *Dorian Gray* (1891)
Stoker, *Dracula* (1897)

Lovecraft, *Tales* (1920s)

Contemporary American Gothic

Stephen King
Joyce Carol Oates
Harlan Ellison
Peter Straub
Thomas Harris, et al.

horror which are psychological—those which explore the terrain of the human heart—almost always revolve around the free-will concept; 'inside evil,' if you will, the sort we have no right laying off on God the Father. This is Victor Frankenstein creating a living being out of spare parts to satisfy his own *hubris,* and then compounding his sin by refusing to take responsibility for what he has done" (*DM,* 62). American Gothic writers embraced this concept as a means of critiquing the American faith in Emersonian self-reliance; we probably see the best evidence of this in some of the tales of Hawthorne, Melville, and O'Connor, who drew characters bearing a remarkable resemblance to Dr. Frankenstein.

(2) *Dracula.* Unlike Dr. Frankenstein, who elects to pursue evil as a conscious choice, Count Dracula meets a fate that "seems totally predestinate; the fact that he comes to London with its 'teeming millions' does not proceed from any mortal being's evil act" (*DM,* 64). For King, *Dracula* is most accurately read as an embodiment of Western culture's fear of sexuality. In Stoker's Victorian society "perverse sexual evil" could not be shown as emanating from the individual. To make sexuality palatable to a Victorian readership, Stoker had to attribute the drive to a source beyond the realm of human control. Thus, the novel features "sex based upon relationships where one partner is largely under the control of the other" (*DM,* 68). King posits a direct line from *Dracula* to the horror genre's deathless fascination with violent punishment as a consequence of sexual indulgence. Furthermore, the novel reinforces the mythos of sexism, as it relies upon primal rape scenes in which women are usually portrayed as helpless victims.[11]

King himself has taken several pages from *Dracula* for use in his own fiction; *'Salem's Lot* is obviously written in homage to Stoker's novel. But perhaps even more interesting is King's interpretation of *Dracula* as a book in which "sex leads to some bad end" (*DM,* 68). Throughout King's canon sexuality is a means for illustrating evil's corrosive potential. Like Stoker, King frequently employs sexuality as a metaphor for a character's loss of moral focus and imminent destruction. Since a healthy sexual response should be an affirmation of life and love between human beings, its perversion serves as an effective vehicle for portraying the loss of one's humanity, a surrendering to sin. In King's fiction, when sex is used as a means of manipulation, its consequences are always evil; when sexuality serves a demented will, the passion of love is turned into the aggression of self-destruction.

(3) *Dr. Jekyll / Mr. Hyde.* The Stevenson novel is at the heart of the split-personality archetype that has dominated the realm of the modern psychological Gothic tale. King employs the text as a vehicle for restating the dominant paradigm of the horror genre: the status quo (Apollonian control)

at odds with the powers of destruction (Dionysian energies). As the Gothic family tree paradigm suggests, nineteenth-century literature is filled with myriad schizophrenic characters; Dickens' Pip / Orlick, Dostoyevski's underground man and Raskolnikov, and Poe's William Wilson illustrate the cross-cultural fascination with the split personality. These examples precede *Dr. Jekyll and Mr. Hyde* by several years, but Stevenson's novel provides the most explicit representation of this psychological affliction. King maintains that the Jekyll / Hyde personality is the most accessible to a modern audience. And Stevenson's dramatization of schizophrenia is aided by his modernistic prose: economy of language and descriptive precision help to lift the novel out of the nineteenth century and into our own. King concludes that Stevenson's book is the prototype for the modern psychological Gothic, influencing work such as Hitchcock's *Psycho* and Robert Bloch's *The Scarf:* "If we look at the Jekyll and Hyde story as a pagan conflict between man's Apollonian potential and his Dionysian desires, we see that the Werewolf myth—in nominal disguise—runs through a great many modern horror novels and movies" (*DM*, 75).

Fairy Tales and Horror Tales

King acknowledges throughout *Danse* that the horror genre has always maintained a special attraction for young people. Children are more capable than adults of "lifting the weight of fantasy" (*DM*, 99) and keeping it afloat; adults appear prone to hernias. But perhaps another explanation for the adolescent fascination with horror, particularly Stephen King's brand of it, is that children are often the central protagonists. A cynical critic might argue that Hollywood and horror novelists are merely exploiting the youth market: consumer demographics indicate that adolescents spend a lot of money. However, I think the issue is more complicated than this, especially in the case of King's fiction.

The vast majority of King's heroes and heroines are either adolescents or adults who have refused to forfeit their childhood bonds. This alone suggests that in King's mind it is the child who remains most capable of surviving a horrific experience and channeling his terror into something useful: "A certain amount of fantasy and horror in a child's life seems to me a perfectly okay, useful sort of thing. Because of the size of their imaginative capacity, children are able to handle it, and because of their unique position in life, they are able to put such feelings to work" (*DM*, 102).

King's contention neatly parallels Bruno Bettelheim's thesis on the importance of the fairy tale as a means for the symbolic resolution of child-

hood fears and anxieties. "In a fairy tale," Bettelheim writes, "internal processes are externalized and become comprehensible as represented by the
figures of the story and its events."[12] Bettelheim emphasizes that by iden-
tifying with the conflicts posed in fairy tales, children uncover resolutions
to their own specific problems and thereby move the fairy tale's meaning
beyond fiction and folklore and into the realm of the therapeutic: "The
fairy tale is therapeutic because the patient finds his *own* solutions,
through contemplating what the story seems to imply about him and his
inner conflicts at this moment in his life. The content of the chosen tale
usually has nothing to do with the patient's external life, but much to do
with his inner problems, which seem incomprehensible and hence unsolv-
able" (Bettelheim, 25). These remarks recall King's comments on the re-
integrative potential of the horror genre.

The horror tale shares a number of other interesting similarities to the
fairy tale. Like the fairy tale, the horror story relies upon primal phobias—
the breakup of familial relationships, death, isolation, separation. In both
genres the reader is forced to engage these issues, confront them, and vicariously participate in attempts to resolve them. Maria Tatar's study of
Grimm's fairy tales indicates that sex and violence are the major thematic
concerns of these tales and that these elements usually surface in the form of
incest and child abuse.[13] As I will detail in chapter 6, child abuse is also a
major theme in King's novel *It,* and evidence of its devastation is perhaps
the most frequently recurring element in his entire canon.

In a novel such as *The Shining* fairy tale references create an analogical
bridge between the events taking place within the text itself and cultural
and historical archetypes. Thus, the issues of abandonment, betrayal, violence, and death take on affective dimensions far larger than those of the
personal issues in the domestic, timebound realm of the Torrance family.
The tales of "Bluebeard," *Alice in Wonderland,* and "The Three Little Pigs"
resonate throughout *The Shining,* giving core scenes in King's fiction a rich
intertextuality. They provide passkeys that open the doors to exotic and terrifying secret places (Alice's Wonderland and Danny Torrance's Room
217); altered states of being that border on the realm of madness (Jack's
slow transformation into Bluebeard, during which he attacks his "golden
haired wife" because of her "betrayal" in failing to obey her husband); and
most of all, the process within which a child's archetypal predispositions
make him vulnerable to the personal flaws of his parents (Danny, like his
brothers and sisters in the fairy tales King references, struggles against the
parental authority that threatens to destroy him as he journeys toward individuation). The symbols and narrative structure of the fairy tales to which

King alludes in *The Shining* fuse the personal relationships, behaviors, and individual histories of the members of the Torrance family with larger, a priori patterns of human behavior.[14]

While King does not directly address specific fairy tales in *Danse,* he does discuss their genre's significance in relation to horror. Many horror films and novels, he insists, have "more in common with the Brothers Grimm than with the op-ed page in a tabloid paper" (*DM,* 131). The monsters and vampires of the horror genre are only slightly removed from those talking animals that are forever dispensing advice in fairy tales. Indeed, many of the Grimm narratives employ the wicked witches and monstrous creatures more commonly associated with the world of horror. Thus, the horror story and the fairy tale rely upon fantastic elements that are not so commonly found in the related realms of myth and folklore. The reader must imaginatively pierce a world that never was and never could be; this is not the case for most tales of mythology and folklore. Furthermore, the surface occurrences in the horror text distort realistic values and expectations to the point that access to a fantastic realm challenges the very foundations of reality.

Not surprisingly, the writers and painters of the surrealist movement— Luis Buñuel and Georges Franju, in particular—were highly intrigued by American horror movies and German fairy tales. They understood that these narratives were dedicated to their own artistic principles: exploring the realm of the irrational, extending reality's meaning through symbology, and overthrowing repression in order to liberate the unconscious. For the surrealists the goal of art was to bridge the gap between man's inner and external realities, between dreams and reality, between the imagination and the world. In effecting a resolution among these states, the surrealists sought to reconstruct a vision of reality that was terrifying and wonderful at the same time—the exact aesthetic combination at work in both the fairy story and horror tale.[15]

Although fairy tales, horror stories, myths, and folk tales would appear to be most appropriately understood as subsets of fantasy, there are subtle distinctions among them. Mythology and folklore tend toward a greater reliance on creating a realistic environment; even the various gods in mythology bear a critical nexus to the mortal world. Primitive man, as Jung was often to point out, was not content simply to watch the sun rise and set; the course of the sun's daily journey "must represent the fate of a god or hero who, in the last analysis, dwells nowhere except in the soul of man."[16] According to Jung, all the processes of nature were mythologized in order to provide symbolic expression of inner psychic drama. This process of projection insists upon the close relationship of mythological being and human psychological character: "The psyche contains all the images that have ever given rise to myths . . . our unconscious is an acting and suffering subject with an inner drama which primitive man rediscovers, by means of analogy, in the processes of nature both great and small" (Jung 1969, 7).

In contrast to mythology's close analogy between divine and human expression, horror and fairy tales tend to move beyond realism and toward exaggeration (thus King's thesis that sociopolitical issues are consigned to a subtextual level, beneath the surface supernaturalism). While the horror and fairy-tale traditions appreciate the importance of realistic elements such as child abuse, they frequently extend the parameters of such subjects. Each form highlights how easily humankind is dwarfed by forces beyond, and indifferent to, mortal welfare. Although the fairy-tale or horror-story protagonist may begin his journey in a normal and naturalistic setting, and may end it in such a setting as well, the world that is discovered in between is always more surreal than real, more irrational than rational, more allegorical than realistic.

Perhaps the greatest distinction between mythology and the fairy tale is one Bettelheim explores in *The Uses of Enchantment:* mythology almost invariably ends in tragedy, while the fairy tale moves toward a happy ending. "The myth is pessimistic, while the fairy tale is optimistic, no matter how terrifyingly serious some features of the story may be. It is this decisive difference which sets the fairy tale apart from other stories in which equally fantastic events occur, whether the happy outcome is due to the virtues of the hero, chance, or the interference of supernatural figures" (Bettelheim, 37). While unequivocally happy conclusions are not always present in the horror genre, the reader will recall King's own belief in horror's central importance as a vehicle for moral affirmation. King's fictional plots generally follow the basic structure of the traditional fairy tale as his child-heroes must at some point do battle against, and eventually vanquish, the evils affiliated with, adulthood. Most often his protagonists, like Grimm's Hansel and Gretel, join together to form strong small-group allegiances to overcome the adult evil that threatens and deceives them. Fairy tales are age-old stories of children confronted by wicked adults in a wicked world. To survive (as the members of the Losers' Club learn in *It*), children must find an alternative to adulthood that will allow them to retain their moral purity.

Aside from referencing the fairy-tale tradition on several occasions in *Danse*, King alludes to at least one specific tale in each of his novels. Some of the more original examples of such evocations are "Bluebeard" in *The Shining*, "Snow White and the Seven Dwarves" in *It*, Grimm's "Faithful John" in *The Dead Zone*, and *The Wizard of Oz* in *Pet Sematary*. But perhaps his most effective use of a fairy tale is his employment of "Cinderella" as a prototype for the novel *Carrie.* Like Cinderella, Carrie is prisoner to her mother's oppression, and her mocking and cruel schoolmates are modeled on Cinderella's evil stepsisters. Both girl-women are victims of sinister home lives that provide no shelter or comfort. Certainly, the agony that Carrie encounters in the schoolyard is as painful as Cinderella's duties in the kitchen and her role as maid for a set of ungrateful siblings. Eventually, Carrie and Cinderella are each provided with a shining, albeit brief, moment at a prom / ball through the kindness of a sympathetic outsider (for Carrie, Sue Snell; for Cinderella, the fairy godmother). As is often the case in King's adaptations, the fairy-tale tradition is pushed to its furthest limits: Carrie's dream night becomes a nightmare unmatched by the transformation of Cinderella's coach into a pumpkin and of her dress into rags. But as Chelsea Quinn Yarbro reminds us, successive versions of "Cinderella" have softened over the centuries. "In one of the original versions of 'Cinderella,' when she is given the chance to be revenged upon her family, she has their noses and hands cut off."[17] Carrie's psychokinetic abilities merely provide her with a range of expression that remains unavailable to Cinderella. Had King written Cinderella's tale, the whole forest would have gone up in flames.

King and Hawthorne: The Gothic Goes Regional

The reader of *Danse* may not agree with all of King's interpretations or even with his assessments of certain texts as being more important than others in shaping the modern horror tradition. But *Danse*'s limitations notwithstanding, one must be impressed with the sheer volume of work King reviews. Recommending *Danse* as a sourcebook for tracing the Gothic line directly to King himself is one of my intentions in this chapter; the inheritance is as varied and wide-ranging as King's own library.

From the naturalists, particularly Theodore Dreiser and Sherwood Anderson, it is possible to sense the dark side of King's American vision: "[The naturalists] wrote of American people living in the heartland . . . of innocence coming heartbreakingly to experience . . . in voices which are uniquely, even startlingly American" (*DM*, 325). King has inherited fairy-tale archetypes from the Brothers Grimm and recast them in a specifically Gothic format. His adaptations have merely moved the locale, as Yarbro notes, from "castles and caves [to] high schools and condominiums" (Yarbro, 62). As is the case whenever a writer consciously creates a literary resonance to another text, fairy tales have helped to enrich King's major fic-

tional premises. And, of course, the greatest literary debt King acknowledges in *Danse* is to the inclusive tradition of the Gothic genre, with all its
permutations and transformative possibilities.

In his essay "King and the Literary Tradition of Horror and the Supernatural" Ben Indick posits that Stephen King "has absorbed and utilized
those qualities which characterize the different types of stories in the horror genre. In his own distinctive style are mirrored the major traditions he
has inherited."[18] As evident throughout this chapter's study of *Danse,* the
potential scope of this thesis in terms of nineteenth-century literature
alone is so vast—from the haunted landscapes of Poe to the vampire legends of Stoker—that Indick has no choice but to overlook critical sources
of inspiration. Perhaps his most glaring omission is King's fellow New
Englander Nathaniel Hawthorne, whose influence King acknowledges
several times in *Danse.*[19] In recalling the origins of the novel *'Salem's Lot,*
for example, King writes that he "wanted to try to use the book partially
as a form of literary homage, . . . working in the tradition of such 'classical' ghost story writers as Henry James, M. R. James, and Nathaniel
Hawthorne" (*DM,* 25).

From Poe, King learned how to visualize the confinement of an interior
atmosphere. *The Shining* would not produce the levels of terror and claus-
trophobic anxiety it does if not for King's awareness of Poe's "Fall of the
House of Usher" and "Masque of the Red Death." King's novel clearly carries something of the bizarre opulence and ominous sense of interior rooms
to be found in Poe's settings, as well as one specific detail—the clock as a
symbolic center of time and psychodynamic energies. Frederick S. Frank reminds us in "The Gothic Romance" that in Poe's fiction "Place becomes
personality, as every corner and dark recess exudes a remorseless aliveness
and often a vile intelligence."[20] With a conscious nod to Poe, King draws
the interior of the Overlook Hotel, with its dark, twisting corridors and history of violence, to reflect Jack Torrance's haunted psyche. Moreover, like
the assorted crypts and chambers that populate Poe's tales, special rooms
exist at the Overlook, most notably the Colorado Lounge and room 217,
where supernatural dynamics are readily apparent, exerting a direct influence on the human world.

Hawthorne's novels and tales, on the other hand, may have helped King
to recognize the value of placing fiction in a wilderness setting and within a
specific historical time frame. The relationship of theme to setting in Poe's
work, while always detailed and relevant, is domestic in nature—murder in
a bedchamber, madness in an isolated mansion, a wife's entombment in her
basement wall. These microcosms are generic Gothic, usually transcending

any sense of historical time and place, conceivably existing anywhere in the world at any moment in time. In contrast, Hawthorne's strength as a regionalist, reflected in his sense of Massachusetts as a repository for historical events as well as a physical entity, is intrinsic to his most important fiction.

King's descriptions of his native Maine and his close scrutiny of character, tradition, and the clash between civilized values and the wilderness find their closest points of comparison in the writing of Hawthorne. The latter's New England forests exercise such a dominating presence in so much of his work that they tend to dwarf the human beings who stumble into them. Hawthorne's woods are environments over which the human world exerts no dominion. Borrowing heavily from the Puritan perspective on uncivilized nature, Hawthorne's woods are settings fraught with danger. Within the uncut trees surrounding their meager enclaves, Hawthorne's young journeymen come to recognize the existence of evil. Hawthorne's conception of nature, as Hyatt Waggoner defines it, is "a symbolic language capable, when responded to imaginatively, of revealing a truth and reality perceived through, but lying beyond, the senses."[21] Hawthorne's journeys into the realm of primitive landscape were really metaphors for journeys into the self. Since Hawthorne's moral aesthetic was so strongly shaped by his Puritan ancestry, it is not surprising that the forest voyage serves to bring his protagonists to a face-to-face confrontation with their own darkest urges—the confirmation of original sin.

Hawthorne's descriptions of moral conflict set in the symbolic arena of New England pines are paralleled in King's treatments of contemporary Maine. For King, Maine is a place of terrifying loneliness, where nature appears to be antagonistic to a human presence, and where men and women often feel the same degree of estrangement from one another as they do from the supernatural creatures inhabiting the woods on the outskirts of their towns. Burton Hatlen, himself a Mainer, perhaps comprehends and appreciates the regional influence on King's work better than any other critic. According to Hatlen, the "myth of Maine" that is gradually unfolding in King's canon is a dark but nonetheless accurate reflection of the state itself: "And Stephen King too knows that there's something chillingly inhuman waiting out in those woods, hiding in the summer maybe, but as soon as the leaves begin to turn it crawls out, and someday when you're out jogging along a back road, or even just riding alone in your car, it stops and puts a cold finger right on your heart."[22]

In *Pet Sematary* Louis Creed's first journey beyond the pet cemetery and into the burial grounds of the Micmac Indians occurs late in November. The absolute sense of an early New England winter, of an environment that is foreign to human habitation and survival, is developed with great success. Aside from capturing the raw flavor of Thanksgiving in the northeast (a phenomenon that remains as foreign to the consciousness of a native Southerner or West Coast dweller as barbecued turkey is to a New Englander), King's description of a cold and dismal landscape corresponds perfectly with Louis Creed's journey to a site that remains in active opposition to his best intentions and personal needs. As Louis makes his way past the deadfall and into the malevolent realm of the ancient Wendigo, a fierce combination of wind and cold assaults him. Certainly, the Maine geography and the climate of this particular night are meant to highlight the fact that the Wendigo is as much at home in this misanthropic surrounding as Louis Creed is not: "The wind was sharper, colder, quickly numbing his face. *Are we above the treeline?* he wondered. He looked up and saw a billion stars, cold lights in the darkness. Never in his life had the stars made him feel so completely small, infinitesimal, without meaning. He asked himself the old question—*is there anything intelligent out there?*—and instead of wonder, the thought brought a horrid cold feeling, as if he had asked himself what it might be like to eat a handful of squirming bugs."[23]

Like Hawthorne's voyagers into the forests, King's characters seldom feel a sense of pastoral harmony with the Maine landscape. His novels are not romantic postcard descriptions of a sojourn in nature; quite the opposite. The rural atmosphere of Maine is frequently a hostile and savage place composed of forces indifferent to human welfare, as well as an environment where malefic supernatural energies reside.

In his treatment of the wilderness, King is even less a transcendentalist than Hawthorne. Within the New World forest, the latter imagined a bifurcated vision: the danger of Faustian temptation as well as the possibility for rebirth and transcendence. As Reginald Cook maintains in "The Forest of Young Goodman Brown's Night," Hawthorne's woods open to reveal the range of possibilities in the human soul, "the form its guilt takes, the contributions of grace and election, the sense of justice, the invocation of mercy."[24] For those characters such as Reuben Bourne and Dimmesdale, whose journeys bring them to a truer measure of their sin and a deeper appreciation of self-deception (along with the humility that attends such revelations), the woods serve as a vehicle for self-enlightenment and growth. In this sense, Hawthorne's New England wilderness sometimes serves in the capacity of moral educator, providing his protagonists with the opportunity to confer new identities upon themselves.

The sinful encounter in the forest, however, does not always liberate Hawthorne's characters. Although they come to associate the woods with evil, Ethan Brand and Goodman Brown refuse to accept the necessary self-discipline and humility that are prerequisites for personal development in Hawthorne's fiction. One might say that Brand and Brown have rejected the advice Hawthorne provides in the sketch "Fancy's Show Box"—that "man must not disdain his brotherhood, even with the guiltiest. . . . Penitence must kneel."[25] These egotists are overpowered by the dark truths they uncover deep beneath the pines and spruce. If not quite tragic, their falls result in a loss of faith in the efficacy of reason. Their solipsistic struggles isolate them; neither Brown nor Brand can overcome the irrational forces residing in the forest and, through symbolic extension, within their own minds. Faced with the realization that their universe is corrupt, these characters become the agents of terror, madness, death, and disorder (Frank 1986, 207).

King's woods also harbor the reality of evil, and like Brown and Brand, his characters seldom triumph in their discovery of it. Usually the encounter with sin in the woods brings no transcendence, only a fate that resembles closely Goodman Brown's "dying hour [of] gloom" (Hawthorne, 148). In *The Tommyknockers* Bobbi Anderson literally stumbles over an alien spaceship buried in the woods behind her house. From the moment she makes physical contact with the protruding edge of the craft, she is drawn to (and doomed by) the evil energies residing within. Although she is warned by the prophetic voice of her dead grandfather (*"Leave it alone, Bobbi. It's dangerous—and you know that, too"*[26]) Anderson has too much in common with Hawthorne's inquisitive journeymen to heed his advice. The physical deterioration that distinguishes the "New and Improved" Bobbi corresponds to her moral disintegration, as she, like Hawthorne's Ethan Brand, willingly sacrifices everything she loves in order to pursue an intimate knowledge of evil.

But Bobbi is not the only person affected by the malevolent force within the woods. As the saucer is gradually unearthed, radiating an invisible pollution, the entire town of Haven falls under evil's influence; the forest extends the perimeters of its powers to include the civilized world. Hawthorne would have interpreted the communal fall of Haven as an opportunity to indulge in "one cry of despair and triumph . . . the communion of your race" (Hawthorne, 146). The collective awareness of sin, however, offers no solace in King's fiction. Haven's moral corruption merely serves to highlight the inherent destructiveness of human society and its essential capitulation in the face of evil's dominion. Thus, King's definition of moral heroism is the exact opposite of Hawthorne's: whereas isolation of the individual from the magnetic chain of the community assures self-destruction in Hawthorne, King insists that only by rejecting all identification with the values of the larger community is it possible for the individual to survive. Jim Gardener, Ruth McCausland, and Ev Hillman are the moral centers of *The Tommyknockers* because of their resistance to the evil that is transforming their town. Indeed, as King articulates in *Danse,* the necessity of repudiating the values of adult society and its collective sins is a core tenet in his fiction and can be traced throughout his canon, starting with *Rage* (one of the Bachman books King wrote years prior to *Carrie*) and extending to the Losers' Club in *It.* I suspect this distinction between King and Hawthorne is best explained in light of the latter's Puritan inheritance: Hawthorne held firm to the doctrine that the individual must acknowledge daily his collective bond with the human community of sin. In Waggoner's words, "No writer has ever placed a higher value on communion and community" (Waggoner, 11). Even Hester Prynne remains, in her lonely isolation, still on the edge of the community, serving it in her own way.

Hawthorne's attitude toward other aspects of the Puritan tradition, however, is not so easily defined. An ambivalence toward New England's history and his own ancestry exercised a tremendous influence on Hawthorne's writing, motivating him to return again and again to test Puritan premises and principles. Hawthorne's fiction examines continually the range and validity of Calvinist cosmology. Although he often detailed the abuses of a narrow Puritan society, Hawthorne also accepted the core Puritan tenet that individuals commit their worst transgressions in refusing to recognize evil in themselves and in failing to exert a greater measure of self-discipline. Its oppressive elements notwithstanding, Hawthorne found much to admire in his New England religious tradition.

Hawthorne's ambivalence toward his regional past resembles King's attitude toward his fictional inhabitants of Maine. While King, like Hawthorne, is highly critical of small-town New England communities and their institutions (the high schools in *Rage, Carrie,* and *Christine;* the socially sanctioned levels of violence and racism in *It;* child abuse in *The Body*), he often places individual Maine men and women in positions that require them to rise above their unassuming and oppressive origins to engage in heroic action. Characters such as Ben Mears (*'Salem's Lot*), Gordie LaChance and Chris Chambers (*The Body*), Jim Gardener (*The Tommyknockers*), Johnny Smith (*The Dead Zone*), Speedy Parker (*The Talisman*), Frannie Goldsmith (*The Stand*), and the members of the Losers' Club share much in common with Hawthorne's quintessential heroine Hester Prynne. Like her, these are individuals of few words, but they are all fiercely independent people in possession of intrinsic and uncomplicated moral codes that remain consistent in the face of societal challenges. Each conforms to the thesis King presents at the conclusion of *Danse,* that morality "proceeds simply from a good heart—which has little to do with ridiculous posturings and happily-ever-afterings—and that immortality proceeds from a lack of care, from shoddy observation, and from prostitution . . . for some sort of gain, monetary or otherwise" (*DM,* 403).

These protagonists have no need for ostentatious behavior; the quiet dignity of their natures is as characteristic of the New England personality as the simple acceptance of the harsh winter climate. Johnny Smith, for example, possesses a tremendous paranormal insight that allows him to know the secret motivations of others. Instead of exploiting this attribute for his own advantage, however, Smith applies it for the benefit of others by saving a group of young men and women from a fire at a local restaurant, helping police to capture a murderer-rapist, and exposing the true personality of presidential candidate Greg Stillson.

King's positive attitude toward the natives of Maine, however, is always qualified by an emphasis on the individual rather than the community. Burton Hatlen recognizes a "powerful ambivalence toward Maine" running through all of King's novels (Hatlen, 50). Recalling Hawthorne, with his mixed perspective on the contributions of New England Puritanism, King seems to understand intuitively that while the small-town Maine environment is capable of producing morally heroic individuals, it can destroy others because of its acute degree of pride of isolation, pressure to conform, and lack of compassion. Harold Lauder, Joe Chamber (*Cujo*), Frank Dodd (*The Dead Zone*), Mrs. Carmody (*The Mist*), and the adults of Jerusalem's Lot, Castle Rock, Haven, and Derry are products of Maine's darker side. Devoid of any genuine love for others, these characters appear to share much in common with the cruel and callous elements King and Hawthorne often affiliate with New England's unsympathetic natural geography and climate. These natives retreat into the self-destruction that attends human isolation in a state with one of the highest suicide rates in America. Their repudiation of humankind is highlighted through the mechanical imagery King frequently associates with each of them, from the motorcycle that eventually seals Harold Lauder's annihilation on a bleak mountainside to the machinery of Joe Chamber's auto-repair shop. As Hatlen concludes, "How many writers before King have so clearly delineated the hard, self-destructive streak that we find in so many Maine people? Edwin Arlington Robinson maybe—but I can't think of anyone else" (Hatlen, 57).

In Hawthorne's *House of the Seven Gables* a legacy of human guilt and sin infests the Pyncheon mansion and continues to manifest itself in generations of inhabitants within the house; the taint even extends to include the larger community of the town itself. The decayed mansion carries with it the symbolic depth of Hester's scarlet letter. It symbolizes all those human motives—avarice, selfishness, egotism—that represent the inescapable reality of the past's influence on the present. Maule's curse is born of successive generations of familial commitment to a tradition of selfish individualism at the expense of compassion and morality. Alfred Kazin highlights this particular point when he suggests that "Hawthorne would have agreed with Marx: the dead generations weigh on the living like an incubus. Unlike Marx, Hawthorne felt that the past, not the future, was his opening to the imagination."[27]

From the Castle of Otranto, to the Usher mansion and the House of the Seven Gables, to Shirley Jackson's Hill House, and right up to the doors of the Overlook Hotel itself, the haunted house has represented, as King reminds us in *Danse*, "an image of authoritarianism, of imprisonment, or of 'confining narcissism' . . . a growing obsession with one's own problems; a turning inward instead of a growing outward. The American gothic provides a closed loop of character, and in what might be termed a psychological pathetic fallacy, the physical surroundings often mimic the inward-turning of the characters themselves" (*DM*, 281). The "imprisonment" or "confining narcissism" to which King alludes is actually the dead weight of the past, especially the dead weight of family heritage. The pride of the founding father who erects a metaphoric and literal house and then demands that his descendants live in it is a central motif used by King's Gothic predecessors—most notably Poe and Faulkner, but Hawthorne as well.

In King's novels *'Salem's Lot, Cujo, The Body, It,* and *The Tommyknockers,* familial moral pollution is indicative of a larger social condition. Entire Maine communities are revealed to be highly susceptible to evil's dominion. The majority of King's nuclear families and the municipalities in which they reside are characterized by a senseless arrangement of vulgar appetites. Motion has replaced direction, impulse has replaced moral choice, and love has been reduced to a process of mutual cannibalism. Parents who are abused by jobs and spouses in turn abuse their children, their offspring thus learn to abuse their siblings and other children, and the cycle continues over the years until it spirals out of control. The legacy of a guilty past, found in the long tradition of the haunted house, is omnipresent in the suburban neighborhoods of King's fiction. Following a particularly gruesome outburst of communal violence, Pennywise resurfaces to stalk Derry's children in the novel *It,* suggesting that the town must somehow compensate for its past moral transgressions by sacrificing a part of its future. In other words, Derry's curse parallels Maule's curse in *The House of the Seven Gables:* the stain of human corruption is passed down from one generation to another, and because the evil is never truly exculpated, each generation is even more debilitated than the one preceding it. Derry is indeed "a feeding place for animals,"[28] possessing all the unsavory aspects of modern America found in King's other fictional landscapes. In Derry, however, the vast corruption King describes in *The Talisman* and *The Stand* is contained in one Maine city, concentrated and festering within individual families and within the various social institutions that are the basis of the community.

Like Hawthorne's Pyncheon house, King's Jerusalem's Lot, Haven, Castle Rock, and Derry embody and engender corruption. Their pasts share similar elements of human cruelty and infamous behavior on a grand scale. Just as the sin that remains unpunished in the Pyncheon legacy affects future generations, the evil that dominates the small Maine towns in King's fiction appears to be generational, the natural consequence of original sin and American citizenship.

That the works of Stephen King should remind us of Nathaniel Hawthorne's should come as no great surprise to anyone who has read *Danse* carefully and recognizes the mythic qualities in the works of both authors. They are both historical novelists as well as novelists of place. King writes in a time and about a region in which the social and cultural conditions resemble those that surrounded Hawthorne. Maine was a part of the state of Massachusetts until 1820, and it can easily be envisioned as being in the same colonial, sylvan, and Calvinistic strangleholds as its southern neighbor. Traditional values, religious beliefs, and a general way of life were as sharply challenged in Hawthorne's Massachusetts as they are currently challenged in King's Maine. Indeed, King is a regionalist in much the same way that Hawthorne was: each sensed that the real meanings behind the history and physical entities of a particular place could be fathomed only after great study—and what better laboratory than one's own ancestral past and regional legacy? As King himself commented in a 1985 interview, "If you're going to live in a place all your life, and if you want to write seriously, you almost have to write about that place" (Underwood and Miller 1988, 150).

King returns over and over to descriptions of his native state, and he does so for some of the same reasons Hawthorne did in writing about New England: these regions are home to a particular people, language, customs, and set of traditions. For both writers, the past is both personal—a matter of family or town history—and a prologue to understanding the present; it is at once a gift and a burden. Both write best about their native region, transforming its particularities into fables. And both understand that the universal themes of great literature—human sin, fear, failure, and endurance—can be rendered truthfully only within settings and through personalities the artist has come to know on a firsthand basis. Much as Hawthorne relied on Puritan New England as a setting for describing and recreating the foibles and sins that are the patrimony of humankind, King views Maine as a deliberate backdrop for his own allegories—one that enables him to utilize specific elements from that culture in his portrayal of the moral conflicts common to us all.

Chapter Three

Evaluating The Bachman Books: *Rage, The Long Walk, Roadwork, The Running Man, Thinner, The Dark Half*

> He saw that all the cars were going to someplace where it was warm, someplace where there was business to transact or friends to greet or a loom of family life to pick up and stitch upon. He saw their indifference to strangers. He understood in a brief, cold instant of comprehension what Thomas Carlyle called the great dead locomotive of the world, rushing on and on.[1]

From 1977 to 1984 Stephen King published five novels under the pseudonym Richard Bachman. The work in at least two of these books predates *Carrie;* King began composing *Rage* and *The Long Walk* when he was a high-school senior. The five Bachman books were written at various points during the first decade of King's career as a writer. But each novel was subsequently revised prior to its release, and the publication dates of at least the last two novels, *The Running Man* (1982) and *Thinner* (1984), extend the Bachman work solidly into King's second decade. While *The Dark Half* (1989) was not published under the Bachman pseudonym, it represents a curious kind of closure of King's relationship with the invented Bachman. An author's note to the novel cites Bachman as an inspirational influence in the book's composition, suggesting that King's own experience with Richard Bachman served as a point of reference for developing the association between writer Thad Beaumont and his alter ego, George Stark. The dearth of interpretive literature available on the Bachman novels[2] lends importance to their inclusion in this critical study.

The Bachman books give rise to several intriguing questions that must be pondered in light of King's meteoric rise in his field: Why would an extraordinarily successful novelist choose to write under a pseudonym? Are these novels valuable works of fiction or merely the flawed products of a young writer struggling to discover his own voice? Would these books command serious interest from critics and scholars if they were indeed written by a Richard Bachman instead of by Stephen King? And to what extent do these narratives possess important resonances to the rest of King's canon?

None of these questions is easily answered. In the 1985 essay "Why I Was Bachman" (which serves as an introduction to four of these novels, assembled under the title *The Bachman Books*) King explains that his decision to publish under a pseudonym was motivated primarily out of a perverse curiosity. Like a child in possession of a wounded bird he has nursed back to health, King wished to see if his fiction could fly without his brand-name help: "Of course we'll never know now, will we? Bachman died with that question—is it work that takes you to the top or is it all just a lottery?—still unanswered." It is certainly true that the Bachman books alone would not have made their author a millionaire, but as King reminds us, "*Thinner* did 28,000 copies when Bachman was the author and 280,000 copies when Steve King became the author."[3]

The single greatest drawback of the Bachman series is that the characters in all the novels are neither well developed nor multidimensional. These books rely almost exclusively upon their plots, which vary in terms of believability and depth; the absence of a Louis Creed, Jack Torrance, Paul Sheldon, or even a Harold Lauder among the characters is sorely missed. These tales do suggest the skill that eventually produced *The Shining, Pet Sematary*, and *Misery*, but the Bachman books are weakest on what is the most enduring quality of King's best work: the characters' interpersonal dynamics and psychological conflicts.

The five Bachman novels are uneven in their capabilities. *The Long Walk* and *The Running Man* are perhaps the best of the group in terms of plot development and sustained suspense. *Rage* in particular suffers from an overstretched reliance on Freudian exegesis. The oedipal hostility of its young male protagonist toward his father and his equally powerful attraction toward his mother serve as the primary justifications for Charlie Decker's spontaneous and cold-blooded murders. Even less plausibly, Charlie's violent rebellion against all authority is not only condoned but personally embraced by his classmate "hostages." In less than a day he has tapped into the collective adolescent rage of his fellow students, and with the exception of only one Nazi-to-be, the class accepts and identifies with Charlie's acts of nihilism, spontaneously according him hero status.

Their weakest psychological and narrative moments notwithstanding, these books are not easily dismissed. So much of what King examines in them is about people being disenfranchised of power on several levels: personal, familial, societal. The central protagonist in each of these texts is a highly frustrated male with a proclivity toward violence and a certain fascination with fame. King suggests that the suicidal impulse that is found to a greater or lesser extent in all of these young men is driven equally by the current emptiness of their personal lives and the quest somehow to transcend this anomie by becoming the center, however briefly, of local and / or national attention.

In order to attain such status, several of King's protagonists employ the medium of television. Consequently, *Rage, The Long Walk, Roadwork,* and *The Running Man* are intense, if sometimes overdramatized, studies of television's capacity for shaping public opinion and transforming individuals. In *The Long Walk* and *The Running Man* the medium functions exclusively as a tool for a repressive government of the future. In both books the rules of journalistic objectivity are abandoned completely; moral questions regarding the legitimacy of the state's actions are never raised, much less explored. The individual is always singled out for moral scrutiny, with an emphasis on citing the punitive consequences for perceived failings. Each expression of individuality or defiance is violently silenced with a bullet; an abundance of such gruesome scenes is filmed and eagerly consumed by an American audience anxious to vent its collective repression through the deaths of its martyrs. The televised "sporting contests" that are the heart of these two books and to which everything else becomes subordinate are sanctioned by a totalitarian regime that desires to impress upon its citizenry the need for conformity and obedience.

The state employs television, a medium oriented primarily toward a huge and potentially volatile mass public, to redirect public pressure away from its daily acts of ethical misconduct and toward the grisly illustrations of what inevitably occurs to those who choose to exist outside the mainstream. This black-and-white perspective of the world is no mere hyperbolization of the medium. As Daniel C. Hallin argued recently, in the past decade American newscasters have tended to capitalize on the "new patriotism" of the Reagan era, reversing a shift toward the more nuanced reporting that resulted from the movements and crises of the sixties and instead presenting the world as a great single-ideology battleground between good and evil—with Americans as the embodiment of good.[4] *The Long Walk* and *The Running Man*'s futuristic portraits of an unholy alliance between the state and television are therefore neither the stuff of fiction nor mere speculations on the future: "In a way, Dan Rather is as much a politician as Ronald Reagan, not personally, but on behalf of his news organization. He goes before the public every day to appeal for 'votes.' And just as politicans have often found that it is more effective to wrap oneself in the flag and praise the wisdom of the People than to get involved in controversial political issues, so in recent years has television" (Hallin, 38–39).

The strength of the Bachman books is found in King's explorations of similar sociopolitical themes and interpersonal conflicts, which in the last two decades have emerged as some of the most significant and serious contributions of his canon. King possesses an acute awareness of the dangers threatening American civil liberties in the age of Jessie Helms and Ronald Reagan. And his fiction has always reflected a certain fascination with—some might call it a paranoia about—the monolithic machinery of American bureaucracy and its ability to complicate and manipulate the lives of individual Americans with remorseless consistency. As the novelist reminds us in the interview that begins this book, "I am not merely dealing with the surreal and the fantastic, but more important, using the surreal and the fantastic to examine the motivations of people and the society and institutions they create."

The Bachman books suggest the world of naturalist literature—particularly the works of two writers who strongly influenced King's career, Frank Norris and Thomas Hardy, insofar as the Bachman tales highlight men and women who are victims of a cruel fate. Sometimes this fate takes the form of bad fortune—for example, the accidental murder in *Thinner*—but most often characters find themselves helplessly lost in an environment that is either indifferent to their welfare or actively opposed to it. Hardy, the author of *Tess* and *Jude the Obscure,* would have found the Bachman novels quite interesting. Like Hardy's Tess and Norris's McTeague, the Bachman characters are distinguished by their sense of entrapment. No matter how they struggle, even those who are survivors in these tales are overwhelmed by inevitable forces—the force of biological nature in *The Long Walk* and *Thinner,* the force of inflexible authority figures in *Rage,* the force of television and its dominating presence in *The Running Man,* and the force of "modern progress" in *Roadwork.* Michael Collings summarizes the naturalistic qualities that give shape to the environments of these texts: "Isolation in turn suggests helplessness, a final motif that unifies the Bachman novels and makes them an inherent part of King's imagined universe. In spite of everything—pain, suffering, death—no one can finally do anything. Characters become enmeshed by social pressure, politics, the external environment; they can no longer control themselves, their actions, or the actions of others" (Collings, 17–18).

These are not novels highlighting the transcendent qualities of either human beings or the societies they create. In this sense, perhaps more than in any other, they reflect the work of a young writer; they are constrained by a narrowing range of possibilities. Perhaps it takes a more mature artist to capture the full dimensionality of human life and render it plausible. But neither are these novels entirely pessimistic. Like so many examples from the naturalist school, these are books that suggest the need for critical alternatives through implication. Moreover, there are moments—albeit ephemeral —in each of these texts when the capacity for human fellowship, so enduring a presence in *The Shining, The Body, It,* and *The Talisman,* provides the main character his only measure of comfort.

Pedagogy of the Oppressed: *Rage*

Early in *Rage,* Charlie Decker, the novel's protagonist, recalls an event from his adolescence. Awakened from a deep sleep during a camping trip with his father and several other adult males, Charlie overhears his drunken father discussing the precise manner in which he would punish any act of sexual infidelity by his wife. He promises emasculation for any man caught with his spouse, but his most vicious retribution would be reserved for the woman: "The Cherokees used to slit their noses. The idea was to put a cunt right up on their faces so everyone in the tribe could see what part of them got them in trouble."[5] As Charlie listens to his father's gruesome speculations, he suffers tremendous cramps from a need to urinate. Later that afternoon, while watching his father slit open the underbelly of a slain deer, Charlie vomits his breakfast.

Understanding the significance of this early scene is crucial to appreciating Charlie's behavior later in the novel. Throughout this book Charlie Decker aligns himself with the oppressed—particularly his young female classmates, victims of sexual oppression—and their struggle against authority, specifically patriarchal authority. In the camping scene just described, Charlie identifies with his mother and the disemboweled deer. Moreover, Charlie's own unconscious incestuous urge aligns him with the hypothetical suitor his father threatens to castrate. The lower abdominal pains he feels each time his father employs, or even makes reference to using, his hunting knife symbolize Charlie's rejection of phallic domination over the feminine. Indeed, when Charlie vomits after witnessing the deer's evisceration, his father eyes him with "contempt and disappointment" (*R,* 16), for his son has obviously failed in this masculine rite of passage. This scorn translates into Charlie's inability to respect authority of any sort. His violent rebellion in his high-school classroom is a challenge to at least three patriarchal entities: the (police) state, the psychiatric / counseling profession, and the school administration. The rage Charlie directs at these authority symbols has its origins in his rejection of his father.

As evinced in works that follow *Rage* (most notably *The Shining, Firestarter,* and *It*), the real monsters in King's canon are always human, and more often than not, they take the form of adult males who erect and maintain elaborate bureaucratic systems of control. Decker's frustration and anger while enmeshed in these systems in some ways presages the experiences of most subsequent male adolescents in King's fiction. Locked inside bodies that society deems in need of domesticating, King's young men are surrounded by restriction and denial. They are the progeny of failed institutions that have not fostered critical inquiry. While in careful preparation for a lifetime of adherence to the status quo, King's angry young men refuse to be processed. And because of the nature of the institutions themselves, King's protagonists, especially in the Bachman books, view violence as one of their few remaining options.

King's portraits of American suburban life are often alarmingly accurate: under the surface, in the modest split-level home with central heating, occupied by college-educated parents and children with potential for future success, lurk some disquieting realities. Charlie knows about rules and authority, but he knows almost nothing of love and affection; he has been taught the necessity of self-control and repression, but not how to channel his tremendous energies into constructive release; and while his school and parents labor to inculcate in him civilized virtues through lectures and books, the alacrity with which they employ violence undermines the sincerity of their efforts.

The classroom hostage crisis that Charlie initiates is partly indicative of his personal and social alienation and partly a mirror to the violence inherent in his father, his community, and his culture. Decker's own actions occur out of an insistence that the authorities confront the truth of their enterprise; no longer can they hide behind the rhetoric of Frank Philbrick's bureaucratic double-talk or the psychobabble of Don Grace. Thus, Charlie's use of violence (perpetrated against adult authority figures; no students are injured or shot) is similar to what occurs with such frequency in the short stories of Flannery O'Connor: it represents a final and deliberate moment when truth seeks to break through the false barriers of personal and social illusion. As Charlie announces to Tom Denver, principal of the high school, "Up to now you haven't had to give much of a rip *how* I felt. But I'm out of your filing cabinet now. . . . I'm not just a record you can lock up at three in the afternoon. Have you got it?" (*R*, 36).

As Charlie's rebellion is centered on the various levels of patriarchal authority, his student-hostages come to direct their own adolescent frustration against Ted Jones. The students appear to recognize and accept Charlie as one of their own; perhaps none of them would resort to his extreme form of antisocial behavior, but they all understand the spirit that has created the hostage situation. The students sympathize with Charlie because they sense intuitively that this is a conflict between the authorities and the disenfranchised. Conversely, they attack Ted Jones because they see him as a representative of what Michael Collings calls "the illusions foisted on children by parents, by school, and by society as a whole" (Collings, 39). Ted is a trenchant reminder to all of them of the hypocrisy and cruelty that is at the center of the patriarchal system Charlie and King attack: "Sometimes, now, it seems to me that Ted was at the center of it all, not me. It seems that Ted goaded them all into the people they were not . . . or into the people they really were" (*R*, 72).

This helps to explain why the class never attempts to criticize, much less physically overpower, their captor. On the other hand, Ted is subject to an array of verbal and physical abuse from nearly every member of the class. Devoid of all innocence, Ted enters the league of the school and state authorities through his refined skills at manipulation and humiliation. He is symbolic of the adult world that all of these children have grown to hate, even though they are in the process of joining it. Indeed, it is interesting that by the end of the novel the hostages have graduated and begun their own transition into adult society. In a letter to the incarcerated Charlie Decker (who has been labelled criminally insane by the authorities who have failed to mold his behavior) we learn that most of Charlie's classmates are on their way to becoming future versions of Ted Jones. The students were capable of recognizing an affinity with Charlie only as long as they remained adolescents.

Highway to Hell: *The Long Walk*

Like the other Bachman books, *Rage* highlights the naturalist influence in King's fiction: the individual is pitted against the social forces of conformity and standardization. *The Long Walk* also focuses on adolescent isolation, but it advances the degree to which the adolescent community is capable of gaining insight into the destructive nature of society and the state. The largely unseen police force that torments and, at one point, attempts to assassinate Charlie Decker becomes the single most dominant entity in *The Long Walk*. In *Rage*, the rage that Decker's classmates direct at Ted Jones remains only partially understood by the students themselves. The reader identifies the connection between their assault and Decker's own repudiation of his society's system of control, but the conclusion of *Rage* suggests that the students themselves fail to move beyond their personal antipathy for Jones to a larger realization of what his personality represents in social terms. The boy-men contestants in *The Long Walk*, on the other hand, are brought to a dramatic awareness of the relationship between their personal destinies and the social environment that shapes and controls the Long Walk.

The real antagonist in *Rage* and *The Long Walk* is a bureaucratic regime sanctioned by a repressive state under a veneer of liberal humanism. Beneath this veneer is a ruthlessness that permeates all of society's institutions. In *The Long Walk* Ray Garraty and the other athletes are watched and monitored by soldiers during every minute of a race in which the participants must neither stop nor fall behind a prescribed pace. When the rules of the game are violated on more than three occasions in any given hour the contestant is executed immediately. This degree of attentiveness highlights the omnipresent nature of the fascist state and its ultimate need to control every facet of a society's existence. The Walk itself is a symbol for the regimented social behavior dictated by the authorities in control: walk to the beat of our drummer or die.

A character called the Major epitomizes the role of the state in this book. Although he is seldom present physically, his presence is always felt by the contestants in the race. He is less a man than a mechanical entity: "you could set your watch by the Major. . . . His face was expressionless and the reflector sunglasses hid his eyes."[6] The Major is clearly a prototype for fascistic personalities in later King novels—Flagg in *The Stand* and *Eyes of the Dragon*, Morgan of Orris in *The Talisman,* Stillson in *The Dead Zone.* All of these military men have sacrificed their humanity to the advancement of a system in which power reigns over morality. Like the Major, these other characters reflect the worst tendencies of the despotic mind: the will to sacrifice individuals in the perpetuation of a system that scorns liberty and individual rights. Garraty's father labels such personalities appropriately in the first chapter, just before he disappears, when he describes the Major as "the rarest and most dangerous monster any nation [could] produce, a society-supported sociopath" (*LW,* 145).

Both *The Long Walk* and *The Running Man* should also be read as somber commentaries on professional American sport and its spectators. The crowds in these novels resemble bloodthirsty mobs wagering maniacally over contests of mayhem and violence. Moreover, as in many contemporary sports, the emotional intensity in King's blood trials incites a degree of sexual arousal within the crowd and the participants alike: "Garraty ran over to the side of the road. The girl saw his number and squealed. She threw herself at him and kissed him hard. Garraty was suddenly, sweatily aroused. He kissed back vigorously" (*LW*, 151). *The Running Man* and *The Long Walk* push the American fetish for competitive sport to its furthest extreme. Primitive drives—sex, survival, violence—are stimulated in each event, and as the danger increases, the urge to indulge these drives intensifies as well. As a result, the crowd is left emotionally drained when the contest is concluded (one might compare their collective exhaustion to that of the audience at an emotionally charged football game played by two equally competitive teams). The brutality of the contest purges the crowd of its frustration and disaffection while leaving it too exhausted to consider the political origins of those emotions.

Even as the respective athletic contests in *The Long Walk* and *The Running Man* are meant to aid the state in its fascistic quest of absolute domination over its citizenry, the individual contestants are presented the ironic opportunity for political insights and action. In the actual physical struggle of these games, King's protagonists penetrate the bleakness of the societies in which they live, of their value systems and power configurations, and seem to acknowledge for the first time the thoroughness of their disaffection. Just as Hemingway's world-weary war veterans Nick Adams, Jake Barnes, Frederick Henry, and Harold Krebs no longer feel connected to their respective societies because of the dirty business those societies have foisted upon them through war experience, King's Garraty and his friend McVries become more socially critical as the Walk unfolds.[7] Not only do they become less and less respectful of the military attendants who deliver verbal warnings and death bullets with mechanical indifference; both boys glimpse an alternative to the spirit of alienation that served as the initial motivation for their entry into the race.

Late in the novel one of the participants, Collie Parker, launches an assault against the soldiers who referee the race. After killing several of them he turns to his fellow contestants and urges them to join in his symbolic coup (*LW*, 306). He invites others to recognize that opportunity for survival against this regime can be taken only by individuals working together to overthrow it. Garraty and McVries unconsciously support this principle throughout the novel, as they are the only participants in the contest who willingly lend aid to the other athletes. As the government seeks to isolate the Walkers into interpersonal competition, the genuine risks McVries and Garraty undertake in support of one another distinguish them from the soldiers, the spectators who line the road scenting blood, and the other Walkers.

Unfortunately, Parker's cry for unity and rebellion proves too ambitious a challenge for McVries and Garraty. In their decision to participate in the Long Walk, these boy-men have unwittingly capitulated to their government's sadistic system of control. Although most of the athletes despise the state, their participation in the Long Walk helps to provide it public legitimation. The fact that the Walkers consciously enter a race that is a "stacked deck" (*LW,* 280) is perhaps the greatest indictment of the society that sponsors the event. But it also indicates that involvement in the Long Walk is motivated by such pessimism about the future—financial, personal, political—that the race represents the one chance for the Walkers to escape the death-in-life circumstances of mature citizenship. As one contestant acknowledges, "I feel qualified to participate in the Long Walk because I am one useless S.O.B. and the world would be better off without me" (*LW,* 285). Consequently, when Parker offers Garraty and McVries the chance to transcend their political impotence and despair, a lifetime's timidity, nurtured under the heel of a despotic regime, forces them to forego the opportunity (*LW,* 307).

At Home for the Holidays: *Roadwork*

George Dawes continues the rebellion of Charlie Decker in *Rage,* only Dawes is several years older, in possession of a greater array of firepower, and frequently extends the strictly personal angst of Decker into global indictments. Of all the Bachman characters, Dawes probably comes closest to Richards's enlightened fury in *The Running Man.* Although their acts of violence may be futile, both men are socially astute enough to understand why they must commit them. And while Dawes is more politically and historically conscious than Decker, the two characters would surely sympathize with one another: like the schoolboy, Dawes's rejection of socially acceptable roles and patterns of appropriate behavior leaves him free to embrace a wholly new construction of reality.

Whereas *Rage* is a novel about the personal anxieties of an adolescent boy and his anger toward authority, *Roadwork* is a commentary on the changing landscape of contemporary America. Dawes's obsession with the construction of an interstate highway that will destroy his home and community is a metaphor for the multileveled arena of social change taking place all around him. He is a man who has come to measure his life in terms of his losses: his youth, his wife's erotic love, his only child (to a brain tumor). But these personal losses merely underscore his existential isolation as an insecure citizen of an unstable world.

The sociopolitical context for this novel of the seventies resonates throughout the text. The novel's backdrop comprises recent reminders of American vulnerability: the energy crisis that incapacitated the nation's lifestyle, the defeat in Vietnam (frequently referenced), and the formation of callous multinational corporate takeovers without concern for loyalties or principles. Moreover, each of these events is juxtaposed with Dawes's sentimentalized memory of how much better the past compares with the disillusioned present. Dawes has lost both his job and his identity in the transition. The frustration that leads to the novel's violent conclusion is centered on Dawes's impotence in attempting to influence the new realities now shaping his life and his country's.

At the same time as *Roadwork* is a bitter cry against the onrush of progress at any cost, it is also a melancholic lament for a version of America that once existed—if not in reality, then at least in the imagination. Dawes yearns for the receding world of familial permanence, secure suburban neighborhoods, American morality abroad, and complacently bourgeois values and loyalties. Everywhere he looks, however, he sees an America in transition, ultimately highlighted in the plastic and concrete of a new housing development (*RW,* 360). Even Dawes's favorite tavern replaces its pinball games with computerized "bowl-a-score" machines (*RW,* 366). Each new change verifies Dawes's isolation in a world that he neither controls nor comprehends. Olivia, the young hitchhiker whom Dawes befriends and beds, is the only character who appreciates Dawes as a principled man, sensing that his values have somehow been violated by forces greater than himself.

Dawes's obsession with an immutable past and his need to strike violently against the symbols that dominate the present (e.g., the heavy construction equipment he vandalizes [*RW,* 439–49]) are illustrated in his way of dealing with the death of his son. Unlike his wife, whose desire to return to college (*RW,* 510) reflects her commitment to the future, Dawes is locked in the past; his terrible loss has not been resolved. He links the memory of his child to a happier and saner period in his own and his society's existence. The child's unexpected and abrupt demise highlights the instability and chaos of the present. The boy's inoperable brain tumor parallels Dawes's feeling of helplessness as a victim of a universe and a society that appear to operate haphazardly, devoid of moral design. The personal loss of his son to an illness that is beyond the scope of Dawes's comprehension becomes the filter through which he interprets recent global events and changes in his community.

The child dies of cancer, a disease that also takes a friend of Dawes's mother-in-law. As Susan Sontag has argued,[8] cancer is the most modern of diseases. It not only continues to deplete the world's population in defiance of science's attempts to conquer it, but it also serves as a metaphor for our times. It is the shadow attendant to the affluent life-style Americans cherish and continue to pursue. In *Roadwork* progress and cancer are inextricably linked: one cancer has killed Dawes's son; another is destroying his home and nation. Both appear to be inevitable conditions, inoperable realities of modern life that Dawes refuses to accept.

Dawes's romantic quest to assert his independence in the face of fate and authority affiliates him with the other Bachman protagonists. The concluding defense of his home—his last enclave in a world without meaning or respect for the individual—makes Dawes a curious kind of patriot; he is defending values that are fundamentally American, particularly the sanctity of private property. Yet, like the rebellions of the other Bachman antiheroes, Dawes's rebellion is ultimately self-destructive, and ironic as well, since his demolition of his house effectively completes the work of the state. In the end, the Bachman protagonists all attempt some version of suicide. As Michael Collings points out, these "characters sacrifice themselves, but nothing really changes. Only the individual's integrity, however distorted it might be, remains to give meaning to death" (Collings, 89). Like Decker, Garraty, McVries, and Richards in *The Running Man,* Dawes performs an act of defiance that is merely a gesture. But it is through that very act of defiance, in which he chooses the time of his death, that Dawes finally exerts at least a modicum of control over a destiny that was never really his to command.

Class Consciousness and Conflict: *The Running Man*

The Bachman books are more fantastic than horrific. Bearing greater similarities to Kafka than to Poe, these tales are less explorations of the supernatural or of terror than they are dark reflections of the present and future conditions of American politics and society. The protagonists participating in these living nightmares may be limited as characters because of the overwhelming conditions against which they must struggle, but King convincingly sketches the circumstances that produce their personal restriction. In fact, the strength of the Bachman novels lies in the use of fantastic events to emphasize a warped social milieu reminiscent of Kafka's fictional microcosm. *Rage* underscores the very real adolescent frustration that is responsible for current levels of violence and drug use and for the dropout rate in the American public school system; *Roadwork* highlights the loss of individuality and personal identity in the complexity of our ever-enlarging, bureaucratic world; *The Long Walk* and *The Running Man* are novels of hopelessness born of poverty and alienation. The national sporting contests featured in the latter two books have little to do with the true spirit of athletic competition and the lessons of good sportsmanship. Instead, they highlight the desperate economic circumstances that literally force young men into such violent "play," while also suggesting a dark collusion between sport and capitalism. These novels, although set in a futuristic America, accurately approximate current living conditions for many inner-city Americans. *The Running Man* in particular may feature a technology yet to come, but the fact that such advances have been employed in order to restrain those who have not benefited from them makes the book a contemporary portrait of the relationship between the oppressed and those who stand the most to gain from their continued oppression.

The Running Man begins where the other Bachman books conclude: in a surreal world where individuals are trapped by economic deprivation. But this novel is even more explicit than the others in indicting the state for its blatant failure to address the suffering of its citizens. The novel's landscape is gleaned from science fiction; it features an environment perhaps best represented in the film *Blade Runner*. Like *Blade Runner*, the novel conveys a vivid sense of the present-day social world through striking images of a postindustrial environment characterized by crowds, excessive technology, and urban decay. Both film and novel emphasize the repressive effects of an advanced technology on the quality of social life.[9]

Throughout *The Running Man* we see a detailed portrait of a polarized society. The hunt for Richards is meant to serve as a distraction from the impending class war fueled by economic disparity. Forced by the reality of his own poverty to participate in the deadly game, Richards is transformed by the Network into a human caricature, the "uptown apartment dweller's boogeyman."[10] Consequently, his death becomes a symbolic purging of the outsider—the metaphorical destruction of the social deviant. The television show "The Running Man" incites class tensions, inviting the middle class to identify and solidify its stereotyping of the lower class. At the same time, Richards's manufactured persona—the urban boogeyman—instills fear in the general populace, rich and poor alike, thereby justifying the need for a despotic police state in order to insure society's "protection."

The Running Man is a terrifying examination of the importance of class

position and wealth as determinants of survival. Ben Richards, because he is
stripped of such privileges, is turned into a public "criminal" hunted by the
very society responsible for his economic plight. His role as persecuted outsider heightens his class consciousness, and he thus wisely follows Killian's
advice to "stay close to your own people" (*RM,* 569). Richards trusts only
those individuals who are from his own disenfranchised class. They in turn
provide him with the loyalty and active assistance he needs to survive. It is
no accident that Stacey and Bradley lend help to Richards without hesita-
tion. As black youths struggling to endure in a divided world, they see
themselves and their people mirrored in Richards's plight.

The interpersonal relationship Richards maintains "with his own kind"
suggests a political survivalism that is unique to the Bachman books.
While McVries and Garraty fail to respond to Parker's call for revolutionary unity in *The Long Walk,* Richards is deeply affected by such a response
when it is articulated by Bradley. Their bond is solidified in a common hatred for the Network; more importantly, these characters come to recognize the need for revolutionary change and willingly sacrifice themselves
to this cause. Bradley's political activism motivates Richards and explains
why the latter chooses not to switch alliances and work for the Network at
the end of the novel. Although he no longer has a familial commitment
once his wife and child are killed, Richards has penetrated to the heart of
his society's moral bankruptcy. To serve this corruption in the role of its
Chief Hunter would be tantamount to scorning the sacrifices of Bradley
and Parrakis.

Thus, Richards's suicidal act of defiance links him to George Dawes in
Roadwork. But whereas Dawes remains entirely isolated, and whereas his
suicide embodies that isolation, Richards's death is far less self-enclosed.
Not only does Richards reject an offer to serve the authorities; he deliberately steers a jet liner into the Network headquarters. Moreover, each time
Richards sends a recorded tape to the Games commission, his message to
the Free-Vee audience is always political in nature, whether he is imploring
the populace to examine the government's massive air pollution cover-up or
cajoling the masses into rebellion. Unlike the other Bachman protagonists,
Richards pushes his social critique beyond himself. Another distinction between *Roadwork* and *The Running Man* is subtle but important: Dawes, acting alone, dies without making an impact on his society; Richards delays the
games only temporarily through his self-destruction, but his suicide nonetheless reflects a political commitment to others and to a world that is larger
than himself.

"Everybody pays, even for things they dint do": *Thinner*

In a curious way *Thinner* inverts the narrative structure common to the other Bachman books. Whereas the protagonists of the other texts begin as displaced individuals whose anger is equal to their alienation, Billy Halleck, the main character in *Thinner,* begins as an entrenched member of his suburban community. Moreover, unlike his Bachman brethren, Halleck embodies the values of this community. That he starts the novel as an obese attorney who owns a big, powerful car and lives with a beautiful wife and daughter suggests the full measure of his entrenchment in an affluent life-style.

However, by the conclusion of *Thinner,* Halleck comes to share a full identification with the other Bachman characters. Like them, he gradually gains insight into the darkness of his society. And in a rejection similar to that of Dawes in *Roadwork* or Richards in *The Running Man,* Halleck completely eschews the middle-class institutions with which he once so strongly identified.

As a consequence of his involvement in the accidental death of a Gypsy woman, Halleck is cursed by her father: the corpulent lawyer is condemned to lose weight until he is reduced to a mere skeleton. As the Gypsy curse takes effect, Halleck discovers that he is no longer an acceptable member of the community; he has become a grotesque outsider. As a result of this change in status, he begins to appreciate for the first time the full range of moral failings that delineate life in Fairview, Connecticut. Essentially, Halleck's curse transforms him into a Gypsy—one who knows what it is like to be rejected because he is different: *"The white man from town lived there,* he thought, *but I'm not sure he's coming home, after all—this fellow crossing the lawn feels more like a Gypsy. A very thin Gypsy."*[11]

As Halleck relinquishes layers of flesh, his eyes are opened to the negative aspects of his middle-class community and his own complacency. As his skeleton gradually reveals itself to his disbelieving eyes, Halleck's psychological sense of self-importance is correspondingly diminished. He once thought of the displaced Gypsies only as a means of confirming his own security and social standing: "We need the Gypsies, because if you don't have someone to run out of town once in a while, how are you going to know you yourself belong there?" (*Thin,* 284). The curse, however, is really a lesson in humility: as Halleck is forced to recognize the flaws in himself, in his marriage, and in his suburban world, the Gypsies—formerly invisible in his eyes—gain in visibility. Billy's plight opens him to the reality of the Gypsies as human beings. His desire to confront Lemke, the man who delivered the curse, is more than a self-preservationist urge; Halleck also seeks to ease his own moral burden. "I want to tell [Lemke] that there was no evil intent. I want to ask him if he'll reverse what he's done . . . always assuming it's in his power to do so. But what I want to do more than anything else, I find, is to simply apologize. For me . . . for you . . . for all of Fairview" (*Thin*, 155–56).

Like Richards in *The Running Man* and Dawes in *Roadwork,* Halleck experiences an expansion of his ethical and political consciousness as a direct result of his personal suffering and circumstances. In the end, like Dawes, Halleck finds himself alone. Deserted by family and friends who prove themselves unworthy, Halleck turns to another outsider, Ginelli, a mafioso thug, for assistance and sympathy. This is significant insofar as it indicates the magnitude of the change in Halleck. He learns that he no longer possesses much in common with the individuals in his former social class. His faith in society and its institutions is so thoroughly weakened that his only source of human fellowship is with a mobster he once represented as legal counsel. Like Richards in *The Running Man,* Halleck's finds relief for his social disaffection only in the company of another pariah.

Thinner bears one final point of comparison with the other Bachman books. This is a novel that suggests human bondage to a cruel and inhuman fate. Although Lemke would have us believe that Billy alone is responsible for the death of the Gypsy woman, Halleck understands the true difficulty of "finally sorting out where an injustice really lay" (*Thin*, 200). He accepts his own "piece of the pie" but also argues convincingly that other agents are involved when a human tragedy occurs—including the absence of dumb luck. Halleck's own acknowledged share of responsibility for the injustice that determines the scope of this novel certainly enlarges his spirit, but in the end he is as much a victim of fate's capriciousness as is the Gypsy woman who elects to jaywalk in front of his car. Like the other Bachman protagonists, Billy Halleck finds himself trapped in circumstances over which he is essentially powerless. Even the destruction of his daughter, the only person in Halleck's life to whom he remains devoted, is the result of yet another accident.

Reading Bachman through a Glass Darkly: *The Dark Half*

The Bachman books are of primary importance to King scholarship because they supply evidence of the writer's earliest concerns. These books served as a kind of laboratory for the young King: in them we trace his growing dissatisfaction with American political life and the machinations of the state, his fascination with developing a mythology of Maine, and an emerging focus on the individual who must confront a chaotic and meaningless world. These are perhaps the three major connecting points between Richard Bachman's work and that of Stephen King. But just as critical to this discussion are the differences that distinguish the Bachman canon from King's. It remains my belief that Bachman supplied King with a necessary alter ego—not just with a pseudonym in an age when publishing schedules make such artificial constructions convenient but, more significant, with a voice to help release some of King's own literary demons. Bachman permitted King to indulge his darkest fantasies and speculations.

More than just mottled backdrops for the narratives, the Bachman landscapes depict a degraded social sphere that stimulates a number of contemporary anxieties. The future, according to Bachman, is devoid of love, stable relationships, and any real degree of sociopolitical freedom. The Bachman novels are bleak and relentless; none ends happily. This world-view, however, stands in solid contrast to the more balanced perspective found in King's other novels. Bachman's despair is only approximated in *Cujo* and *Pet Sematary*. The rest of King's canon offers at least some measure of redemption, and his best books—*The Shining, The Stand, The Dead Zone, The Talisman, It,* and *Misery*—employ that redemptive potential as an effective counterbalance to the limits that impose themselves upon the individual.

This is not to argue that Bachman's vision is somehow separate from King's, but the Bachman work is best interpreted as representing a pessimistic side of King's psyche, an elaboration of the perspective that has led King to predict with chilling certainty that "our technology has outraced our morality. And I don't think its possible to stick the devil back in the box. I think that it will kill us all in the next twenty years."[12] Bachman remains unmoved by the power of love, the force that absolutely dominates King's best and most persuasive fiction. In short, the Bachman novels were written by the mind that would also produce Randall Flagg and Annie Wilkes—a mind who understands intimately the nihilistic impulse.

If Bachman can be seen as King's dark twin, their relationship forms an intriguing parallel to that between George Stark and his creator, Thad Beaumont, in the novel *The Dark Half*. In both instances the pseudonym functions as a dark (but apparently necessary) alter ego for the artist, an avenue for venting his most violent and pessimistic inclinations.[13] The details surrounding the invented union between Stark and Beaumont are explicitly rendered, and they clearly underscore King's intimate awareness of his own relationship with Bachman. Even information relevant to those individuals who knew about, protected, and eventually revealed King's pseudonym[14] corresponds closely to the fictional events that occur in *The Dark Half*.

Beaumont struggles to deny his relationship with Stark. Although he claims that "*Except in books, I've never killed anyone*" (*DH*, 140), this attempt to distance himself from his alter ego is the barest of rationalizations. In fact, Stark has his origins in Beaumont's psyche, literally and metaphorically. He is Beaumont's fetal twin as well as an extension of the writer's psychological id: "Thad thought of George Stark and shuddered a little. . . . He had, after all, built George Stark from the ground up" (*DH*, 143). Beaumont has not only indulged his dark urges in Stark's fiction; he has also profited financially from his popularity. No wonder, then, that Beaumont exhibits such a genuine reluctance to "bury" Stark in a mock-graveyard publicity stunt (*DH*, 28).

The inclusion of Wendy and William, Beaumont's identical twin children, is meant to suggest further the symbiotic relationship of Stark and Beaumont. Because each twin responds to every action of the other, Stark is an extension of Beaumont himself. The two appear to share even a capacity for mental telepathy. As Stark's real-life murder spree grows more visceral and extensive, Beaumont comes slowly to acknowledge the extent of their union:

"Stark might be calling from somewhere in New York City, but the two of them were tied together by the same invisible but undeniable bond that connected twins. They *were* twins, halves of the same whole, and Thad was terrified to find himself drifting out of his body, drifting along the phone line, not all the way to New York, no, but halfway; meeting the monster at the center of this umbilicus, in western Massachusetts, perhaps, the two of them meeting and merging again, as they had somehow met and merged every time he had put the cover on his typewriter and picked up one of those goddamned Berol Black Beauty pencils" (*DH*, 200).

The Dark Half fails as a novel because of the ambiguous quality of its central relationship. Although King makes a great effort to establish profound psychic correspondences between Beaumont and Stark, their union remains vague and unconvincing. While King means their nexus to be rendered in concrete and believable terms, the reader is never able to accept it as serious or plausible. The very emergence of Stark as a physical being, born from the discarded fetus in Beaumont's brain and then emerging from a false grave prepared for him in a Castle Rock cemetery, tends to weaken severely the character's link to the rich tradition of literary doppelgangers.

Unlike Stevenson's *Jekyll and Hyde,* whose split transformation is occasioned by scientific explanation, or Poe's William Wilson, whose alter ego is so effectively portrayed because he is invisible to everyone but himself, King's Stark is, confusingly, an independent agent yet fatally dependent upon Beaumont. This contradiction in the character is never clarified or resolved for the reader. Perhaps with this problem in mind, Christopher Lehmann-Haupt pointed out in his early review of the novel that "the hard work of explaining the plot's logic may account for why *The Dark Half* is unusually talky and cerebral for a thriller by Stephen King."[15] One moment we are asked to view Stark as a secret sharer of Beaumont's most private inclinations; the next minute these two men are as different from one another as a suburban professor and an urban street punk. What makes *The Dark Half* such a frustrating book is that these inconsistencies are not sufficiently explicated.

In his examination of the interrelationship between reader and novel, Edward Bullough argues that a work of fiction is most successful when the reader interacts with it is so completely as to be almost convinced the art is reality. The fine separation between the reader's involvement and his or her recognition that art is separate from real life (what Bullough calls "psychical distance") is necessary to ensure that the reader is drawn into a work of art to the point of "the utmost decrease of distance without its disappearance."[16] Thus, while the reader is ideally to maintain a disinterested perspective on the fiction, the narrative must make the reader care about the plot and the characters, their situations, values, fates, and credibility. While King is elsewhere often masterful at bridging the gap between reader and text, *The Dark Half* violates Bullough's theoretical principles because King never reduces the aesthetic distance enough to make the reader believe in, much less care about, the legitimacy of the Beaumont-Stark relationship. The reader senses that this novel's potential, like that of the fetus in young Beaumont's head, was never fully realized; its idea simply required a greater evolution in order to sustain itself.

In spite of the many similarities between Stark and Beaumont, *The Dark Half* revolves around the conflicts that serve to separate them. Bachman and King, I suspect, were never antagonists to the same extent. King has remarked in assessing the Bachman work, "If I had thought the Bachmans were bad books, or if I was publishing them out of a sense of vanity, then I wouldn't allow them to go out under any circumstances."[17] Bachman offered King the opportunity to explore a side of himself that is far removed from his image as a dedicated father and husband who is also an active participant in the community of Bangor, Maine. In the end Bachman served as a means of liberating King's art. If *The Dark Half* offers any real autobiographical insights into the relationship King shared with Bachman, it suggests that the more hopeful perspective contained in the fiction published under King's own name may have been possible only after Bachman had had his say. To whatever extent Bachman may have been King's adversary, he appears to have been a necessary one.

Chapter Four:
Science and the Apocalyptic Imagination: *The Talisman* and *The Tommyknockers*

It was clear that if I had an ideal reader anywhere in the world, it was probably Stephen King; and it was also clear to me that the reason for this was that his aims and ambitions were very close to my own. . . . [The] experience of first reading King was like that of suddenly discovering a long-lost family member—of finding a brother, really—and that is no exaggeration.[1]

Peter Straub's reflections on Stephen King, with the latter perceived in the dual roles of reader and writer, would be interesting and noteworthy even if the two men had never decided to coauthor a novel. That *The Talisman* (1984), a work so centered on family (both nuclear and extended) and on fraternal relationships, should emerge from their joint effort gives added significance to Straub's comments. A good portion of *The Talisman* concerns family: the quest to aid a dying mother / queen in her fight against cancer, the uncovering of the sobering truth about the deaths of a father and an uncle, and the discovery that a twin brother who died in infancy exists in a parallel universe. Jack Sawyer, the twelve-year-old boy who is at the center of these concerns, forms unexpected familial relationships with two men and a beast he encounters in his travels across America and in the mythological Territories—Speedy Parker, Richard Sloat, and Wolf. Although not related by blood to Sawyer, Speedy clearly serves as a surrogate for Jack's lost father, and Wolf and Richard make up for Jack's lack of of siblings.

According to Douglas Winter, the collaboration between King and Straub had been planned since 1977, the year when the two distinctive and successful writers first met in London and commenced their friendship. The story line for *The Talisman* was not established until Straub returned to the United States in 1980, but from that point on the book apparently unfolded quickly. Both men took turns writing alternate sections and experimenting freely with each other's established style and voice (Winter 1984, 158–59). As Straub recounts, "the book is full of little tricks between us where we're trying to fool the reader into thinking the other guy wrote it" (Underwood and Miller 1988, 172).

Although the last hundred pages of the novel are anticlimactic, labored, and in need of severe condensing, the remainder of the book is remarkably well plotted and fluidly paced. Straub's and King's joint writing voice in this book is seamless; I don't think it is possible to distinguish, at least from style alone, which of the two writers contributed a given chapter or section. This is no small accomplishment, especially since the author of *Ghost Story*, with its Jamesian diction and symmetry, produces strikingly formal prose, whereas King is known for his loose and colloquial style of narration. I suspect Straub and King nourished one another's writing in this enterprise; surely a book the size of *The Talisman* would not have been written in so short a period of time and at such a level of quality had the two writers not found major points of similarity along the way. Moreover, each learned something from the other. Straub felt that the collaboration made him more aware of narrative possibilities, "as if some rough spots were knocked off because of the closeness I had to the way Steve works." If Straub's narrative range was broadened through King's influence, the latter found himself paying greater attention to stylistic details: "I can't remember ever writing anything and being so conscious about what I was writing" (Underwood and Miller 1988, 173).

The Talisman borrows heavily from epics as diverse as Dante's *Divine Comedy* and Tolkien's *Lord of the Rings*. The concept of the hero was important to the coauthors, and in preparation for writing *The Talisman* they read several books about the epic hero, the meaning of the hero, stages of heroic development, the Christ figure, and apotheosis (Beahm, 286). King himself is deeply attracted to the epic design; *The Stand* (1979) prefigures *The Talisman* and is also about a westward journey across the United States, while *It*, which follows *The Talisman* two years later, is also epic in its dimensions, measuring a town's historical battle between good and evil. I will have more to say about the epic tradition and its connection to *The Talisman* later in this chapter. The significance of this tradition notwithstanding, the single most important literary influence on King and Straub's collaborative vision is not a formal epic at all but a colloquial narrative about a distinctly American adventure.

"Where the Water and Land Come Together": *Adventures of Huckleberry Finn* and *The Talisman*

From *The Talisman*'s epigraph to its concluding citation from *Tom Sawyer*, Mark Twain's inspiration pervades the narrative King and Straub published exactly 100 years after the release of *Huckleberry Finn*. Although his name is Sawyer, *The Talisman*'s adolescent protagonist has little in common with Twain's romantic idealist of the same name, whose sense of adventure is always greater than the risk involved. Jack Sawyer's real kin is the orphan-child friend of Tom Sawyer, Huck Finn. Huck's experiences on the Mississippi would allow him to empathize with the trials and brutality Jack encounters on his own American adventure. While Tom Sawyer's terrors are primarily self-constructed, Huck and Jack need to work constantly at repressing their imaginations. Terror is no mere abstraction for either of these boys; the real world provides them both with more than enough stimulation. One suspects that had Huck Finn had access to *The Talisman*'s Territories, he would have migrated there frequently (the very word *Territories* is used in conscious homage to Twain, although Huck Finn's territories are always more psychological than geographical, more mythical than real).

Like his fictional prototype from the nineteenth century, Jack Sawyer begins *The Talisman* under someone else's control. Huck must ascribe to the civilized virtues of Miss Watson, while Jack is transported, against his desires, from one end of the country to the other: "His mother was moving him through the world, twitching him from place to place; but what moved his mother?"[2] Like Twain's narrative, *The Talisman* highlights, through the metaphor of a geographical journey, the struggle of a young boy and his effort to pursue goodness in the face of worldly evil; a quest to retain a spirit of hope in spite of terrible experiences; and most important, a young man's attempt to maintain his identity and purpose in the face of forces that would strip him of both.

Huck's journey takes him south through Twain's and America's past. There Huck discovers a patriarchal world of violence and stupidity—a world amply characterized by Col. Sherburn, a man of mock gentility who defines his manhood by killing an unarmed drunk under the barest of provocations, and by the Duke and King, who rely upon their cultured hypocrisy to trick people out of their dollars and dignity. In *The Talisman* Jack's journey is west instead of south, but the violent portrait of America he discovers in both the Territories and contemporary America is profoundly reminiscent of Huck's landscape. (Moreover, *The Talisman* should be seen as a continuation of the general social critique traced throughout the Bachman novels in chapter 3.) The rural America Jack encounters bears much in common with the towns and villages Huck and Jim visit along the Mississippi. *Huckleberry Finn* and *The Talisman* are wide-angle portraits of humanity at its worst. Kindness and generosity are seldom found, while ignorance and greed are seemingly rewarded.

Smokey Updike and the Oatley Tap epitomize Jack's experiences on the road. The boy finds himself in a bondage (he keeps referring to the metaphor of the pitcher-plant) that neatly parallels Huck's servitude at the hands of the Duke and King. Huck and Jack are trapped by virtue of their innocence and vulnerability, manipulated by men without scruples who are interested only in obtaining power and lining their pockets.

In the societies delineated by Twain and by King and Straub, the dominant value system is embodied by *The Talisman*'s Morgan Sloat / Morgan Orris. This helps to explain why Jack feels Morgan is always somehow capable of monitoring his progress westward: the entire geography Jack traverses, like the shore world in *Huckleberry Finn*, is littered with individuals who wish to subject Jack to economic and/or psychological exploitation. As Jack quickly discovers, both the Territories and America itself are governed by some version of the Morgan ethic. The American capitalist has been setting the tone for society since the start of this country, and in exporting the doctrine of oppressed labor to the Territories, Morgan Sloat represents the most contemporary illustration of capitalist imperialism.

In light of this pessimistic portrait, it is not surprising that both *Huckleberry Finn* and *The Talisman* should also highlight the unholy alliance between religion and money. In *Huckleberry Finn* the word of God is used to justify even slavery, the most inhuman of acts, while in *The Talisman* a warped religious vision rationalizes the psychosexual exploitation of children in Sunlight Gardener's home.

In contrast to the bleak social backdrops for both *Huckleberry Finn* and *The Talisman*, the spirits of Huck and Jack are continually renewed by contact with black father figures. Nigger Jim and Speedy Parker exist outside the forces of alienation and violence that characterize the larger white culture in both books. Speedy is a blues musician, while Jim is a primitive mythologist. The music and folklore that have enriched these men are far removed from the sterility of Morgan Sloat and the society whose values he has both internalized and further warped. As a consequence, Jim and Speedy are immune to the dying spirit of the white world; they present an alternative vision rooted in nature and folk tradition. Speedy and Jim are uncorrupted by the mood of capitalist America, and they have none of the anguish that besets the men and women of the wasteland—the inhabitants of Twain's shore world and of the Oatley Tap.[3]

From conversation and interaction with Jim and Speedy, Huck and Jack gain strength against the despair that pervades their respective worlds. The climactic scene of *Huckleberry Finn* occurs when Huck elects to forsake the moral posturing of his society and "go to hell" rather than return Jim to the institution of slavery: "It was awful thoughts, and awful words, but they was said. And I let them stay said; and never thought no more about reforming. I shoved the whole thing out of my head; and said I would take up wickedness again, which was in my line, being brung up to it, and the other warn't."⁴ Several scenes in *The Talisman* parallel this moment, as Jack is forced to accept responsibility not only for Speedy (when the latter is injured on the California beach in chapter 40), but for Wolf and Richard Sloat as well. Significantly, Jack must assume the role of shepherd when Wolf is pulled from the Territories to modern America and, conversely, when Richard Sloat travels with Jack through the Blasted Lands in the Territories. Although these duties severely inconvenience Jack in his quest for the Talisman, they signal another level of maturity and ethical development in his personality. Just as Huck selects human compassion over social and religious dogma, Jack risks his life and his quest by refusing to abandon either Wolf or Richard. The journeys down the Mississippi and across America parallel one another insofar as they are really about the moral educations of Huck and Jack. The quests for Jim's freedom and the Talisman are finally inextricably related to this ends: before Jim can truly be free, Huck must understand the real value of freedom; before the Talisman can work its healing magic, Jack must possess a set of moral principles that makes him worthy of its powers ("Uncle Tommy had been fond of quoting a Chinese proverb that went: *The man whose life you save is your responsibility for the rest of your life.* Never mind the ducking, never mind the fancy footwork; Wolf was his responsibility" [*Tal*, 248]).

There are undoubtedly other points of comparison that link *The Talisman* to *Huckleberry Finn,* but the final one that should be raised here is the emphasis placed upon historical transitions in both novels. During the 1880s the tension between the belief in change and the awareness of the destructiveness of change was unavoidable. Twain was interested in drawing a preindustrial portrait of nineteenth-century America, even as he was forced to acknowledge the inevitable violation of an agrarian ideal. *Huckleberry Finn* is set at that moment when the artistic hope for a balance between industry and nature, between progress and conservation, was lost. Unlike Jack Sawyer in his voyage through America, Huck and Jim are often provided with moments of pastoral tranquility on the river (Jack finds such moments only in the Territories). Yet these periods of harmony within nature are always ephemeral—threatened by other men, social institutions, and especially the intrusion of progress itself in the form of the steamboat that literally breaks up their floating home. In that illustration of an uneasy historical shift, Twain places his voyagers in the most precarious of situations: abruptly set adrift in the middle of the night. The scene is shocking, terrifying, but most of all filled with implication, suggesting that all the extravagant possibilities for independence and romantic joy projected upon the American landscape since the age of discovery might be as easily and inexorably snapped as a raft in the path of a steamboat. It was as if Twain, as Leo Marx argues, with little conscious awareness of the convention, somehow discovered the tragic thread that runs through the fabric of complex pastoralism.[5]

Beneath the surface of Twain's adventure story is a subtext concerning America's transition to a new age of industrial capitalism; the novel initiates Twain's skepticism about industrial civilization and his faith in the kind of world that humans create. Straub and King have likewise projected upon the literal landscape of *The Talisman* a commentary on three unique historical epochs: contemporary America in the mid-1980s (Jack traveling westward along the interstates), the distant American past (the eastern Territories and Outposts), and a sobering projection of an America to come (the Blasted Lands). *The Talisman,* even more explicitly than *Huckleberry Finn,* is a discourse on the destruction of the pastoral ideal and its technological aftermath. In America's cities and suburbs, Jack and Wolf cannot dream of honesty and wholeness; only in the Territories is some measure of psychic unity still available. And as was the case in Twain's pastoral America, there exists the awareness that the Territories are an endangered landscape; that the Blasted Lands, following the very progress of civilization itself, are expanding outward. Inherent in this perception is a sense of tragic inevitability that somehow is never fully counterbalanced by Jack's personal survival or the Talisman's magical properties. It is, however, this aspect of *The Talisman* that effectively links the novel to *Huckleberry Finn, Walden, Moby-Dick,* the stories of Hemingway and Faulkner, and the poems of Robert Frost: all are unflinching, characteristically American examinations of the implacable advance of history.

A Deregulated Journey through "Reagan's America"

In discussing the political subtext of *The Talisman,* Peter Straub has observed that its grim picture of American society and values is a "description of 'Reagan's America'. . . . The book does seem to be about the death of the land, the terrible poisoning of the land."[6] If this novel is indeed critical of, and inspired by, "Reagan's America," it is no coincidence that the dark evils of Morgan Sloat / Morgan Orris emerge from the west coast and head east, roughly paralleling Ronald Reagan's progression from political ascendancy in California to the U.S. presidency in Washington, D.C. There can be little doubt that the authors shaped Morgan in Ronald Reagan's image, at least in terms of how these men realigned the political and environmental agendas of their respective worlds. Sunlight Gardener is modeled after the television evangelists of the religious Right.

As a specific indictment of the Reagan legacy, *The Talisman,* perhaps again elaborating upon a central metaphor found in the Bachman books, employs cancer as a means for highlighting a deteriorating social and physical environment. The novel dramatizes the following statistics, which certainly reflect Reagan's general philosophy of governmental deregulation and callous indifference toward the environment (James Watt, the bureaucrat who once justified the selling of vast tracts of National Park forestland to private developers, was, after all, Reagan's initial appointment as Secretary of the Interior): "A recent report by the Hudson River Sloop Clearwater shows that there are more than 500 factories and sewage treatment plants that together dump hundreds of pounds of suspected carcinogens like formaldehyde and trichloroethylene into the river each year. And while most of the dumping is performed under permit from the state, there are dozens of spills each year that exceed permit levels."[7] Jack's mother, Lily Cavanaugh, is dying of an illness that is reflective of her time and place. Her cancer is both a physical manifestation of the polluted landscape across which Jack trudges and a symbol of a morally polluted society. As events that take place in the Territories echo occurrences in modern America (and vice versa), Queen DeLoessian, who is also sick, is likewise the visible symbol of her world's slow collapse because of Morgan's growing influence. King and Straub have merely altered the sex of the Fisher King legend: the King's illness, as Weston notes, like Lily's and Queen DeLoessian's, is symptomatic of a cultural wasteland.[8] Jack, in his role as Jason (the Territories word for "Jesus") is given the allegorical task of renewing these dying worlds and restoring their spiritual health.

The pristine beauty of the eastern Territories is meant to contrast sharply with what modern technology has created in merely a century of transforming the American landscape. The Blasted Lands, on the other hand, are the only indication that the Territories may well be both a reflection of the nuclear tests conducted by the army in Arizona and Nevada and a dark prognosis for America's larger future. King and Straub indict the highly rational minds that produced nuclear weaponry for the highly irrational consequences in terms of animal and vegetable mutations.[9] Perhaps this is the reason the Blasted Lands are depicted so vividly in *The Talisman;* the authors required little imagination, given the examples of Hiroshima and Nagasaki, to envision the results of radiation poisoning, the aftereffects of a nuclear nightmare that King at least feels will be technological man's legacy to the earth: "As the train pulled past the animals, Jack saw that the testicles of the male had swollen to the size of pillows and sagged onto the ground. What had made such monstrosities? Nuclear damage, Jack supposed, since scarcely anything else had such power to deform nature. The creatures, themselves poisoned from birth, snuffled up the equally poisoned water and snarled at the little train as it passed. Our world could look like this some-day, Jack thought" (*Tal*, 470).

Morgan Sloat would transform the Territories into another version of the American wasteland, and Wolf's highly developed sense of smell is a con-stant reminder that corporate executives such as Sloat are bringing America ever closer to the realization of Jack's future fear. Tied to the earth by virtue of his vulpine genes, Wolf is unable to adjust to industrial America; his yearning to leave the wasteland fuels and parallels Jack's evolving apprecia-tion for the Territories. It is significant in itself that Jack's closest friend in his journey is half man and half beast, implying that Jack's sensibilities have enlarged beyond the human (and rational) sphere to the extent that he has come to respect all living beings. Jack's trek across America, the lush Terri-tories, and the Blasted Lands helps to transform his consciousness. Before he can restore the wasteland, he must first learn to appreciate what has been sacrificed in its place. Wolf's aesthetics are instructive to this end. By the conclusion of the novel Jack is as radical a twelve-year-old environmentalist as America has seen since Huck Finn pronounced that there "warn't no home like a raft."[10]

Jack's love of the Territories' air and delicious foods, his willingness even to accept the magic inherent in Migration, indicate that he, unlike his friend Richard Sloat, is no rationalist. Because of Jack's willingness to accept the possible, he is in a position to grapple effectively with the various terrors he encounters, both human and supernatural. When evil does manifest itself in the various archetypes portrayed in King's writing, only those characters with the imagination to transcend the "ossified shield of rationality"—to recognize and accept evil for what it is—stand a chance in fighting it.[11] Thus, while Richard cowers in shocked disbelief when confronted with the supernatural horrors of the Blasted Lands, Jack trusts in their reality and in his perception of it and is thereby empowered to overcome his own fears and rational urge toward denial. This ability proves especially important in the chapter "Jack and Richard Go to War," in which Jack must battle in close contact with Morgan's grotesque legions.

Jack's understanding of the world is not grounded by Sloat's incessant need to explain the inexplicable. In fact, King and Straub are so critical of Richard Sloat's practical rationality that it serves to mirror the distorted emphasis on control and structure used to characterize Sunlight Gardener and Richard's father, Morgan. Richard adheres to a belief that there must be a logical arrangement to the world, that science imposes laws and maintains a certain basis for order. His is the voice of the eighteenth-century man, further refined and bolstered by the phenomenal advances of the modern age. Unfortunately, such logic is also responsible for the Blasted Lands and a severely polluted American landscape. Jack's sensibilities, however, are essentially medieval; he is a child of poetry and magic. As Jack's contact with greater levels of social corruption grow, his connection to the mystery and magic of the primitive world, represented by Speedy and Wolf, expands accordingly. *The Talisman* posits that the world-view of a poet or fantasist is needed if the wasteland is to be renewed. Indeed, this perspective might not be so impractical after all, King and Straub appear to argue; the very survival of the Earth may well depend upon just how seriously we are willing to pursue such aesthetics.

The Talisman and the Epic Tradition

Unlike the devastation of the landscape associated with Sloat and his influence, Jack Sawyer is affiliated with the world of nature and the primal energies that reside in the Territories: "he would have been astounded if told he had wept several times as he stood watching those great ripples [of grasses] chase each other toward the horizon, drinking in a sight that only a very few American children of his time had ever seen—huge empty tracts of land under a blue sky of dizzying width and breadth and, yes, even depth. It was a sky unmarked by either jet contrails across its dome or smutty bands of smog at any of its lower edges" (*Tal*, 189). Jack / Jason is not only the prince of this land, fighting, like a medieval representative of Arthur's court, to reclaim the order of the crown; he also comes to embody the life spirit that animates the Earth itself. Sloat seeks to disrupt the regal line of succession in the Territories. In a novel that hinges upon as many medieval conceits as *The Talisman* does, it is appropriate that all of nature should turn against such men. Thus, the ocean fish protect Jack in his quest toward the Talisman (chapter 40) because they recognize him as the legitimate heir to the Territories' throne.

Early in *The Talisman*, as Jack makes his way across Ohio, he comes face-to-face with the recognition that he is no longer a typical American adolescent. In a suburban mall parking lot, Jack is confronted by three teenage girls and their football-hero boyfriend: "They were leggy in their tight jeans, these confident little princesses of the tenth grade, . . . One of the princesses glanced at him and muttered to the brownhaired girl beside her. *I'm differ-ent now,* Jack thought: *I'm not like them anymore.* The recognition pierced him with loneliness" (*Tal,* 204). Jack's immediate understanding of the dis-tance separating these young women from himself is sparked by more than just hair and perfume. By the time he meets these "little princesses of the tenth grade," Jack is poignantly aware that they belong to a world he has been forced to abandon. Yet even as he is made to feel his loss, he also senses that his difference has made him somehow stronger, investing him with qualities that are greater than the boy he would have been had he remained in New Hampshire with Lily. At this moment of isolation and humiliation, Jack is already in possession of an inner strength that could never be com-municated to the three girls or their jock boyfriend: "Something in Jack Sawyer's face was both strong and forbidding—something that had not been there almost two months ago, when a much younger boy had set the small seafront town of Arcadia Beach to his back and had begun walking west" (*Tal,* 310).

The roadways of America and the Territories have abused Jack, but they have also taught him how to survive. In the tradition of epic heroes through-out Western culture—from Homer's Achilles and Odysseus to Tolkien's Frodo—Jack learns not to be afraid of conflict, that human vultures must be personally confronted if evil is to be held in check. Thus, by the end of the novel Jack has become the polar opposite of the victim boy-child the reader remembers from the Oatley Tunnel, standing in the dark, afraid of shadows, clutching his toothbrush. Throughout *The Talisman* Jack is warned of the obvious dangers awaiting a young boy alone on the road. But no one mentions that such direct experience also toughens the individual who is able to survive it. When Jack meets Osmond early in the book, his "fear and loneliness combined in the sharpest, most disheartening wave of unhappiness he had ever known. *Speedy, I can't do this! Don't you know that? I'm just a kid*" (*Tal,* 110). One of the most persuasive elements in *The Talisman* is the degree to which this early attitude toward the world is trans-formed as Jack's journey brings to him an evolving sense of self-confidence and mental hardiness. Speedy dispatches Jack on this cross-country errand without money (he later gives Sawyer a guitar case full of it), without the aid of an automobile (Speedy has access to both cars and drivers, and on his own (even as Speedy follows him westward) because the black man knows that the quest-romance demands a hero in possession of an authentic sense of selfhood. Just as the four representatives from the Free Zone, following Mother Abagail's instruction, must cross the mountains into Las Vegas on their own without food and modern conveniences in mental preparation for battle against Randall Flagg in *The Stand,* Speedy likewise seeks to strengthen young Sawyer. Like Homer's Odysseus, Jack learns to lie and disguise himself, not out of an evil intention to defraud but because he must learn how to survive in a hostile environment. The powers of the Talisman pale in comparison with the transformation that occurs in Jack while he is on the road; in fact, the Talisman remains useless until its owner can prove himself worthy of its use.

As in many of the epic narratives that shaped the writing of *The Talisman*—Dante's *Divine Comedy,* Virgil's *Aeneid,* Milton's *Paradise Lost,* Ovid's *Metamorphosis,* and Tolkien's *Lord of the Rings*—the hero must pass through hell on his journey to selfhood and the salvation of the two queens. Sunlight Gardener's Home for Wayward Boys is *The Talisman*'s equivalent of the underworld. Rudolph, the home's dishwasher, insists that Gardener himself is a "devil from hell" (*Tal,* 336), and when Jack and Wolf flip into the Territories from the home's lavatory, hell is exactly what they find. As Dante had to descend literally through the levels of hell as an integral part of his journey to paradise, Jack must endure physical and psychological torment while a prisoner in Sunlight's home. The section dealing with Jack and Wolf's incarceration at Gardener's is located literally at the center of the novel. This is appropriate, as it signals a clear break, distinguishing Jack Sawyer, who began this quest against his will and full of trepidation, from Jack / Jason DeLoessian, whose spirit Jack really comes to embody while a prisoner at Gardener's home. Not only is the Jack we see there willing to fight to protect himself and Wolf; he likewise possesses a mental toughness that enables him to refuse, even under the duress of torture, to provide Sunlight with answers to his requests for information. That Jack endures the violent loss of Wolf (a homophobic trauma that would destroy the stability of most American adolescents) and continues his journey only highlights Sawyer's attributes as an epic hero: he emerges from the hell of Gardener's captivity a stronger individual, resolute in his commitment to the task that awaits him.

The underlying theme of Dante's *Divine Comedy* is that love is the force that holds the universe together and links the individual fragments of creation to its God. Love is the motivating force behind Dante's spiritual pilgrimage. But for Dante the concept of love is no mere abstract principle; it is a focused psychic experience on one specific object. Dante's deep commitment to Beatrice starts him on the road to salvation; his love for her guides him through the darkness of his own soul and toward "the love that moves the sun and other stars."

Dante's journey is reflected in what Jack learns in the course of *The Talisman*. It is love that motivates Jack's quest for the object. But the personal commitment to his mother that serves as his initial stimulus enlarges in the course of his journey westward to include other people, even other worlds. The movement of the novel, again corresponding to the epic tradition, is from the personal toward the universal. At the moment when Jack finally bonds with the Talisman, he is no longer Jack but some sort of mystical axis, like the Talisman itself, bringing the individual elements of the universe together as a unified whole. In contact with the Talisman, Jack gains insight into the meaning of the spiritual principles that underscore not only human life but also the life of the universe: "*He was God. God, or something so close as to make no difference*" (*Tal*, 591–92). The quest for the Talisman, however, is always more than the journey to a specific place to secure a single object; it is the fulfillment of a fundamental Christian principle—that life can only be measured in terms of the love it inspires. As a Christian epic *The Talisman* takes as its subject the soul's—and by extension, society's— pilgrimage from despair to salvation. As Dante must learn humility and selflessness (the sin of pride is the one most difficult to exculpate in purgatory) if he is to progress in his moral evolution, Jack Sawyer must come to the point at which he is able to give up to Richard what he has come so far to secure: "The weight of the Talisman suddenly seemed immense, the weight of dead bodies. Yet somehow Jack lifted it, and put it in Richard's hands. . . . Jack realized that sensation of weight had been only his imagination, his own twisted and sickly wanting. As the Talisman flashed into glorious white light again, Jack felt his own interior darkness pass from him. It occurred to him dimly that you could only express your ownership of a thing in terms of how freely you could give it up . . . and then that thought passed" (*Tal*, 598–99).

The entire novel adheres closely to the elaborate paradigm Joseph Campbell associates with the heroic adventure in *Hero with a Thousand Faces*, but nowhere is Campbell's influence more apparent than in Jack's character transformation. Campbell traces two kinds of recurring heroic personalities: in the domestic fairy tale the child prevails over his personal oppressors, whereas in the quest-romance the "world-historical, macrocosmic hero" brings back from his adventure the means for the regeneration of his society (Campbell 1949, 37–38). King and Straub appear to have created in Jack Sawyer a composite of these two heroic strains. Even as Jack remains an outcast, he gains possession of an active, articulated will. He comes to

determine a subject position in the world, and his quest is of his own voli-
tion. The search for the talisman unveils the boy's godly powers, "revealed
to have been within the heart of the hero all the time" (Campbell 1949,
39). In turn, the evolution of his identity, the individuation that is a consequence of his experience, forms a nexus to the maintenance of a universal
order. The broader interests of the communities Jack represents—his familial one in America and, later, the DeLoessian kingdom in the Territories—
are served by the success of his adventures. Jack's major benefit to the larger
social worlds in this novel takes the form of the essential connectedness established between the individual and his community. In the tradition of the
cosmogonic hero, he becomes "one of the world redeemers, the so-called in-
carnation, in the highest sense. His myth opens out to cosmic proportions.
. . . The boon that he brings restores the world, . . . releasing the vital energies that will feed the universe" (Campbell 1949, 246, 349, 352).

Jack's quest is successful because through the course of his journey he has
been internalizing the "healing message" of the Talisman. His unions with
Speedy, Wolf, and Richard teach him about love and friendship. In contrast
to the egocentric Morgan Sloat, Jack does not seek power for himself: "*I
don't want to be God,* I ONLY WANT TO SAVE MY MOTHER'S LIFE!"
(*Tal,* 592). The quest for the Talisman, like the search for the Grail or
Beatrice's love or the Seventh Ring, is as religious in its nature as it is
mythic. Concluding back in New Hampshire on the night of the winter sol-
stice, *The Talisman*'s cosmological message signals the advent of hope.
Jack's mother is reborn on the day that signifies the annual rebirth of creation: "a wondrous odor spilled out with the gray-golden cloud, an odor
sweet and unsweet, of flowers and earth, wholly good, yeasty; a smell of
birth, Jack thought, though he had never attended an actual birth" (*Tal,*
642). An appropriate ending for a narrative that locates itself firmly in the
tradition of the Christian epic—within the reassurance that the universe is
not haphazardly arranged, that life can be lived constructively and with purpose, and that evil operates within the purview of our control.

The Nuclear Forum Continued: *The Tommyknockers*

Early in *The Tommyknockers* Jim Gardener awakens from a night of
alcohol-induced sleep "not far from the Arcadia Funworld Amusement Park
in Arcadia Beach, New Hampshire" (*Tom,* 85). Not only is Gard's seaside
bed near the very spot where *The Talisman* begins and ends, but as if to solidify the intertexual connection thoroughly, Gard then encounters a young
boy named Jack who is playing alone on the beach (*Tom,* 91).

It is not surprising that these two novels should share such obvious cross-referencing, as King began serious work on *The Tommyknockers* in the autumn of 1982, only months after Straub and he had commenced coauthorship of *The Talisman*. Moreover, it is worth noting within this context that King was himself responsible for *The Talisman*'s thematic premise (Winter 1984, 158). Issues of nuclear weaponry, radiation poisoning, and the apprehension associated with an energy source whose waste byproducts are still potently radioactive thousands of years after the power has been used exerted so great a personal influence on King that he felt the need to project his concerns in both *The Talisman* and *The Tommyknockers*. The writing in these two books suggests that King, like his protagonist Jim Gardener, was nothing less than obsessed with nuclear proliferation—particularly from 1977 (the year he conceived the core story line for *The Talisman*) through 1987 (when he finished work on *The Tommyknockers*). As King told an interviewer shortly after the publication of *The Tommyknockers:* "In the case of *The Tommyknockers,* what I was writing about were gadgets. I had to write this book to realize that all of these things—the Minute Man, the Skyhawk, the Polaris submarine—are nothing but gadgets. If we kill ourselves, that's what we're going to do it with: a lot of Disneyworld gadgets of the sort that kids build with chemistry sets" (Beahm, 292).

The debate that takes place between Gardener and Ted, the nuclear power representative, in chapter 5 is not only an exact dramatization of academic cocktail-party pretentiousness and power politics (his long personal association with the English department at the University of Maine has served King well); more important, it also presents the thematic dialectic embodied in the rest of the novel: Are the benefits of the nuclear genie worth the risk of his potential wrath?

The Tommyknockers, through the unoriginal science-fiction premise of invading aliens and their leaking spacecraft, is actually a unique antinuclear document refuting Ted's claim that "nuclear is the only alternative" (*Tom,* 74). Because the nuclear theme dominates the scope of this novel, the reader is always cognizant of nuclear energy when King describes the exotic, invisible power radiating from the Tommyknockers. In exchange for the "little accidents" at Chernobyl and Three Mile Island, posits Ted, nuclear "solves the problems, all the problems" (*Tom,* 108). Like Ted's nuclear miracle, the Tommyknockers provide an unlimited source of energy and problem solving. But as humans are exposed to the fallout that attends these benefits, they suffer the effects of radiation poisoning: tooth and weight loss, spontaneous bleeding, uncontrollable vomiting, brittle bones, fatigue, disruptions in menstruation, and the eradication of less complex biological life: "*This is how it would be—this is how it* will *be—if one of their asshole power plants ever does melt down. . . . Is this a spaceship, Bobbi? Or is it a great big containment housing that's already leaking? It has, hasn't it? That's why these woods are so quiet, and that's why the Polyester-clad Neurologist Bird fell out of the sky on Friday, isn't it?*" (*Tom*, 374). As Bobbi gradually uncovers more of the alien spaceship, the Tommyknockers' radius of influence and pollution increases accordingly. And as the ship's lethal air spreads beyond the digging site to affect the town of Haven, five miles away, the townspeople suddenly find themselves in possession of a tremendous, albeit terrible, technology. Haven is coopted slowly, following Bobbi's example, as the lure of "unlimited power" corrupts the town's citizens into "the dance of untruth" (*Tom*, 236).

Thus, the entire novel becomes a thinly disguised parable of nuclear energy and the willingness of modern communities to risk human safety and the sanctity of the land for the corporate promise of clean and cheap energy. The mystery of the altered appliances in Bobbi's house and yard parallels the esoteric physics necessary to produce nuclear fusion. By implication, Gard and Bobbi no more understand the exotic energy sources inspired by the Tommyknockers than the average American comprehends the dynamics of a nuclear reaction. Even the Tommyknockers themselves, as Bobbi acknowledges once her metamorphosis is completed, do not fully comprehend their advanced technology. Her confession that "We're builders, not understanders," typifies human ignorance in the complex arena of nuclear physics: "There are wavelengths. But beyond that, we don't understand it very well" (*Tom*, 480). Her self-revelation becomes an unsettling but appropriate analogy to many of the human technocrats currently making policy decisions on nuclear facilities and gadgetry. As Barry Commoner has eloquently stated, "No optimistic assurances, no government guideline, can give us release from a profound fact of modern life—that the environment exacts a price for the technological intrusions upon it. . . . The modern automobile, or the nuclear reactor, is indeed a technological triumph. In each is embodied the enormous insights of modern physics and chemistry, and the exquisite skills of metallurgy, electronics, and engineering. Our success is in the construction of these machines; our failure is in their operation."[12]

Initially, even Gardener greets the arrival of the alien power source as a benign and positive occurrence: "the Tommyknockers weren't monsters or cannibals; they were like the elves in that story about the good shoe maker" (*Tom*, 163). Gard's early interpretation is a metaphor for the general public's initial—and naive—attitude toward the nuclear industry. Just as Ted the Power Man assures those at the cocktail party of nuclear power's safety and viability, the emerging nuclear utilities promised the world a new era of freedom from fossil fuels. Only after the real and potential disaster at Three Mile Island did popular opinion begin to shift, forcing the Western world to the realization that commercial nuclear power carries a drawback—in terms of health, safety, and waste byproducts—for every one of its assets.

One of Gardener's great fears regarding the legacy of nuclear power is that "some twenty-fifth-century archaeologist" will uncover the "spent fuel rods that were stacking up in big hot piles" (*Tom*, 58). His apprehension is ironically realized in Bobbi's excavation of the alien spacecraft. Bobbi and he have discovered history's "hot pile" buried deep in the woods, and in his "sickening excitement" (*Tom*, 45) to get inside the ship's hull, Gard is no more aware of the danger or capable of controlling it than is his hypothetical future archaeologist who stumbles across the site of buried fuel rods. And this is precisely King's point about nuclear energy: it continues to be a force essentially beyond human manageability. It remains a capricious energy source—as capricious as the human fall, produced by a three-inch protrusion of metal in the ground (something one "could have walked past three times a day for forty years and never stumbled over" [*Tom*, 14]), that led to the discovery of the spaceship. For King, there are only fateful consequences to the production of nuclear power. *The Tommyknockers* poses an ominous warning to those modern men and women who persist in trusting blindly in the "miracles" of science. As Jim Gardener understands unequivocally, the future must inevitably uncover whatever the past has left behind.

Haven, Maine: On the Road to Derry

King's portrait of the social community in *The Tommyknockers* represents a large portion of the book. Haven is both a continuation of King's critique of the rural Maine town (vividly explored in the earlier book *'Salem's Lot*) and an anticipation of the more elaborate (in terms of a richer historical and geographical matrix) social milieu of Derry in *It*. In *The Tommyknockers*, as in *Lot* and *It*, King sets up an opposition between a megacharacter, the town, and several central characters who seek to subsume their identities and freedom within its great communal persona.[13] In each of these novels the town as a community revolves around some locus of decay: in *It*, the Derry sewer system; in *Lot*, the Marston House; in *The Tommyknockers*, the ship in the woods. Individual members of the community are drawn to, and influenced by, the evil they generate and from which the plague of death emanates and spreads. As in one of King's favorite films, George Romero's

Night of the Living Dead, the afflicted townspeople—the alcoholics, the sexually perverse, the amoral, the men most prone to violence—become the walking dead who have sacrificed their reason, vision, and morality for inclusion in a group identity: "Their *two* minds: the human one and the alien one. Always there came a point where the becoming might degenerate into madness—the madness of schizophrenia as the target minds tried to fight the alien group mind slowly welding them together . . . and then eclipsing them. This was the time of necessary acceptance" (*Tom,* 237).

Against this collective antagonistic energy King places several protagonists who represent the life force in their stubborn refusal to capitulate to the unified will of the town. In *Lot* this band of renegade survivors consists of Ben Mears, the child Matt, the doctor, and Callahan the priest. In *It* the small band of child-adults in the Losers' Club is all that remains to battle the town's avatar. In *Tommyknockers* Ruth McCausland, Ev Hillman, and Jim Gardener are alone in their estrangement from the communal psyche that has engulfed Haven. And Ruth, for those who would criticize King's women characters, is far more courageous than either Ev and Gard; her fight is without the benefit of a protective metallic shield to insulate her from the polluted Tommyknocker "fallout."

By his own admission, King did not have an easy time in writing *The Tommyknockers* (Beahm, 292). That the novel took five years to complete may reveal a great deal in itself. *Tommyknockers* is, finally, an artistically unsatisfying book, even as it sustains a fascinating metaphor for history's most apocalyptic crisis. Lacking an effective moral center to counterbalance the pervasive corruption of the Tommyknockers, the novel faces squarely the age conceived by nuclear physics and finds in its darkness few avenues of hope.

Although well-intentioned and a humanitarian, Jim Gardener wallows in self-pity and an alcoholic haze for better than three-fourths of the novel. He shares many of the self-destructive qualities that eventually doom Jack Torrance in *The Shining:* "I saw what was happening to you . . . to a lesser degree I saw what was happening to the others, but *I still went along with it*" (*Tom,* 478). King himself has acknowledged this comparison, and his comments underscore a fundamental problem with the novel's narrative focus: "Jim Gardener does bear some resemblence to Jack Torrance from *The Shining,* except that I think Jack is a better man. In the same situation, Jack Torrance would have blown the whistle one hell-of-a-lot quicker than Jim Gardener does, because Jack actually has his shit together; it was the hotel that bent him back and forth until he broke" (Beahm, 292). The moral centers in *'Salem's Lot, The Talisman,* and *It,* by contrast, contain individuals who are both open to experience yet purposeful in their commitments. Until it is very nearly too late, Gard is a man without purpose, jaded and exhausted. Even his fierce antinuclear stance never matures into any kind of responsible radicalism. Although in possession of a wealth of information that defines his antinuclear position, Gard never moves beyond the role of angry and isolated gadfly, except when he participates in several protest marches in front of plant facilities.

Hillman and Gardener qualify as King heroes more by accident than by design. They both recognize the need to *"do something . . . to make up your mind to do the right thing"* (*Tom,* 28), yet neither man is very inspiring or convincing in the choices he pursues. While they manage to rescue David from his interstellar limbo, their good actions are dramatically and narratively contrived, and even these pale in the face of evil's enormity. The good people in this book are all destroyed, and the best of them, Bobbi Anderson, is turned into a grotesque parody of her former self. The novel concludes with Gard's lifeless body literally being swallowed by the reanimated Tommyknocker spaceship. His late attempts to thwart the design of the "interstellar gypsies" have unwittingly served it: released from its centuries-old grave, the ship is now conceivably free to haunt other worlds elsewhere, or even to return to Earth. The characters' quest to "do something right" in this book never quite carries an active conviction that transcends Ruth McCausland's inventive "message," which is itself a statement of despair. Although written simultaneously, *The Talisman* and *The Tommyknockers* are finally worlds apart.

Critics are fond of establishing and maintaining categories for writers; this sometimes helps to make the authors' fictional canons more comprehensible, but usually it represents the critics' desire to advance particular theoretical paradigms or angles of inquiry. King is most often placed in the genre of horror literature, and sometimes in the realm of fantasy or the fantastic; very seldom is he affiliated with the tradition of science fiction. This is initially surprising, as he frequently employs many of the themes and artifacts typically associated with the genre. On the other hand, King will never produce the "hard" science fiction demanded by aficionados of the genre; he is unwilling, for example, to explore the workings of scientific machinery or to establish a plausible degree of technological expertise to explain futuristic speculations. Even in *The Tommyknockers,* the novel from King's canon most clearly indebted to the science-fiction genre, the writer is always more interested in the social and personal implications of an advancing technology than he is in the actual technology itself. "My own philosophy," King remarked after the release of *The Tommyknockers,* "has always been that I don't care how the gadgets work; I care how the people work" (Beahm, 291).

In *The Talisman* and *The Tommyknockers* King borrows from the realm of science fiction, but it is always for his own purposes. The exclusion of King in critical discussions of science fiction is probably appropriate. His "tales of science" no more provide technological solutions for the technological problems raised than they posit the improvement of human society as a result of scientific advancement. His fiction continually parodies the hubris of scientific utopians, the Brave New World mentality of those who envision the future in terms of a technological panacea.

The inclusion of a technological dimension throughout King's canon merely adds another level of pessimism to an already dark perspective on contemporary American life. The sophisticated gadgetry featured in several of his short tales and novels merely highlights aspects of human estrangement and our general willingness to relinquish control over our personal lives and shared physical environments. The true terrors in King's fiction emerge from society as well as from science. They are best summarized in Jack Sawyer's sobering observation about the Blasted Lands, that "Our world could look like this someday" (*Tal,* 471). The distance between what King perceives fictionally and what modern America is doing to itself environmentally (and morally) can be seen to narrow on a daily basis. One of King's own great fears—personal as well as fictional—is that Sawyer's "someday" may well be today.

Chapter Five

Ship of Ghouls: *Skeleton Crew*

When rationality begins to break down, the circuits of the human brain can overload. Axons grow bright and feverish. Hallucinations turn real: the quicksilver puddle at the point where perspective makes parallel lines seem to intersect is really there; the dead walk and talk; a rose begins to sing.[1]

All artists have personalities and distinctions that give shape to their art; no one is equally skilled at everything. Artists who attempt to stretch beyond their innate powers command respect but frequently risk failure. The problem is compounded by the vagaries of audience expectation. Every artist who presents work for public consumption has an image, and for careerist reasons must change it only with extreme caution.

I suspect that King's greatest achievements, like those of his early mentor William Faulkner, will continue to be his novels. While loquaciousness and a tendency toward looseness in plot are major liabilities in some of his longer fiction, King nonetheless appears to require a broad venue in order to best develop characters and themes. The short story is pressed to its limits in his hands; King's are often too derivative of blood-and-guts horror fiction, overly sentimental, or just plain silly. On the other hand, several of his short tales are paragons of precision and psychological terror. When a reader finishes an exquisite example, such as "Last Rung on the Ladder" or "The Monkey," King's failings elsewhere in the genre can be immediately forgiven.

In *Stephen King, The First Decade* Joseph Reino begins his examination of King's first collection of short stories, *Night Shift* (1978), with the assertion that the book is "a representative anthology of Stephen King's short fiction with dramatic situations so interestingly rendered that curiosity is immediately aroused" (Reino, 100). Reino's assessment is also applicable to several selections from King's second collection of short fiction, *Skeleton Crew* (1985). Michael Collings and David Engebretson insist that *Skeleton*

Crew is the better collection of the two, "more consistent in quality than *Night Shift,* more descriptive of King's versatility as a writer."[2]

Skeleton Crew contains a wide and uneven range of material. In "The Monkey," "The Raft," "Nona," and "The Reach" King has never been more adroit in handling narrative pace and psychological subtexts. In "Here There Be Tygers," "Cain Rose Up," "The Wedding Gig," "Mrs. Todd's Shortcut," "Uncle Otto's Truck," "Survivor Type," and "Gramma" his plotting is less exacting, his themes less sophisticated, his conclusions telegraphed and predictable.

Skeleton Crew, however, offers a representation of the major themes and issues discussed elsewhere in this book and given more elaborate consideration in King's longer fiction. There is, for example, work that exposes the dangers inherent in scientific technocracy and religious zealotry (the novella *The Mist*); stories that are representative of the science-fiction genre ("The Jaunt," "Beachworld," and "Word Processor of the Gods"); simple morality fables, like many of Poe's tales, in which acts of criminal behavior return to haunt the perpetrator, suggesting that an offense against another is also an offense against oneself ("Uncle Otto's Truck" and "The Wedding Gig"); and tales that are most rewarding when their subtextual properties are pursued: "The Raft" as a study of the rite of passage from childhood freedom to the terrors of adulthood, and "The Monkey" as a psychoanalytic tale examining the deleterious consequences of self-repression and guilt.

Reino makes careful note of King's tendency to link individual stories in *Night Shift* through patterns of repetition: "a phrase, quotation, theme, or question repeated with dramatic effect not unlike the well-known incremental techniques of traditional ballads on tragic themes" (Reino, 100). This proclivity is likewise evident in *Skeleton Crew,* as several stories carry a variation of the refrain "Do you love?" Sometimes raised as a terrifying self-indictment ("Nona"), sometimes uttered in absolute certitude ("The Reach"), the phrase functions within a variety of interesting contexts, and its potential meaning shifts in a manner appropriate to the context in which it appears.

In "The Raft" the question arises as Randy, the young central consciousness in the narrative, is about to be swallowed by a gelatinous creature that floats upon the surface of Cascade Lake. When he first poses the question "Do you love?" it comes from within the warm recollection of summers past, and his answer is affirmative. But by the end of the narrative—and this is in keeping with the plot's progression from Randy's response to a naive and simplistic college dare to his serious confrontation with death and loss—Randy's query, as well as the answer he receives, have changed in tone. His final address is to the hydromonster itself, and it expresses a desperate hope for a last moment of kindness rather than a dreamy wish for personal fulfillment. The answer, however, as if in Melvillian confirmation of nature's essential indifference toward the human world, is provided by a loon's scream "somewhere, far across the empty lake" (*SC*, 270).

On a more affirmative note, "The Reach" concerns another variant of the same question. Stella Flanders' journey into the Reach is not the lonely death experience that Randy undertakes. In place of his "empty lake," Stella discovers a community of souls from her past—a society of the dead, who seek her not for punishment or out of malevolence but because of the enduring power of love. In spite of the cold and snow that surround Stella, her death is neither isolated nor painful. In fact, the conclusion of the tale indicates that her last journey completes the natural cycle of life and, at the same time, begins another one.

In addition to some variant of the phrase "Do you love?" lakes are a conspicuous presence in many of the tales in *Skeleton Crew*. In *The Mist* the white cloud that carries in it the mutant results of the Arrowhead Project comes in directly over a lake, as does the terrible summer storm that appears to precipitate the mist's arrival. The lakes in "The Monkey," "The Raft," and "The Reach" come to represent much more than mere bodies of water; they evolve into symbols for the unknown or the unconscious mind. In each of these stories the lake serves as a barrier to the protagonist's past or future that he or she is forced eventually to traverse. The character's physical crossing of the lake—walking across the frozen ice in "The Reach," swimming the water in "The Raft," or using a rowboat to get to the lake's epicenter in "The Monkey"—corresponds to a psychological crossing, the symbolic welding of two distinct eras in time (usually present and past). Thoreau discovered metaphoric correspondences to himself in the mystic waters of Walden Pond; likewise, King's *Skeleton Crew* characters experience some sort of transformation in their water crossings or journeys. But whereas Thoreau's lake usually signified the most affirmative elements in his nature, King's waters tend to mirror the dark side of the human psyche—its secret sins and lost vision.

The short story has one great advantage over the novel: its forced concision creates an intensified effect. Because it can be read in one sitting rather than over a series of days or weeks, the short story leaves a more powerful imprint on the mind. This seems particularly true of short fiction that is ever mindful of its psychological implications, its efforts to reveal a specific condition or personality disorder. The stories analyzed in this chapter were selected not only because of "the grace and finesse with which they are narrated and their ultimate terrors skillfully unveiled" (Reino, 103), but also for the value of their psychological complexity. "The Raft" and "The Monkey" in particular are two of the finest examples of psychological terror to be found in American literature. In this present era of "slash-and-gore" horror films and fiction, readers who lament the passing of the psychological Gothic, fully realized in the tales of Hawthorne and Poe, would do well to examine "The Monkey" and "The Raft" carefully. Like "Roger Malvin's Burial," "My Kinsman, Major Molineux," and "The Black Cat," these two King stories are best appreciated as allegories of the human heart. Their terrors, although couched in highly personalized contexts, actually veil subtle truths about the dark realities of the human condition. "The Raft" and "The Monkey" underscore the struggle to prevail over forces that have, finally, less to do with supernatural phenomena located outside the self than with the mind's own destructive impulses. "The Reach" endures as one of the most optimistic and certainly the gentlest tale ever narrated by Stephen King. If novels such as *Pet Sematary* and *The Shining* pose a view of the afterlife in terms of Dionysian energies aligned with evil, "The Reach" offers a positive counterpoint: that death does not signal the end of human love but rather its perpetuation. *The Mist,* the longest work in the collection, continues the technocratic critique King raised in the early Bachman books, *The Stand, Firestarter,* and, of course, *The Talisman* and *The Tommyknockers.* Like these novels, *The Mist* indicts the misdirected experiments of a technology that is ultimately beyond the understanding of those who created it. Often cited especially by students as a favorite King text, *The Mist* moves as swiftly as a summer thunderstorm from the security of familial domesticity to the nightmare of a world completely upended.

The Clouding of Human Minds

With the notable exception of an albino tentacle that is severed in battle at the loading dock behind the Federal Foods supermarket, the supernatural special effects of *The Mist* are not in evidence for a full two-thirds of the novella. This is a remarkable achievement in itself, given that the characters and the reader are both profoundly conscious of a supernatural presence for nearly the entire length of the narrative. King holds his reptilian and crustacean creatures in abeyance to force our attention onto the tale's real abhorrence: the behavior of human beings who suddenly find themselves confronting adversity and tragedy.

Ironically, as the pearl-white mist shrouds the market microcosm in a soupy fog, those who are trapped inside unveil their true personalities.

Stripped of their social veneers as a result of the circumstances in which they find themselves, the men and women of *The Mist* exhibit the full emotional spectrum of human responses—from avarice and immobilizing fear to unselfish compassion toward complete strangers. In the controlled microcosm of the supermarket, which becomes the scene of slowly unfolding levels of terror and the hysteria of mass despair, King measures the courage and coping skills of his protagonist-heroes.

Some of the men, frustrated in their helplessness, decide to test themselves physically against the creatures who inhabit the mist. Norm, Jim, and Myron, the stockboys, initially respond to the situation with a blind male bravado that is unguided by reason. Others, we are informed, "had lapsed into a complete stupor without benefit of beer, wine, or pills. The hard cement of reality had come apart in some unimaginable earthquake, and these poor devils had fallen through" (*SC*, 96). Brent Norton, the New York lawyer, on the other hand, refuses to see the cracks in the "hard cement of reality" and clings to a desperate rationality, even as he witnesses proof of the irrationality outside. Devoid of any imaginative capacity, he and his "Flat Earther" group are unable to abandon the complacent order that has sustained their place in the world. Norton's hyperrational stance in defiance of the novella's surreal developments is shown to be no more viable a response than Mrs. Carmody's emotional ranting. Whereas Norton completely shuts out the new reality occasioned by the mist, Mrs. Carmody has no difficulty accepting the changes brought about by its arrival. However, it is her medieval interpretation that is suspect.

Most of the characters in *The Mist* thus demonstrate a deficient understanding of, and response to, the adversity they are forced to encounter. For most, the reality of the mist highlights the failure of the human mind to interpret accurately what the senses supply it by way of empirical evidence: "Norton was imposing a mental gag order on himself. Myron and Jim had tried by turning the whole thing into a macho charade—if the generator could be fixed, the mist would blow over. This was Brown's way. He was . . . Protecting the Store" (*SC*, 73). The fact that the creatures who emerge from the mist resemble pterodactyls and other primordial life forms from the deep sea suggest a further connection to the behavior of the humans inside the food market. As Hitchcock's disruption of nature can be seen as a comment on the human world in his classic film *The Birds*, King implies that the bestial level of social interaction that takes place inside the supermarket is reflective of the primeval devolution occurring just outside its glass doors and windows.

Several of the characters, however, manage to face the mist without illusions or the need to deny their fears, and for them this communal tragedy presents the opportunity for personal growth. Focusing their attention and energies on the welfare of others rather than indulging their own terror, Hattie Turman, Ollie Weeks, Amanda Dumfries, and the novella's first-person narrator, Dave Drayton, cope best with the deteriorating situation around them. When Amanda and Dave decide to make love in what proves to be a final moment of quiet on the first night, it is a spontaneous act that underscores the need for human interdependency, the bond that is forfeited by the other characters who remain inside the market: "We lay down then, and she said, 'Love me, David. Make me warm.' When she came, she dug into my back with her nails and called me a name that wasn't mine. I didn't mind" (*SC*, 103).

Amanda and David, along with those who support them, rise above the self-centered arrogance that informs the attitudes of Norton, Carmody, and the Arrowhead Project, which is responsible for producing the monsters. The mist's very existence must be attributed to basic human negligence: the failure to care enough about the welfare of others and the environment we share. Near the narrative's conclusion Dave Drayton posits that "it was the mist itself that sapped the strength and robbed the will" (*SC*, 122). This is not exactly correct. The degree of weakness and lack of will that Drayton references is finally not caused by the fog; the real lack of will in this story concerns public failure to monitor sufficiently a technocracy that has been given too many tax dollars and not enough accountability. The culprits of the Arrowhead Project, as Douglas Winter points out, "remain as faceless and opaque as the mist itself" (Winter 1984, 100). The mist, then, is a metaphor for the clouded vision that inspired the Arrowhead Project as well as for the moral ambiguity that later engulfs those inside the market and leads to Mrs. Carmody's rise to power.

The Psychology of "The Monkey"

What does the little toy monkey in this story represent? This question is, of course, critical to unraveling Hal Sherburn's relationship with the monkey, much less the story's core meaning. Is the simian toy some sort of dark talismanic device that is a harbinger of death? Or does it maintain a more specifically personal connection to Hal? The tale supports both interpretations. The fish that are mysteriously killed when the monkey is entombed at the bottom of Crystal Lake would appear to indicate the randomness of evil. Yet the fact that the toy is intimately connected to Hal, linking him to his childhood and events that occurred over 20 years ago, suggests that the monkey is also some sort of psychological signifier to Hal's past. I wish to pursue this latter interpretation, not only because it is the richer but also because it stands in opposition to Douglas Winter's approach to the text as an illustration of "outside, predestinate evil" (Winter 1984, 227).

One of King's greatest skills as a writer is his ability to describe the terrors associated with childhood, particularly the shadowy guilts that frequently attend a child's initial experience with death. In *It,* for example, the personal guilt that is established after the murder of Bill Denbrough's younger brother becomes a motivating force in the older boy's relentless pursuit of It. And in *The Body* Gordie La Chance assumes the onus of his older brother's death in light of the cold indifference that characterizes his parents' state of bereavement. In these two texts King implies that for children the mystery of death is even more complicated than it is for adults, for in their confusion and innocence children often assume a measure of personal responsibility.

Drawn back to his "home place where [Hal and his brother] had finished growing up" (*SC,* 144) for his Aunt Ida's funeral, Hal finds himself highly susceptible to the unhappy memories of his childhood, which revolve around the deaths of loved ones. In his anger and grief after the accidental death of his best friend, Johnny, Hal had believed that a toy monkey was somehow responsible, and he had buried it in a deep well located on his aunt's property. Although the boy had had no direct influence on Johnny's fall from the treehouse, he had been both traumatized by it and, more important, filled with tremendous guilt. Hal had been both secretly relieved that "it hadn't been his turn [to die]" (*SC,* 147) and dimly conscious of how easily it might have been: "Johnny had been climbing the rungs up to his treehouse in the backyard. The two of them had spent many hours up there that summer" (*SC,* 145). Unable to articulate these feelings because of their complexity and his own desire to repress them, Hal had projected them onto the toy monkey—"it was the monkey's fault" (*SC,* 145)—and buried his own guilt, like the monkey thrown down the shaft, deep within the "dark well" of his psyche. This psychological nexus is supported years later when Hal finds himself drawn back to the "rock-lined throat" of the cistern, in which he sees "a drowning face, wide eyes, grimacing mouth . . . It was his own face in the dark water" (*SC,* 144).

The recent death of his mother-surrogate aunt, the journey back to his former home, and his current struggles as husband and father serve to reactivate all of Hal's submerged adolescent anxieties, which have never been adequately resolved. Thus, the monkey "resurfaces" from the well as Hal's past terrors are brought into juxtaposition with his present crises. Hal is "losing Dennis" (*SC*, 143), his oldest son, and his relationship with his wife is equally strained: "Just lately she took a lot of Valium. It had started around the time National Aerodyne had laid Hal off" (*SC*, 143). That the monkey returns at this point in his life is an indication of Hal's lingering childhood vulnerabilities. His insecurities about his career, his marriage, and his parenting are reminders of the powerlessness he knew as a child.

Hal's monkey is a psychological signifier of his repressed past. We have traced how his condition was exacerbated by Johnny's accidental fall from the treehouse, but Hal's initial level of guilt had actually been established years prior to that incident. The monkey itself had first been discovered in the back of his father's "long and narrow and somehow snug back closet" (*SC*, 150). Hal had felt the urge to return repeatedly to this closet, "trying, as best [he] could, to somehow make contact with [his] vanished father" (*SC*, 150). In an unnerving parallel to King's own personal history, Hal's father, "a merchant mariner, had simply disappeared as if from the very face of the earth when [Hal] was young" (*SC*, 144). As is often the case with small children whose parents divorce or die, the boy had grown up feeling as though he were somehow personally responsible for his father's disappearance, perhaps believing that his parent's actions were the result of something he had done or failed to do as a son. It is significant that Hal had discovered the monkey only after repeated visits to his father's closet and that the appearance of the toy had coincided with the deepening of Hal's sense of personal loss and guilt.

The monkey is thus linked to Hal's psychological disturbances, and each time Hal is made to experience death, his condition worsens. The sudden and terrible losses of his mother, his babysitter, his best friend, and his brother's playmate would have been difficult for any child to accept, even with the assistance of loving parents and a professionally trained counselor. Hal, however, had had no one to advise him on interpreting these tragic events, and his subsequent pain and confusion had easily been translated into guilt. Unable to sustain a barrier between himself and these dark accidents of fate (Johnny's fall and Beulah's murder) and natural conclusions to life (his mother's brain embolism and Aunt Ida's stroke), Hal had felt responsible for their occurrence. In the mind of this assaulted child, the monkey had become an extension of his hyperdeveloped conscience. His efforts to create a physical distance between himself and the toy had been symbolic of his own self-avoidance. For almost three decades Hal had repressed his guilt, channelled it into the buried monkey. As an adult, when Hal is forced to address these old, submerged feelings, the monkey resurfaces (in addicts' jargon, Hal has never gotten the monkey off his back): "There was the guilt;

the certain, deadly knowledge that he had killed his mother by winding the monkey upon that sunny after-school afternoon" (*SC,* 159).

As an adult, Hal is in a more advantageous position to acknowledge and confront the deep psychological disturbances he misapprehended as a child. But to accomplish this he would probably need the help of a psychotherapist to bring to consciousness that which has been repressed, so that personal integration and wholeness might become a real possibility. Unfortunately, he never seeks or receives such assistance; he has only the unqualified love of his youngest son, Petey, to help him shoulder the psychic burden that the monkey represents. His commitment to Petey enables Hal to weather a tremendous storm (symbolic of his inner personal strife) in order to reinter the toy in "the deepest part of Crystal Lake" (*SC,* 167). Hal puts trust once again in his capacity for self-discipline. Like the well on Aunt Ida's property, the lake is another metaphor for Hal's unconscious mind, and at the end of the tale Hal's guilt is once more pushed back into its "deepest part." Significantly, however, on this occasion the monkey (Hal's guilt) proves much more difficult to repress. Hal must risk his very life in his struggle to "get rid of the monkey for another twenty years" (*SC,* 169). While the story appears to imply in its optimistic conclusion that this may well be the case, any student of Freud would concur with Hal's own self-diagnosis: that unless he experiences the type of release that would be obtained by acknowledging and confronting his long history of guilty associations, the monkey and all that it signifies is "*just going to come back and come back and that's all this is about. . . .*" (*SC,* 161).

Allegorical Rites of Passage

King begins "The Raft" with this sentence: "It was forty miles from Horlicks University in Pittsburgh to Cascade Lake, and although dark comes early to that part of the world in October, and although they didn't get going until six o'clock, there was still a little light in the sky when they got there" (*SC,* 245). Thus he places the reader immediately at the heart of the story, revealing a hyperconscious awareness of time that lends a breathlessness to the narrative's pace. From the distance separating Pittsburgh and Cascade Lake, to the late hour when the journey commences, to the autumnal finalities associated with late October, the narrowing perimeters of time are made almost palpable for the reader. The syntax of the sentence itself— which contains two dependent clauses, one right after the other, that both begin with *although*—suggests the potential danger inherent in whatever action these characters have elected to undertake. Their motives are as yet unknown, but there is already a foreboding quality, conveyed by the opening sentence's suggestion of the deliberateness of the choice to venture out in spite of the ominous changes taking place in the landscape. This evocative opening also forms a nexus to the full symbolism of the tale's deepest meaning: we will soon learn that the characters featured in this sentence are in the "October" of their adolescence, on the verge of adulthood. Although we share in their naïveté at this point in the narrative, the opening sentence embodies the story's metaphor of chronological entrapment. These young people are about to lose touch with the great freedoms of childhood—deathless summers, irresponsibility, and personal immortality—as their futile attempt to thwart time's advance is mirrored in a growing psychological desperation.

What begins in the first few pages of "The Raft" as a whimsical salutation to summer (*SC,* 248) deepens into a highly allegorical indictment of the rite of passage into maturity. The tale is about nothing less than the transitional terrors associated with growing up in America. As a child Rachel recalls swimming out to the white raft, but once there she remained "for damn near two hours, scared to swim back" (*SC,* 247). The hydromonster partly symbolizes universal childhood fears, in particular those associated with the unknown. In this context the raft comes to represent an intangible transitional barrier that separates innocence from experience, adolescence from adulthood. Randy confirms this when he remarks that the raft "looked like a little bit of summer that someone forgot to clean up and put away in the closet until next year" (*SC,* 247). Just beyond the raft, however, inhabiting the deepest waters of the lake (which serves, as in "The Monkey," as a means for visualizing the human unconscious), is the amorphous hydromonster—the manifest symbol of the imminent adulthood that each student must face.

The hydromonster, as "latent with symbolism as Melville's white whale" (Winter 1984, 172), represents the cannibalistic impulses King affiliates with the adult world throughout his canon. Moreover, the adjectives used to describe it—"circular," "masculine," "mute," "purposeful," "even-shaped," "lithe Naugahyde," "criss-crossing"—all suggest elements of containment and/or rigidity. I will have more to say in the next chapter on the subject of how the adults who populate King's fictional world frequently oppress young people, physically and psychologically, and how evidence of this can be traced throughout King's canon, from *Carrie* to *It.*

In light of the broad definitions of negative adulthood presented in King's fiction, it is interesting that the one constant in the majority of his adult characters is their aptitude for betrayal. The young adults in "The Raft" come to exhibit some of the negative traits of adulthood in their interpersonal behavior. As the story unfolds, all of the relationships, same-sex as well as heterosexual, deteriorate. Randy and Deke have been college roomates for three years, but Randy does not trust his friend around women, and when Deke glances at Randy, "it [is with] more loving familiarity than contempt . . . but the contempt [is] there, too" (*SC,* 252). The two boy-men are similar only in terms of their mutual insensitivity toward Rachel and LaVerne. The girl-women are treated either as children to be silenced or threatened, or sexual toys who must always make themselves accessible. For most of the story the females are reduced to male fantasy objects, little more than breasts and bottoms, and they vie consistently for Deke's attention. Even in the midst of their peril, they perceive themselves solely as sexual competitors, turning exclusively to the men for any measure of comfort. Randy also discovers that his best friend and his girlfriend are lovers; they have thus betrayed both him and Rachel. Randy contemplates all this while trapped on the raft. At one point he acknowledges to himself that "the black patch on the water scared him. That was the truth" (*SC,* 252). Much is suggested in this double-edged association between the hydromonster and truth. Does "that was the truth" merely indicate Randy's honest acknowledgment of his fear? Or does it mean something more—that in the presence of the black patch Randy gains sudden, truthful insights?

Literally stripped of their clothes, all of the child-adults, and Randy in particular, are also stripped of their illusions. Even Randy's sole moment of comfort in LaVerne's sexual embrace proves transitory at best: she is literally swept from underneath him at the very moment when "the tactile sensations were incredible, fantastic" (*SC,* 266). Randy's losses seem to be orchestrated by, or at least centered in, the hydromonster itself. It lures him to study its "flaring nuclear colors," falsely deceiving him into believing that "perhaps the thing could fix it so there was no pain; perhaps that was what the colors were for" (*SC,* 269). At one point or another in each of our lives we share Randy's blind faith that the world of adulthood will somehow be if not a triumphant experience, at least a manageable one. But the reality of the aging process always brings disillusionment and concludes in death, even as we try, like Randy, to believe that there must be some way to "fix it so there [will be] no pain."

In the concluding pages of "The Raft" Randy clings to a series of kaleidoscopic memories from adolescent summers: "the feel of summer, the texture; I can root for the Yankees from the bleachers, girls in bikinis on the beach . . . the Beach Boys oldies" (*SC,* 267). These memories of boyhood, however, are no more a shield against the dark realities of adult life than is the raft an adequate barrier against the hydromonster's assault. The physical deaths that occur in this tale, albeit grotesque and graphic, pale in their capacity to evoke terror and sympathy from the reader when measured against the story's subtext of innocence betrayed. In his last hours of life, bereft of human comfort and anticipating his own demise, Randy learns what we all must in light of the harsh realities of aging: that the cocoon of innocence—symbolized appropriately in Randy's romantic urge to "say good-bye to summer, and then swim back" (*SC*, 248)—is lost once we have emerged from it.

Do the Dead Sing?

Stella Flanders' 95-year-old imagination is death-haunted. From the beginning of "The Reach" to its conclusion, her life is seen in reference to those she has buried. In fact, Stella's reach has very little to do with the actual "water between the island and the mainland" (*SC*, 489); it is, instead, the spiritual swell that continues to link her to the men and women of Goat Island who were her family and friends: "*Your blood is in the stones of this island, and I stay here because the mainland is too far to reach. Yes, I love; I have loved, anyway, or at least tried to love, but memory is so wide and so deep, and I cannot cross*" (*SC*, 493).

Content to have spent her entire life never having journeyed across the Reach to the mainland, Stella is now an old woman whose past is more meaningful than her present; the island dead have been whispering to her long before she sees her first apparition. Although she shares an apparently warm relationship with her living son and grandchildren, for the length of the story Stella's only topic of communication with them concerns the past and those who are dead. Douglas Winter postulates that "When Stella Flanders embarks upon her journey, she understands what she is leaving behind in the 'small world' on this side of the Reach: 'a way of being and a way of living; a feeling'" (Winter 1984, 10). This is not precisely accurate, for while Stella does relinquish the present and her commitment to those still alive on Goat Island, she does not abandon her past, as Winter suggests, but rather rediscovers it in her reunion with those she has lost. Indeed, although she maintains a connection with the dead that grows increasingly stronger in the course of the narrative, she indulges her recollections not out of weakness or morbidity but because they remain a conduit to love. This is why death poses no real fear for Stella; she knows that "it don't hurt . . . All that's before" (*SC*, 504). Her past is not left behind when she chooses to

cross the Reach, as her "small world" is reanimated in contact with the island's dead: "He was holding his hat out to her in a gesture that appeared
almost absurdly courtly, and his face was Bill's face, unmarked by the cancer that had taken him" (*SC*, 502).

The story's optimism is sustained by the nucleus of a small town, and
this is critical to understanding Stella's attitude toward her existence: "I see
enough of what goes on in cities on the TV. I guess I'll stay where I am" (*SC*,
492-3). Stella's perspective on her Maine home is unique in King's canon.
With the possible exception of *The Dead Zone*, in which we see a community working in unison to capture a rapist-murderer stalking local women,
King's general treatment of small-town America is neither flattering nor
equivocal. In contrast to the citizens of the malefic microcosms of 'Salem's
Lot, Haven, Castle Rock, and Derry, the Goat Island inhabitants in "The
Reach" take care of one another, view their neighbors as integral members of
an extended family, and continually emphasize the importance of caring interpersonal relationships:

> *"Children,"* she would tell them, *"we always watched out for our own. We had to, for
> the Reach was wider in those days and when the wind roared and the surf pounded
> and the dark came early, why, we felt very small—no more than dust motes in the mind
> of God. So it was natural for us to join hands, one with the other.*
>
> *"We joined hands, children, and if there were times when we wondered what it was
> all for, or if there was any such a thing as love at all, it was only because we had heard
> the wind and the waters on long winter nights, and we were afraid."* (*SC*, 499)

Stella's appreciation that her own identity is inexorably linked to the
larger social community reflects the more affirmative side of King's social
self. In a conversation I had with him prior to the interview in chapter 1,
King mentioned that his choice to remain a resident of Bangor, Maine, was
based partly as a result of his commitment to the community itself as a place
that has nurtured both his family and his fiction. Although his novels and
stories pose a rather bleak portrait of communal life in America (see chapters 3, 4, and 6 of this book), King's own personal feelings toward Bangor
seem to closely resemble Stella's feelings about Goat Island in "The Reach."
King continues to give back to the town in which he lives: he remains an active presence in Bangor's political life, he has given numerous public lectures at the local university at Orono, he has supported benefits to raise
money for Bangor's neediest, and he recently contributed funds to buy
baseball uniforms for the town's Little League.[3] Whenever a director seeks
to film an adaptation of one of his texts, King always lobbies hard to set the

film in Maine in an effort to share some of his financial success with his fellow citizens: "For years I've desperately wanted to get film crews into Maine. There are parts of Washington County where twelve weeks of shooting could generate more income than the place sees in a year."[4] In another man of King's wealth and stature, these activities might appear to be token gestures, but in his case they genuinely reflect his awareness of his responsibilities as a citizen and a human being.

In *The Reach* Stella Flanders understands that the only hope for men and women in the face of nature's awful cruelty is the degree of commitment we give to one another: "They stood in a circle in the storm, the dead of Goat Island, and the wind screamed around them, driving its packet of snow, and some kind of song burst from her" (*SC,* 504). Her character embodies a side of Stephen King that is seldom noted either in popular reviews of his fiction and films or in scholarly analyses. She represents the life force that sustains each of King's small-group relationships—from that of Danny, Wendy Torrance, and Hallorann in *The Shining* to that of the members of the Losers' Club in *It.* The heroes and heroines in King's fiction do not triumph as a result of their personal independence or complacent withdrawal from corruption. Their endurance is based upon the degree to which they have not sacrificed their humanity and upon their quest to find others with whom they might entrust their love. Stella Flanders never really fears a reunion with those who have died, because for her the dead wear sympathetic faces and retain the most important capacity with which human beings are endowed. As King wrote in *Danse Macabre,*

the horror writer is not just a writer but a human being, mortal man or woman, just another passenger in the boat, another pilgrim on the way to whatever there is. And we hope that if he sees another pilgrim fall down that he will write about it—but not before he or she has helped the fallen one off his or her feet, brushed off his or her clothes, and seen if he or she is all right, and able to go on. If such behavior is to be, it cannot be as a result of an intellectual moral stance; it is because there is such a thing as love, merely a practical fact, a practical force in human affairs. (*DM,* 403)

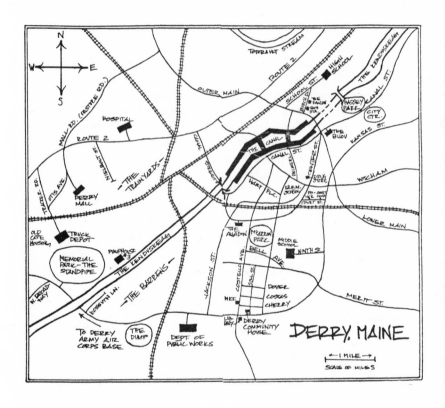

Chapter Six
Art versus Madness: *It* and *Misery*

"In Derry people have a way of looking the other way."

(It, 455)

It is not only the longest novel Stephen King has so far published; it is also, by King's own admission, the magnum opus of his two decades of work.[1] It is a novel that embodies many of the issues, themes, and narrative stylistics King has been employing since *Carrie*. In fact, throughout *It*'s rolling narrative several themes, characters, and even objects from earlier books recur or make cameo appearances, like the recurring themes and characters in Faulkner's Yoknapatawpha County cycle. For example, a younger version of *The Shining*'s Dick Hallorann is a member of the heroic rescue team that manages to save several lives from the inferno at the Black Spot. Even Christine itself, the 1958 Plymouth Fury that terrorizes Pittsburgh in the earlier novel *Christine,* is resurrected from the auto graveyard to ferry Henry Bowers to his early-morning assignation attempt at the Derry public library.

But perhaps the most intriguing parallels are between *It* and the earlier King novella *The Body*. Both texts explore the loyalty of childhood friendships; both are narrated from the perspective of adults looking back on their youths; and both feature innocent adolescents on a voyage to experience and change, all the while under siege by violent or negligent parents and gangs of older juvenile delinquents. Even Milo's dump in *The Body* bears a marked resemblance to Mandy Fazio's junkyard in *It*. What really makes these books a terrifying excursion into modern American life, however, is King's attitude toward the social environments of Castle Rock and Derry, along with his scathing indictment of their adult inhabitants.

In the course of his literary career, King has experimented with a wide variety of haunted arenas. He began with an oppressed girl in *Carrie,* then moved to a hotel in *The Shining,* a car and a dog in *Christine* and *Cujo,* respectively, and a burial ground in *Pet Sematary.* In *'Salem's Lot, The Body,* and *It* in particular, his attention is carefully focused on a single city as he portrays evil's embrace of an entire community. In *It* the physical geography

of Derry, Maine, like that of Castle Rock, is meant to reflect the moral ty-
pography of the town and its history; it is a place where there is little that is
kind or beautiful. Instead, the pollution of Derry's extensive canal system
defiles and overwhelms whatever is life-sustaining or aesthetically pleasing,
serving as an appropriate metaphor for Derry's value system: "Canal Street,
where most of Derry's bars were ranked like felons in a police lineup, paralleled the Canal on its way out of town, and every few weeks or so the police
would have to fish some drunk's car out of the water, which was polluted to
drop-dead levels by the sewage and mill wastes. Fish were caught from time
to time in the Canal, but they were inedible mutants" (*It*, 192).

A central thesis in *It*—that an entire town can become a haunted
landscape—surely owes its origins to *'Salem's Lot* and *The Body*. But *It*
soon parts company from these two earlier books insofar as the later novel
is a much more elaborate and historical analysis of Derry's dark sociology.
Neither *'Salem's Lot* nor *The Body* endeavor to delve into the complex matrix of historical and economic evils that taint Jerusalem's Lot or Castle
Rock. In this sense, then, *It* is a far more ambitious work than either of its
predecessors. The novel seeks to portray and explain thoroughly the
interrelationship between the town of Derry and the monster It, a creature
that sustains the city's economic stability (upon his return to Derry, the
adult Bill Denbrough is shocked by evidence of Derry's affluence, moder-
nization, and size) while preying upon its vulnerable youth. Indeed, the
union between It and Derry is so intimate that the monster's 27-year
feeding cycles are linked to levels of violent activity within the town. As
Mike Hanlon, the self-ordained historian of Derry / It, speculates in one
of his journal entries: "It is as if a monstrous sacrifice is needed at the end
of the cycle to quiet whatever terrible force it is which works here . . . to
send It to sleep for another quarter-century or so. But if such a sacrifice is
needed to end each cycle, it seems that some similar event is needed to set
each cycle in motion" (*It*, 641).

The Sociology of *It*

In the "Smoke-Hole Ceremony" Richie and Mike witness the birth of It
in an era that roughly corresponds to the age of prehistoric America. Mike
postulates that "It's *always* been here, since the beginning of time . . . since
before there were men *anywhere* . . . It was there then, sleeping, maybe,
waiting for the ice to melt, waiting for the people to come" (*It*, 763). In
most of the inanimate, malevolent centers in King's fiction—from
Christine, to the Micmac burial ground, to the Overlook Hotel, to the

Tommyknockers' spaceship—a connection and / or identification with the human world is absolutely necessary to animate their malefic energies. King may well be suggesting that evil exists only as a theoretical construct without human beings—and that it only becomes real when we humans, with our greeds, liabilities, and unchecked urges, serve as its hosts.[2] The fact that the spaceship carrying It in its primordial stage "lands right where the downtown part of Derry is now," (*It*, 763) suggests the absolute link between the genesis of It (and its cryptic allusion to original sin) and the human town that will settle upon It.

Following Mike Hanlon's suggestion in chapter 10—that the adult members of the Losers' Club should reacquaint themselves with the town they shared as children and eventually abandoned—Eddie Kaspbrak returns to gaze down into the Barrens. It is a place of junglelike vegetation located on the perimeter of Derry, where as children Eddie and his six friends found companionship and happiness. The Barrens is appropriately named, for in spite of the landscape's lush environment, it houses one of the central thresholds that It employs—usually assuming the physical form of a clown named Robert Grey, or Pennywise—to surface from its sewer lair to stalk Derry's children. This threshold is actually a cement cylinder that connects with the maze of drainage and sewage pipes that honeycomb Derry's underground. Stamped on top of the steel cap covering this pipe, Eddie remembers, are the words "DERRY DEPARTMENT OF PUBLIC WORKS" (*It*, 358). The cap becomes a kind of calling card in the relationship between Derry and It, a metal welcome mat that is symbolic in its language: the concrete cylinder is a conduit to the bowels of Derry as well as to the home of It. This is the place where Derry, through the hunger of It, "works" on its "public," the young citizens of the town.

Mike Hanlon is the first to recognize that the town and Pennywise share a reciprocal bond: "It's become a part of Derry, something as much a part of the town as the Standpipe, or the Canal, or Bassey Park, or the library. Only It's not a matter of outward geography. . . . Somehow It's gotten inside" (*It*, 503). The various masks that Pennywise wears in luring children to their grisly deaths are symbolic of the masks that disguise and distort the true history of Derry itself. Underneath the veneer of Rotary Clubs and dusk curfews established out of concern for its children is Derry's reality, a history of persecution of outsiders—from blacks (as Hanlon's father reveals in his remembrance of the Black Spot), to the children who play in and around the town, to Adrian Mellon, who is murdered because he is a homosexual. Like the town's children, the gay and black communities of Derry exist outside the social mainstream. This puts them in the position to comprehend the workings of Derry more clearly than the rest of the town at the same time as they are the victims of its violent prejudices. Anyone weaker or living outside the adult white male community is immediately vulnerable to Derry's sanctions. As Hanlon discovers in his quest to record the truth of Derry's history, the town's reputation not only is guarded by the patriarchal authority of such Derry organizations as the Legion of White Decency but also reflects the protective biases that white males have always employed in maintaining their dominance in Western culture.

In his book review of *It*, Lloyd Rose argues that the novel fails because the real world of Derry, "with its racists, homophobes, wife-beaters, and sadistic teenage bullies," is more frightening than the supernatural evil of It: "King doesn't really have the literary strengths necessary for straight novel-writing. And although he does a credible job with Derry—at times it's like Lake Wobegon with dry rot—the more convincing Derry is, the less believable is the creature haunting its sewers. And when we face the creature, the town becomes unconvincing and far away. Rather than blending, the real world and the supernatural one keep elbowing each other out."[3] This comment reflects the typical inability of critics to view King's fiction as a body of literature that is in any way a serious portrait of, or commentary on, contemporary life. The main problem in Rose's analysis is his misapprehension that Derry and It can be discussed individually, that they are somehow two unique entities. They cannot be separated; Derry must always be considered an extension or manifestation of It, and vice versa. From this perspective, the real and supernatural worlds in the novel do not "keep elbowing each other out"; rather they are statements about one another and the necessity for understanding each in light of their coexistence. This fundamental interrelationship is detailed throughout the novel. The massacre of the Bradley gang is a splendid illustration of this; it also represents some of the best writing in King's career.

The Derry men who take part in that afternoon event are not motivated to kill the Bradleys out of any sense of justice over the law's violation or out of self-preservation. Nothing quite so noble; they are merely engaging in the sport of hunting down others who have attained national reputations. As in Faulkner's treatment of Percy Grimm and the racist crowd he manipulates in *Light in August* and "Dry September," the slaughter becomes a community event spoken of as a "party" and a "carnival" (*It*, 654), complete with souvenirs and picture taking. King means for the reader to see that nothing in the long litany of Bradley criminal offenses can quite measure up to the moral apathy of the Derry men who kill them. It is for this reason that Pennywise, a member in good standing of the Derry community, emerges as a central participant. The levels of violence and brutality that characterize the slaughter, coupled with the quasi-sexual enthusiasm of the citizens who participate in it, strikingly parallel the same qualities in Pennywise's attacks on Derry's children. The warped glee that attends the clown's participation is a barometer for understanding how all the Derry men feel about their own involvement: "Said that clown was leanin out of the window so far that Biff couldn't believe he wasn't *fallin* out. It wasn't just his head and shoulders and arms that was out; Biff said he was right out to the knees, hanging there in midair, shooting down at the cars the Bradleys had come in, with that big red grin on his face. 'He was tricked out like a jackolantern that has got a bad scare,' was how Biff put it" (*It*, 654).

The Derry men who massacre the Bradley gang with a hail of bullets rely upon a level of community cooperation that is never approximated elsewhere in the novel. It is interesting, in light of this social interaction, that It, in the guise of Pennywise, feels secure enough to venture beyond its usual haunts of sewers and canals and allow itself to be seen by Derry's adults in direct daylight (usually, It is invisible to the adult world). Perhaps it is not only security that draws Pennywise out into the open but also his own level of excitement—which, as the above quote indicates, is so intense that It could not bear to participate vicariously only. In a community most accurately defined by its general condition of human apathy, isolation, and moral amnesia, this single event from Derry's dark history, which brings together so many of Derry's citizens in single-minded purposefulness, inspires Pennywise into a frenzy of open involvement. But as is often the case in this relationship, the clown also inspires the townsmen themselves to greater levels of violent behavior. The association between Derry and Pennywise extends to the point that each of the men who remembers seeing Pennywise describes the clown as being in possession of a gun identical to his own; this suggests that the clown is a reflection of the town itself, if only subconsciously—a mirror to the violence that is inherent in Derry's manhood: "The one glimpse I caught of him, it looked like he had a Winchester bolt-action, and it wasn't until later that I figured out I must have thought that because that's what *I* had. Biff Marlow thought he had a Remington, because that was what *he* had. And when I asked Jimmy about it, he said that guy was shooting an old Springfield, just like his. Funny, huh?" (*It*, 653–54). The affiliation between Derry and Pennywise is most similar to that between a host and parasite. On occasion, however, as the Bradley narrative illustrates, this analogy breaks down, as Pennywise is shown to be capable of giving back to the town something of what It usually takes.

A Novel of Children and Child Abuse

More than a study of the dark history of Derry, more than an analysis of the current state of the town or of It as an evil force inextricably linked to human behavior, *It* is a novel about child abuse. As Mike Hanlon notes in one of his diary entries, "Here in Derry children disappear unexplained and unfound at the rate of forty to sixty a year. Most are teenagers. They are assumed to be runaways. I suppose some of them even are" (*It*, 158). Throughout the narrative, repeated patterns of adult-to-child violence and neglect become dominating memories for main characters—including the members of the Losers' Club as well as those of Bowers' gang.

The theme of child abuse is an obsessive one in King's fiction. In part, the novelist would seem to be responding to the current national interest in the issue, as reflected by the American media. While child abuse has always been part of family life, only recently have Americans been forced to appreciate the extent to which it occurs and to question the stereotypes formerly associated with it. Until the recent emphasis on reporting child-abuse cases and taking action in support of the victims, child abuse was often conveniently and wrongly assumed to occur only among the lower classes as a direct expression of their poverty and lack of education. Most Americans are now beginning to understand that it is a problem, like alcohol and drug addiction, that cuts across class lines and socioeconomic strata. The widespread awareness of this issue has provided King the opportunity to portray a modern evil in a form that his American readership can recognize immediately. But perhaps even more important, for King's fictional purposes, is that child abuse is an effective means of highlighting the gap that separates adults from children. Children are abused by their parents throughout *It*— from Eddie Kaspbrak's mother-invented illnesses to Alvin Marsh's barely restrained incestuous urge. The extent of child oppression, as Hanlon notes, is excessively high in Derry, indicating that there are certain social conditions in this town that make child abuse the norm rather than an aberration.

King never explains fully why the children of Derry are Pennywise's primary prey. It is suggested late in the book that their imaginations produce a greater level of fear, and the associated secretions make them a more tender meal. But a more likely explanation is that the town's citizens do not appreciate their own children, and Pennywise, as a mirror to the town itself, merely carries this antipathy to its logical consequence. In any event, it is fitting, in light of It's preference for children, that the monster's most effective mask should be that of Pennywise the Dancing Clown. A clown is supposedly a character created for the delight of children—part cartoon, part emanation from a coloring book. But clowns are also associated with children in adults' minds, and It is an "adult" monster. A clown's image is often terrifying to a young child, who may be frightened by the lurid colors and the realization that the clown is indeed someone—most often an adult—wearing a disguise. That Pennywise is not what he seems underscores the facts that Derry is not the upstanding community it appears to be and that the town's citizens, particularly its parents, are neither nurturing nor benevolent toward their children.

The various shapes It assumes in its reign of terror always reflect in some way the silver and orange of Pennywise the clown, its core avatar. But usually It chooses forms unique to the individual child under attack, fashioning a visage of symbolic terror related to the child's personal past or future. For Mike Hanlon, It is an orange bird with silver lines, reminiscent of the reptile that haunts a Rodon movie he has seen recently as well as the creature that flew overhead during the events his father witnessed as a young man at the Black Spot. For Eddie Kaspbrak, It assumes the shape of a leper, "wearing the ragged remains of some strange silvery suit" (*It*, 313). The leper is a dark manifestation of Eddie's asthma, as the leper's decomposition centers on his face, particularly the nose. Beverly Marsh's apparition of It appears as the witch from the fairy tale "Hansel and Gretel," but the witch is also her father and Pennywise blended into one: "She turned, swirls of red hair floating around her face, to see her father staggering toward her down the hallway, wearing the witch's black dress and skull cameo . . . " (*It*, 572). The connection is significant, for like the children in "Hansel and Gretel," Beverly has been betrayed by her father. Her whole attitude toward men has been shaped by his abuse and neglect. As such, Alvin Marsh is used by Pennywise as an effective tool to terrorize Beverly. His refrain "I worry about you Bevie . . . I worry a lot," punctuated by blows with his fists, connect this woman-child not only to the dark paternity in "Hansel and Gretel" but also to the sadistic masculine figures in her life—starting with her father and including her husband Tom and, eventually, Pennywise the clown.[4] Stan Uris first encounters Pennywise in the form of the two dead children who drowned in the town Standpipe. Twenty-seven years later, Stan will choose to die in water rather than face It a second time. For Bill Denbrough and Richie Tozier, the clown is a werewolf wearing a Derry High School jacket that barely contains the orange pompom buttons of the clown's suit underneath. The high-school jacket, which may be a symbolic link to the immediate futures of Bill and Richie (they will both attend high school in four more years) further affiliates the clown with Derry itself, this time with one of its primary institutions. In each case the clown ties itself directly to the victims it pursues; for instance, the name Richie Tozier is stitched on the bloodstained high-school jacket of the Neibolt Street werewolf (*It*, 379).

Few writers, with the possible exceptions of Dickens, Dostoyevski, and Golding in *Lord of the Flies,* portray the world of childhood and adolescence—particularly in terms of the nascent psychopathologies that are often manifested in the transition stage of adolescence—better than King. Henry Bowers, Patrick Hockstetter, and Victor Criss are refinements of the vicious side of American youth, which King has examined thoroughly in "Sometimes They Come Back," *Carrie, Christine,* and *The Body.* Devoid of tenderness and the capacity to love, these savage children spend their days repeating grades in school and devising methods of spreading torture and destruction. They are always products of abusive and frequently broken families, and the levels of anger and hostility with which they greet the world reflect the parental legacy they have inherited. It is thus little wonder that Pennywise is drawn to employ Bowers in his service. Even without the clown's corrosive influence, Bowers's madness is symbolic of Derry itself. Indeed, throughout the novel his capacity for hatred, his proclivity toward violence, and his relentless quest for vengeance against the Losers' Club reveal him to be yet another of It's avatars. As Hanlon realizes, "It's using Henry. Maybe the others too, but It's using them through Henry" (*It*, 940). Bowers stalks the Losers' Club in 1958 as well as in 1985 in a manner that takes its obsessiveness from Pennywise himself. The clown has the capacity to appear anywhere out of nowhere—from sewers and toilets to the canals and the Barrens itself. Bowers likewise haunts the Derry landscape with the goal of isolating children, at first to inflict beatings and humiliation (e.g., Eddie's broken arm) but later, as Bowers becomes more of an instrument for It's will, to perform acts of murder (e.g., his attempt to kill Beverly in 1958, when she is caught fleeing her father, and to murder Mike Hanlon in the Derry library in 1985).

However King means us to interpret the evil that is represented by It, the fact that the creature is a shape-changer above all else would seem to link it to the rich mythology surrounding Satan and his legions of evil. One need only consider King's elaborate research into the Indian legend of the Wendigo for the publication of *Pet Sematary,* or the metamorphosis of *The Stand*'s Randall Flagg into animals affiliated with various netherworldly gods, to appreciate the writer's vast comprehension of demonic mythology and tradition. In *Pet Sematary,* for example, King adheres closely to scholarship in the area of Indian folklore; his Wendigo is a remarkable approximation of the cannibal / form-assumer that was believed to haunt the burial grounds of several Indian tribes in the Canadian northeast. The time of year in which *Pet Sematary* is set reflects King's awareness that in Indian folklore the evil spirit exerts its strongest power during cold spells and snowstorms.[5]

The transmogrifying capability of the Wendigo evil, however, achieves its greatest representation in *It*. In this novel King approximates the medieval perception that evil—in the form of the fallen Satan, who preceded the creation of man—exercised the ability to modify its shape to one essentially human (e.g., the witch Beverly encounters, Eddie's leper, the wolfman of Neibolt Street, Pennywise) but always with some bestial features (wings, claws, a tail). For instance, the grand Duke of Hell, Baal, is usually given the ability to make himself invisible and to change his physical form in order to trick those who come in contact with him. Of particular interest, in light of It's final metaphorphosis into a spider, is that Baal's strongly built torso is often pictured ending in spider's legs.[6]

All the shape changing that occurs in *It* leads to It's ultimate self-revelation as a pregnant mother spider—perhaps yet another partial reflection of the individuals in the Losers' Club, for although many of these children are growing up without fathers, each has a mother, as does the female It. Furthermore, the fact that the spider is pregnant may be connected to the fact that no adult member of the club has been able to conceive a child. But the spider itself—aside from being an insect that traps its victims in a web, just as It seeks to trap and feed upon the children of Derry—is also an insect that works alone, and herein is the one hope the Losers' Club has for destroying It's evil. The club's members are unified by friendship and love—the elements that will ultimately produce It's destruction, as Pennywise inspires and thrives upon human isolation and hate.

Completing the Circle: Children to Adults and Back Again

On their own, each member of the Losers' Club is victimized by Bowers, the teenage hood, and his gang. Ben has his stomach marked for life and is almost murdered on the last day of school in 1958, Richie and Bill lose their dam, Mike Hanlon is beaten and finds himself in danger of being murdered by stoning, Eddie has his arm broken and might have been more severely injured had the police not arrived to rescue him, and Beverly knows that if she is caught in the Barrens she will be raped or killed. The Derry children caught alone by Bowers are vulnerable and doomed, as they would be in encountering It. But working together in support of one another, the adolescents of the Losers' Club gain the courage and power to vanquish foes who are their physical superiors.

A wellspring for the collective energy that radiates from the Losers' Club is their shared commitment to one another and to the other children of Derry. The Losers view themselves as engaged in a righteous quest for all the victims of Derry's oppressive history. As each member of the club knows from personal experience, there is no single group more oppressed and expendable than Derry's children. The strength of the seven adult-children who struggle against It lies in their ability to join their individual imaginations to create the psychic potency of a group dynamic. The birth of the name Losers' Club, for example, occurs immediately after Richie, Beverly, and Ben work together to thwart Bowers during an alleyway attack in the summer of 1958: "And so that was where they went . . . or where they escaped. Richie would think later that it set a pattern for the rest of the summer" (*It,* 359).

As if in prophetic response to Richie's assessment, the rock fight in the Barrens a month later echoes this scene. Not only are are the members of the Losers' Club united in their battle against Bowers's tyranny, but Bowers himself is linked directly to It; King refers to him as a "bloated poisonous spider" (*It,* 691). These two pivotal scenes involving the Losers against Bowers are preludes to the third battle, which will occur later that summer against It. In the rock fight the group is unified in spirit and enlarged in number, for Hanlon's intduction into the club increases its membership to seven. The number seven has magical implications, and each member of the group seems to sense it: "Bill looked from Mike to Richie. Richie met his eyes. And Bill seemed almost to hear the click—some final part fitting neatly into a machine of unknown intent" (*It,* 700). In the preliminary battle against Bowers, Bill emerges as the leader and spokesperson for the Losers' Club. He confronts Victor Criss in a rock-fight showdown, and he is the one with enough bravado to claim the Barrens for the group. The Losers' solidarity gives definition to their community of seven. As Richie is first to recognize, it sets not only the "pattern for the rest of the summer" but also a pattern for the rest of their lives.

Reunited 27 years later in Derry, the adult Losers realize that the memory of what took place years ago is only partial, that memories of events fade quickly as a child moves on to adulthood and forgetfulness. An encounter with a werewolf or an animated statue of Paul Bunyan might so terrify an adult as to render him or her immobile (e.g., Audra enters a state of catatonia after viewing It as spider). But because of their capacity for endurance and a plastic sense of the past, children are sometimes in a better position to absorb the terrifying shocks they experience. In 1985 the magical properties associated with childhood subsist primarily in dim recollections for the now-adult members of the Losers' Club. The reactivation of memory, centered on a return to childhood, will be required if these adult-children are finally to vanquish It. Thus, the collective power of the adult version of the Losers' Club can be defined as the sum of the members' individual memories from 1958. This helps explain why most of these memories occur to the individuals in the company of the whole group.

In his essay "Rising Like Old Corpses: Stephen King and the Horrors of Time-Past," Leonard Heldreth argues that "King sees the past as a look back into insanity. . . . Individuals are menaced as much by their previous selves and actions as they are by external evils." While Heldreth's thesis is an accurate barometer for understanding events in a novel such as *The Shining,* his argument is severely weakened when applied to *It.*[7] In this latter novel, memory serves a twofold purpose. First, it brings the individual back into contact with his or her past, thereby creating a channel between the adult recollecting an experience and the child actually experiencing it: "Years later, as Ben recounted this, Bev suddenly cried out, startling all of them—they were not so much listening to the story as reliving it" [*It,* 861]. Second, memory establishes further and more deeply the psychology of the group. As we have seen, the Losers are people who are much less dynamic as individuals than they are as participants in a small-group relationship. Each personal memory becomes a shared history, allowing the individual narrator to help fill in the gaps belonging to others in the collective. This process also works in reverse; individual narrators are aided in their attempts to connect with events from the past by the group's comprehensive analysis and commentary. This activity of piecing together a collective past (which takes place throughout the novel, but essentially begins when the Losers return to Derry in 1985) provides the adults with a complete composite of It and the summer they shared. The bond of sympathy that forms as a result of their "talking out" a formerly insulated series of personal terrors and tragedies produces a level of transcendence for the group as a unit, as well as a new sense of security for each individual disclosing what had formerly been a strictly personal encounter with It. The act of making the personal public—of allowing sympathetic others to activate their sympathy—somehow manages to create a degree of personal liberation; the individual is no longer solely responsible for shouldering the onus of guilt or pain: "'But we did *something,*' Mike said quietly. 'At some point we were able to exercise some sort of group will. At some point we achieved some special understanding, whether conscious or unconscious'" (*It,* 516).

In *It* the recognition of, and bonding with, the personal suffering of others allows the adult members of the Losers' Club to enlarge their own spirit of redemptive sympathy. The individual and the collective grow stronger as a result of their personal reflections on the past. In an article entitled "Good and Evil in *The Shining*," Burton Hatlen posits that "the Good in King's world is represented only by small groups of people who (barely) cling together in the face of an encroaching darkness, rather than by any supernatural power which can serve to counterbalance the forces of destruction."[8] Hatlen's understanding of goodness in King's universe is tied to a network of human compassion: the value of human community must outweigh the lure of selfish urges toward power and dollars. Rarely do King's novels include a force of good, other than the potential relationship that can exist among human beings; but often there is an unmistakable undercurrent of a supernatural good that lends support to human relationships. This positive dynamic is not capable of shaping world events in the way that the Wendigo or the Overlook Hotel or It can manipulate reality. But what the good force does in King is often to remind characters of their responsibilities and commitments—to the better parts of themselves, to their friends and families, to others. Some such force is at work on Dick Hallorann in *The Shining*, helping him overcome his initial wish "that the cup had never been passed his way" (*Shin*, 317) and sending him forth to rescue the Torrance family. A similar force appears in *Pet Sematary* through Pascow's spirit when it warns Louis Creed that "Your destruction and the destruction of all you love is very near, Doctor" (*PS*, 87).

The individual members of the Losers' Club return to Derry of their own free will. Many of them have much to lose—important occupations and spouses who need them. But survival in King's world always demands risk on the part of the individual. In return for that risk, his characters often rediscover love, and equally important, an ability to recapture the past through more than just memory. To do battle against It a second time, the adults must rediscover their connection to childhood, becoming, at least in their imaginations, children again: "*The only thing that really remains is to finish going through it, to complete the job of catching up, of stapling the past to present so that the strip of experience forms some half-assed kind of wheel.* Yes, *Mike thinks,* Tonight the job is to make the wheel; tomorrow we can see if it still turns . . . the way it did when we drove the big kids out of the gravel-pit and out of the Barrens. '*Have you remembered the rest?*' Mike asks Richie*" (*It*, 702).

In *It*, and throughout most of King's fiction, youth is not just a force of physical vitality but also a psychic reservoir. As King argues throughout

Danse Macabre, the energies of youth are recognized best in the imaginative capacity to believe, to dream, and to dare. The Ritual of Chüd, as Bill discovers the second time he employs it, is a synthesis of the most laudable aspects of childhood faith mixed with the adult capacity to turn this faith into something workable: *"No more Losers, no more cowering in a hole in the ground and calling it a clubhouse, no more crying in Georgie's room . . . believe in yourself, believe in the heat of that desire"* (*It,* 1057).

The adults in Derry have lost the capacity for acting courageously out of faith—basic moral faith in self-decency as well as a larger societal ethic. Children, whether because they don't know any better, or because they really have nothing to lose, or because their appetites for adventure are not easily satiated, are not jaded into the cynicism that too often is the inheritance of advancing years. Chüd, then, is nothing more than Danny Torrance's shine: at its essence it is a current of love that flows magically among individuals who have not forfeited the power that represents the best part of being young. Perhaps Richie Tozier best expresses this concept as he recalls the Smoke-Hole ceremony: *"The energy you drew on so extravagantly when you were a kid, the energy you thought would never exhaust itself—that slipped away somewhere between eighteen and twenty-four, to be replaced by something much duller, something as bogus as a coke high"* (*It,* 734). In 1985 the magical properties associated with childhood exist primarily in memory for the members of the Losers' Club. But in the Derry public library on the eve of their descent back into the sewers of It, the Losers complete the journey back through memory and time: "Bill felt an exalting sense of power. He was dimly aware that he had an erection, and that every hair on his head was standing up straight. The sense of force in the completed circle was incredible. All the doors in the library slammed shut in unison. 'I remembered,' Beverly said. She looked up at Bill, her eyes huge, her pale cheeks wet. 'I remembered *everything.* My father finding out about you guys. Running. Bowers and Criss and Huggins. How I ran. The tunnel . . . the birds . . . It . . . *I remember everything'"* (*It,* 900–901).

The circle imagery at work here and throughout the remainder of the book is meant to suggest both the power of the Losers acting in unison, having finally reconnected with one another, and the unified strength associated with their collective return to the past. When a magician wishes to create magic, he draws a circle around himself, and it is from within this bounded area that powers can be called into play that are lost outside the circle. Joseph Campbell has studied the importance of circle imagery in a variety of cultures throughout history. He concludes that the circle maintains universal magic, suggesting the timelessness of human life. His description of the circle's symbolic properties conforms precisely to the experience the Losers encounter in their Derry reunion: "Everything within the circle is one thing, which is encircled, enframed. That would be the spatial aspect. But the temporal aspect of the circle is that you leave, go somewhere, and always come back."[9]

Throughout his fiction, King employs circle imagery as evidence of supernatural power. Surely, the series of spirals and circles associated with the pet cemetary and the Micmac burial ground in *Pet Sematary* represent one of the most ambitious and successful examples of this. In *Pet Sematary,* however, circular imagery suggests negative energy; Louis Creed spirals further into the bondage of the Wendigo each time he crosses the perimeters of the Micmac burial ground. In *It* something quite different is at work; the image of the wheel or circle is meant to highlight the adult-to-child journey that the Losers must undertake in order to ensure their survival. Other circular implications appear in a variety of instances and in a myriad of permutations. Most notably, the adults remember the physical circle they had created in the Barrens as children after their first encounter with the spider. With their hands joined at Stan's urging, they had pledged loyalty to one another and taken a blood oath to return if Pennywise should ever reappear in Derry. In their second battle against the spider, as adults, they require the same spirit of unity: "It was the force of memory and desire; above all else, it was the force of love and unforgotten childhood like one big wheel" (*It,* 1092).

In *Hero with a Thousand Faces* Campbell maintains that the circle stands "for the kinship group, the clan, the tribe. . . . it contains the secret of the transformation of heavenly into earthly forms. The hearth in the home, the altar in the temple, is the hub of the wheel of the earth, the womb of the Universal Mother whose fire is the fire of life" (Campbell 1949, 42). As King indicated in the chapter 1 interview in this book, Beverly's role in *It* is that of "Universal Mother," and her presence is likewise reminiscent of Campbell's transformative wheel. In serving as the feminine center for the sexual initiation of each male in the Losers' Club, Beverly essentially forms a circle around herself and her six lovers, making certain that each of the boys is protected within the perimeters of their shared love and experience. The magical circle that Beverly draws around her lovers is meant to contrast with the pregnant It, whose 27-year cycles of violence and murder imitate the circular patterns of Derry's history.

Certainly, one of the most important circular symbols in the novel must be the wheels of Silver, Bill Denbrough's repossessed bicycle, which he must learn to ride again if he hopes to complete the full imaginative cycle of his journey back to adolescence, and to save Audra's life as a consequence. The bicycle, significantly oversized, is symbolic of Bill's great powers. Silver's name not only suggests the Lone Ranger's trusted steed but is also the substance in the slingshot projectile used by the Losers to wound the werewolf at Neibolt Street. Riding atop Silver, Bill appears as a gallant warrior; he summons the imagery of a god, perhaps Mercury or Bellerophon, the rider of Pegasus. Like Pegasus, Bill is a symbol of poetic inspiration. In spite of his stutter, Bill's powers—moral and literary—are his legacy as an adult.

It is particularly interesting, in light of the novel's plethora of circular shapes and recurring patterns, that Silver's wheels should propel Bill Denbrough along the street at a reckless rate of speed. The bicycle ride is a clear allusion to the child Bill had watched riding a skateboard on the first day of his return to Derry: "He rode as Bill had suspected he would: with lazy hipshot grace. Bill felt love for the boy, and exhilaration, and a desire to *be* the boy. . . . The boy rode as though there were no such things as death or getting older" (*It*, 597). Dressed as the adolescent boy he now vividly remembers, with the catatonic Audra riding close behind him, Bill rides his old bicycle on a journey back through the streets of his youth, connecting the skateboarder to a younger version of himself. This final "ride to beat-the devil" takes him back through all the fears he had as both a child and an adult before facing It on each occasion: "He saw the yawning darkness where the street had been, heard sullen water rushing down there in the tangled darkness, and laughed at the sound" (*It*, 1136). Perhaps because he must still rescue Audra from the abyss of her own terror, the courage of the past few weeks has not yet faded into memory for Bill as it has for the other survivors of the Losers' Club. That he can now laugh at what once terrified him suggests that he has completed the circle from child to adult and back again. Moreover, the reader senses that Bill's journey will not fade into dull memory in quite the same manner as it has for the others. As discussed later in this chapter, Bill's occupation as a writer promises to sustain the adult-child connection: "*he thinks that it is good to be a child, but it is also good to be a grownup and able to consider the mystery of childhood . . . its beliefs and desires. I will write about all of this one day, he thinks*" (*It*, 1138).

Form Mirrors Content: Stylistics of Survival

Paralleling the thematic quest to form a parabola linking past with present, the narrative of *It* alternates in point of view between 1958 and 1985. As the adult Losers attain a more complete memory of their personal and composite pasts, it is appropriate that King's narrative style should mirror the expansion of their collective consciousness. King ceases to provide calendar dates in chapter 19, so that the place and hour define the relative moment as past and present fully synthesize. As the quest to destroy It intensifies, forcing the Losers to recall their adolescent encounters with the monster, the specific time frames of 1958 and 1985 blur, becoming nearly inseparable.

From chapter 20 until the end of the book the alternation between the two eras accelerates as they gradually merge into one, reflecting a geographical and historical intersection. In addition to the novel's semiotic recreation of past events, the reader encounters many of the traits that Fredric Jameson has affiliated with postmodern discourse. Among these are the use of pastiche and collage as structuring devices; the emergence of a polyphonic textual structure; and most important, a displacement of history by historicism, in which the past is reinterpreted and reconstructed in the present.[10] The varying time references of individual chapters flow into one another, making memory and reality synonymous. This flickering narrative style intensifies to the extent that sentences starting in one history are finished in another; thus the literal journey into the sewer and the metaphorical joining of past and present in the minds of the Losers are embodied in the structure of the text. Indeed, by chapter 22, "The Ritual of Chüd," it is impossible to distinguish between the events of 1958 and 1985. The second confrontation with It so closely resembles the first that the two battles meld, both in the minds of the participants and in the form of the narrative.

In his 1929 critical analysis originally entitled *Problems of Dostoevski's Art,* Michail Bakhtin argues that the Russian novelist's major literary contribution is the origination of the "polyphonic novel." Among the various aspects Bakhtin associates with this narrative form is the conscious attempt to transcend time, linking past to present in a process of simultaneity:

"The ability to exist simultaneously and the ability to stand side by side or face to face opposite one another is for Dostoevski the criterion for differentiating the essential from the nonessential. Only those things which can conceivably be presented simultaneously, which can conceivably be interconnected in a single point in time, are of the essence and enter in Dostoevski's world; . . . [Dostoevski's characters] remember from their past only those things which have not ceased to be current for them and which continue to be experienced in the present: an unexpiated sin or crime, an unforgiven insult."[11]

Bakhtin ascribes the polyphonic novel exclusively to Dostoyevski, arguing that the Russian author's work represented a significant break with nineteenth-century narrative tradition. By limiting his frame of reference to the Continental novel, however, Bakhtin excludes the work of nineteenth-century experimental American novelists such as Hawthorne and Melville. *Moby-Dick, The Confidence Man, Benito Cereno,* and *The House of the Seven Gables* also illustrate Bakhtin's concept of a polyphonic novel. Stephen King's *It* comes out of the American Gothic tradition, which (as discussed in chapter 2) includes Melville, Hawthorne, and Faulkner. It is important to recognize that King's book owes its experimental orientation more to a distinctly American legacy than to an exclusively European influence.

Certainly, Faulkner's contributions to the development of the modern novel were important influences on the narrative structure of *It*. In many of Faulkner's best novels actions in the present are held in suspension by an interrupted narrative that allows the events of the past to become reanimated, thus creating what Bakhtin defines as "materialized history," in which "time becomes, in effect, palpable and visible."[12] King's purposes in *It* parallel Faulkner's in novels such as *The Sound and the Fury, Light in August,* and *Absalom, Absalom!* insofar as both writers believed that survival and identity, for individuals as well as for social communities, were possible only when the past was acknowledged and viewed in direct relationship to the present. Through the interplay of time and place, as he expands memory from the individual toward the collective, King engenders in *It* a fictional narrative drawn from a variety of historical consciousnesses. In a manner that recalls Bakhtin's description of the polyphonic novel, King superimposes one time upon another, inventing a present through a vision of the past. Just as Faulkner dispenses with the typical characteristics found in conventional narratives in order to provide the reader with a deeper and multifaceted understanding of history, King employs a polyphonic narrative—incorporating time dislocations and convergences, and multiple and subjective perspectives on a shared past—to highlight the dialogism the Losers use to defeat the monological It.

Throughout King's canon evil manifests itself as a monological presence. Whether it takes the shape of a religious fanatic, the fascistic authority of Randall Flagg, or the social conformity dictated by the Tommyknockers and It, evil thrives in a rational, highly ordered world. King's malefic incarnations are devoid of imagination; they subsist in closed, self-contained systems that never compromise their empowerment. Evil in King's fiction always tries to make its knowledge the only knowledge. It manipulates, restricts, and silences opposition. And usually the narrative itself, while projecting such a consciousness, is appropriately reduced to a single authoritarian voice. The very choice of It's name, a third-person neutral pronoun, underscores its condition as a nonaddressable entity. In *'Salem's Lot, The Tommyknockers, The Stand,* and *It,* the evil is represented in the unity of the townspeople and the malefic avatar—a monological merging in speech, thought, and action: "The voice had told him [Henry Bowers] about the day's work while he knelt beside Butch with the knife against Butch's neck. The voice had explained everything. . . . The voice would take care of him—he sensed that. If you took care of It, It would take care of you. That was how things had always been in Derry" (*It,* 948, 949).

In contrast, the forces of good in King embody Bahktin's principle of metafictive dialogue. As evident throughout *It,* King's concept of moral goodness relies upon a multifaceted perception of reality. In the unique voices and personalities of the Losers and in the various healthy, predominantly male associations found throughout King's canon, we find viable alternatives to evil's self-enclosure. Jeanne Campbell Reesman argues that generally, when maleficence is defeated in King's fiction, a small group of people must band together in a democratic and participatory union to counterbalance evil's monarchy. Through dialogue among one another, these characters find a way to save themselves and their communities:

"Nearly all scenes with the Losers are dialogues; the novel's brief early reliance on narrative exposition is replaced by heavy use of dialogue. Interior monologue is replaced with something new, something like "interior dialogue" with other characters. This becomes especially important in the concluding scenes. Repeated confessions, telling and retelling of events, remembering and sharing—all telling is important to the group. When Mike Hanlon calls back the Losers to come back to Derry and face It again, the dramatic revelatory scene in the Chinese restaurant forms a model for many scenes to come, as the Losers begin to remember, to speak, and to address the past and its evil influence upon their present lives. All important decisions to act are henceforth made in dialogue."[13]

Moral survival in King consistently requires an enlargement beyond the self and toward a recognition of otherness, and the narrative structure affiliated with interpersonal unions mirrors this expansive quality. Thus, the monologic authorial voice employed to describe It and used also by the spider to describe its own solitary condition is ever distinct from the communication formed by the Losers' dialogical plurality: "It wanted . . . to break their mental communication. If that ceased, [Denbrough] would be utterly destroyed. To pass beyond communication was to pass beyond salvation; he understood that much from the way his parents had behaved toward him after George had died. It was the only lesson their refrigerator coldness had had to teach him" (*It*, 1055).

For King, the breakdown of causality and chronology, of creating discourse as differentiated and polyphonous as possible, creates an openendedness of meaning that resists It's urge to appropriate and institutionalize thought. The Losers strive to keep a sense of otherness alive as a mark of the resistance of experience and subjectivity to It's attempt to socialize language—the means by which alienation and loss of identity are continuously situated and resituated in Derry.

King's Looking Glass: Portraits of the Artist

Indisputably, much of Stephen King's popular appeal in the last two decades is due to the fantastic events that take place in his fiction. His writing, no less than Tolkein's or Lewis's, is often centered on magical occurrences. But the magic in King's world is never restricted to the domain of the supernatural. Several of King's protagonists are writers (autobiographical, to various degrees), always in possession of certain powers of transcendence—talismanic properties directly affiliated with the skill of their profession. As King acknowledges in the interview in chapter 1 of this book, "Wherever you go in my little part of the landscape, the writer is always there looking back at the reader. So, what I have written about writers and writing in the last five years or so has been a real effort on my part to understand what I am doing, what it means, what it is doing to me, what it is doing for me."

In June 1989 King was asked by *The New York Times Book Review* to select a character in fiction he would most like to travel with and to explain why. His response was "Sherlock Holmes—it would be fascinating to view American life through his deductive eyes."[14] The writers in King's canon seem to be kin of Sherlock Holmes: they are like instinctive detectives of life, seeking the truth through deductive reasoning in a world where madness threatens to reign.

There are two writers in *It*—Mike Hanlon, who keeps a journal that records Derry's history and speculates on its connection to Pennywise, and Bill Denbrough, who writes fiction on the same topics: "All those novels. Derry is where they all came from; Derry was the wellspring" (*It*, 219). Let us consider Hanlon first, as he is the pivotal character around whom the Losers as adults initiate the journey back to childhood.

Hanlon is not merely a recorder of Derry's nefarious past; he also is its moral conscience. His journal keeps the terror of It in focus, monitored, and

eventually contained. The act of journal writing does several things for Mike
Hanlon. First, remembering the words of his deceased father reinvigorates
his relationship to him and to a past they must interpret together. Hanlon's
father, while not a writer himself, was one of Derry's first historians, "col-
lecting old clippings about the town. It [was] his hobby" (*It*, 719). Father
and son share a sense of the importance of history—that the past is a subject
that must be studied if humankind is to survive in the present. Like the poet
in folklore and mythology, Hanlon uses his skill as a writer to recreate the
past in order to understand it and discover its moral lessons for the present.
Second, the act of writing allows Hanlon to make associations among the
historical events that have occurred in Derry and to use this information to
trace a pattern to It's behavior (he is the one who recognizes, for example,
that there is a cycle to which Pennywise's activities conform). His careful research enables him to distinguish Derry's daily patterns of criminal behavior
from evidence of Pennywise's larger design: "It's come again. I know that
now" (*It*, 470).

Each of the four Derry interludes in the novel is a direct excerpt from
Hanlon's journal and represents an attempt to recapture moments from
Derry's long association with It. Hanlon's writing essentially parallels the
journey of the Losers in their effort as adults to remember the past. At the
end of the second interlude, Hanlon writes to the point of exhaustion and
literally falls asleep inside the pages of his notebook. While he is asleep,
Pennywise visits him to leave a symbolic balloon with Hanlon's face painted
on it, perhaps indicating that Hanlon's act of composing has brought the
clown increasingly into focus. As a record of his father's rendition of events
that transpired at the Black Spot, Hanlon's writing gives birth to memory,
and Pennywise is reborn.

The recollection of his father's narrative stirs Hanlon's remembrance of It
as a giant bird in the Ironworks. The act of putting that narrative in writing
creates a permanent connection in Hanlon's mind: "I wrote until long after
three this morning, pushing the pen faster and faster, trying to get it all out.
I had forgotten about seeing the giant bird when I was eleven. It was my father's story that brought it back . . . and I never forgot it again. Not any of
it. In a way, I suppose it was his final gift to me" (*It*, 471). But what makes
Hanlon think of his father's story as "a terrible gift . . . but wonderful in its
way"? (*It*, 471). "Terrible" suggests his recognition of Pennywise as a dark
presence in Derry that has cut across historical eras and generations (it is immediately after this interlude that the Losers reassemble for their second assault in the sewers). "Wonderful" suggests his appreciation of the legacy of
defiance that is embodied in his father's Black Spot narrative. The history

recorded in Hanlon's journal, in other words, is not merely a record of Pennywise's wanton evil; it also contains the memory of individual acts of endurance and resistance against that evil.

Hanlon's need to write down his father's narrative allows him the opportunity to connect his own experience at the Ironworks, where Pennywise had appeared as Rodon, to his father's recollection of a bird hovering over the burning at the Black Spot. Both these occasions illustrate the terror and collusion that are part of evil's design, but they likewise indicate that it is possible to subvert this design. At the Ironworks and at the Black Spot, individuals thwart the power of Pennywise. As a child Hanlon fires tiles at the bird, so severely wounding it that it abandons the attack against him. At the Black Spot, Dick Halloran, Trev Dawson, and Hanlon's father work together to save the lives of others, risking their own in the process. These examples of heroic self-discipline and group cooperation against the mindless brutality of It are unified in Hanlon's journal into heroic action: in spite of evil's sinister manipulations, individual men are shown to be capable of undermining its plan. Hanlon's research thus reveals Pennywise to be something less than omnipotent. Moreover, in studying the history of the Black Spot, Hanlon discerns that through a commitment to think not as selfish individuals but as members of a collective responsible for the welfare of others, it is possible for a group of individuals to weaken Pennywise. In their righteous battle against It, the members of the Losers' Club are reminiscent of the black men who had struggled against the racist power structures of Derry. And like the blacks who had founded the nightclub in flagrant rejection of Derry's atmosphere of racial intolerance, Hanlon, a generation later, refuses to condone the town's subtle attempts to cover up the oppression of its children.

Mike Hanlon must be seen as the central character in this novel. Through his daily journal entries he has maintained close contact with It for the past 27 years. Hanlon elects to remain in Derry to "keep the lighthouse" (*It*, 512), even as the others leave to make their fortunes elsewhere; he recognizes when it is necessary to summon his adult friends; and because of his role as the clear-eyed historian of Derry, he emerges as the leader and organizer when the Losers first return to the town. Mike's journal has provided him with the unique perspective of juxtaposing Derry's past and present. For him It's violence is no dim recollection, as it is for the others, who must make the long journey back through the corridors of their own memories. Because he has studied continually the relationship between his own past and Derry's history, Hanlon is more attuned to the psychological needs of the Losers and helps them prepare for their final encounter with It. He also is in possession of the plan of action that must be followed to recreate the magical circle the group had formed as children. He senses intuitively, for example, that Denbrough, even more than the others, will be forced to journey back into time. In preparation, Hanlon purchases a can of oil and a bicycle-tire repair kit; he anticipates Silver's reemergence (*It*, 607).

Although Bill Denbrough is the acknowledged leader of the group, Hanlon plays an equally significant role. He serves as a kind of high priest–initiator, encouraging the adult Losers to trust in their individual and collective consciousnesses of the past. He eases his friends into acknowledging the relationship between the past and present-day Derry, helps them to trust in the belief that Pennywise will be vanquished for a final time, and provides the example of his own self-sacrifice as a means of encouraging similar behavior in the others: "Bill remembered the fact Mike had so quietly pointed out: the six members of the Losers' Club who left Derry had quit being losers. Mike had stayed behind and was still behind" (*It*, 606).

Like his own father, who is summoned from memory into a living presence through the act of writing, Hanlon's life and career are best defined by his unflinching loyalty and courage. Although he is not physically available for the final battle against the spider / It, Hanlon has prepared and led the Losers' Club to the point that Bill Denbrough is able to take over. Hanlon gently leads Denbrough back across the landscape of time, back through memory, until Denbrough recalls for himself the exact "preconditions for the use of magic" (*It*, 610) first invoked 27 years ago.

As Hanlon employs his journal to understand better the events of his own history and the cycle of It's involvement with his town, Bill Denbrough uses writing as a means of actively confronting the fear that represents the very heart of Derry's past and present. Denbrough's writing is a means of maintaining contact, of not forgetting, as well as a vehicle for exculpation: "Bill sometimes wrote stories. . . . He did this a bit more frequently since George's death. The pretending seemed to ease his mind" (*It*, 333). Denbrough writes tales that explore the unmentionable in Derry; in so doing, in retaining the courage to expose the lie, he gains a sense of strength and affirmation. These are the elements so desperately missing from Derry's civic life. Because of the town's failure to face itself—to acknowledge its own darkest urges and secrets—evil is allowed the opportunity to flourish. Denbrough is the "soul" of the Losers' Club: he is its natural leader who has suffered more than the others (his brother George has been killed by It and he feels the guilt of responsibility) and who possesses, because of his role as a writer, a keen awareness of moral absolutes and the importance of maintaining them. Pennywise remains most frightened by Denbrough's powers.

It appears to recognize that while Denbrough's stutter makes him the least articulate of all the children, his imaginative capacity, deepened and honed as a result of his occupation as a fiction writer, makes him the most dangerous: *"The writer was the strongest, the one who had somehow trained his mind for this confrontation over all the years, and when the writer was dead with his guts falling out of his body, when their precious "Big Bill" was dead, the others would be Its quickly"* (*It*, 1018).

Like the other members of the Losers Club, Denbrough cannot remember exactly the events that transpired 27 years ago. But as Hanlon helps him to acknowledge, he will need to recreate the Ritual of Chüd, a sort of linguistic contest between monster and man. Denbrough's skill as a writer helps in this quest, as his imaginative capacities recapture "these memories waiting to be born" (*It*, 140). As Hanlon's journal work illustrates, Denbrough learns that a writer must be willing to face his memories honestly and without flinching; this active struggle is his only hope for gaining control over them.

Denbrough and Hanlon are the moral centers of *It*. And if we accept King's premise that *It* is an epic journey through an urban underworld,[15] then Denbrough and Hanlon are related to the epic hero in Western civilization. The protagonists of the best epic poems—Odysseus, Aeneas, Dante—embark on voyages that are revelatory of their very selves, and the fullness of humanity is mirrored in their quests. Like Odysseus, who discovers himself through his wanderings, his pain, and his courage, Denbrough and Hanlon, through their own epic quest, learn moral lessons about coping with adversity. King's two characters also exemplify the epic hero's resourcefulness in exploring the full range of his emotional and intellectual attributes.

All of the writers in King's fiction occupy roles similar to that of the hero in the epic tradition: to reassert order in the midst of chaos and destruction. While these individuals may not possess the supernatural abilities of a divinity, they do possess the powers to create and control. King's writer-protagonists, like Dante in the *Divine Comedy,* remind us continually that they are merely human, not supernatural, beings; and since they are perhaps the most human of all the heroes in King's canon, their experience has as much relevance for us as it does for them.

In his discussion of the relationship between myth and modernism, Joseph Campbell maintains that the epic hero's real moral legacy is found not in his individuality but in his commitment to the body of society as a whole, since he derives his manners and techniques of living from the group. In *Hero with a Thousand Faces* Campbell argues that the modern age has extolled the self-determined individual, thus creating a fragmented society in which gods and myths disappear. As noted earlier in the discussion of *The Talisman,* King has sustained a fascination with Campbell's thoughts on the relationship between the quest-romance hero and the community from which he emerges and returns. Hanlon and Denbrough, as leaders of the Losers, share the same knowledge that Campbell extols in the epic hero: alone, the individual will is too often misdirected; conversely, the urge to better the condition of others restrains the pull toward egotism. Like *The Talisman, It* is a novel that not only echoes the fundamental structure of the mythic quest as Campbell defines it but also reaffirms the very essence of its thematic content. Campbell's wish to see myth and a group identity reintegrated in modern times is at least partially fulfilled in this novel of epic proportions.

Another Portrait from the Gallery: The Artist in Misery

On two separate occasions in his 1987 novel *Misery,* Stephen King makes reference to John Fowles's fine first novel, *The Collector.*[16] King's book is indebted to *The Collector* on a variety of levels, most obviously because it recreates Fowles's plot: a lonely and misdirected individual, motivated not by a desire for money or sex but by a curious admixture of admiration and rage, kidnaps and torments an innocent artist. The differences that distinguish these parallel plots, however, are truly startling, as King inverts the Gothic male villain / chaste maiden prototype to which Fowles so deliberately adheres. *Misery* is a novel of its time insofar as its woman character is not cast in a passive role. Annie Wilkes may be viewed as an unfortunate victim of her own mental illness, but she is also a victimizer. Like the masculine rakes and rogues who preceded her in the tradition of the eighteenth-century Gothic romance, Annie is this tale's Gothic villain, and her aggressive impulses are frequently described through the imagery of rape. In the opening scene of the novel, for example, Paul awakens briefly from the unconsciousness of a drug overdose to discover his captor laboring to resuscitate him: he "smelled her on the onrush of breath she had forced into him the way a man might force a part of himself into an unwilling woman" (*M,* 4).

There is little question that King's Annie Wilkes and Fowles's Ferdinand Clegg / Caliban are seriously deranged individuals. Annie exhibits nearly textbook symptoms of a manic-depressive personality. In her manic phase she is capable of indulging her captive, Paul Sheldon, with tenderness and sympathy; her depressive stage takes her to the opposite extreme, as she besets Paul with vicious acts of wanton cruelty that always threaten to culminate in murder-suicide.

Fowles's antagonist resembles Annie in a number of remarkable traits. Both Caliban and Annie seem sharply aware that their social status is inferior to that of their guests. Paul Sheldon is a famous and wealthy "smart guy" novelist, while Miranda is an exquisitely beautiful and cultured daughter of a doctor. Annie and Caliban resent deeply the class differences separating them from their captives, and often inflict verbal and physical punishment as a consequence. Moreover, Annie and Caliban have severely warped attitudes toward sexuality, which symbolize the degree of repressiveness inherent in their personalities. The only manuscript of Paul's new novel, *Fast Cars,* is burned by his captor because of its obscene language; and Annie's amputations of Paul's body parts are symbolic emasculations (after she severs his ankle in the most gruesome scene in the novel, she discloses that she had considered substituting his "man-gland" [*M,* 251]). Similarly, when Miranda attempts to seduce Caliban after several glasses of sherry, he is rendered impotent. He is only aroused later, after he drugs her and takes several pornographic photographs of her bound and gagged while wearing high heels. Although his illness is perhaps not illustrative of a textbook maladjustment (he is less erratic than Annie, his personality is more consistent and regulated), Caliban is a wellspring of misogynistic hostility beneath his mannered and sober exterior: "Once I let myself dream I hit her across the face as I saw it done once by a chap in a telly play. Perhaps that was when it all started. . . . She was just like a woman. Unpredicatable. Smiling one minute and spiteful the next."[17] Just as Annie indulges a certain personal obsession in possessing her writer as though he is an exotic bird, Caliban is in love with Miranda as a human butterfly that will enrich his collection. Both captors seek to own beauty, to control and ultimately to destroy what fascinates them. This quote from Miranda's journal aptly defines the situation of both captives: "The sheer joy of having me under his power, of being able to spend all and every day staring at me. He doesn't care what I say or how I feel—my feelings are meaningless to him—it's the fact that he's got me" (*Fowles,* 150).

Although Annie and Caliban are terrifying individuals, their terror does not emerge as a result of their fantastic urge to indulge obsessive behavior. What is truly terrifying about *The Collector* is that it is a story about the masculine desire to dominate women. It is, without qualification, a novel with a strong feminist subtext, warning explicitly against the patriarchal proclivity to view women as fantasy objects. Sharing the tragic destiny of so many women down through history, Miranda must die because her captor has not learned how to live. Caliban acknowledges the seductiveness of his sexist urges and even manages unconsciously to indict the gender bias that inspired them: "All right, you think I'm not normal keeping you here like this. Perhaps I'm not. But I can tell you there'd be a blooming lot more of this if more people had the money and the time to do it. Anyway there's more of it now than anyone knows. The police know, I said, the figures are so big they don't dare say them" (*Fowles, 67*).

Unlike *The Collector, Misery* has no feminist overtones; it is a novel about the destructive, potentially castrating nature of women. Although her mental instability is never in doubt, Annie Wilkes is one of the few women in King's canon who possesses real power, and she does not know how to handle it responsibly. Aware that her authority is in constant jeopardy—from the police, or from Paul himself as he regains his strength to rebel against her—Annie's every action reflects her need for domination. And to this perversely independent end, she is willing to sacrifice everything: the farm animals, a state policeman, Paul himself, her nursing career, and eventually, even her own life.

The Collector features a young painter struggling tentatively with her own definition of what it means to be an artist; *Misery,* on the other hand, is about the consequences of artistic fame. Paul Sheldon is a veiled autobiographical portrait of King himself; both writers struggle to attain critical recognition in genres (romance and horror, respectively) that are often too restrictive and thus easily disparaged. From this perspective, Annie Wilkes must be seen as a composite of all the conflicting forces—from the demands of an expectant audience to the disparaging remarks of academic critics and reviewers—that seek to confine the art of Sheldon / King into reductive and therefore safe categories.

But *Misery* is not a safe book. It ultimately transcends *The Collector* in the sense that Paul is able to triumph over the will of his captor, while Miranda is sacrificed to it, a victim of her own femininity. More than two-thirds of Miranda's journal entries center on recollections of a fellow artist, G.P. (George Paston). This older male mentor-lover is carefully revealed as a father figure in Miranda's existence, particularly in terms of her slavish quest to win his acclaim. From her journal we learn of G.P.'s favorite artists, his theories of art and life, his moods and eccentricities. As Fowles develops these entries, the reader actually comes to know more about G.P. than about Miranda. The extent of her documentation is significant because it shows the degree to which she has been dominated by his influence. Although G.P. has succeeded in deepening Miranda's sense of aesthetics, he has done so at the expense of her self-confidence, forcing her into a subservi-

ent position, especially in terms of her identity as an artist. As he once revealed to her, "The art of love's your line: not the love of art" (*Fowles,* 149).
By negating Miranda's status as both an artist and a mature woman, G.P. is
merely another version of Caliban. As her independence is weakened,
Miranda becomes all the more dependent upon him. We witness no better
illustration of these points than when Miranda is presented with her first
and only real opportunity to free herself from Caliban's domination. Instead
of using the axe to dispatch him after inflicting a serious head wound,
Miranda retreats from the sight of Caliban's blood; she goes soft at the
thought of his pain. While her compassion is certainly an admirable virtue,
it also underscores her inability to take control of her own destiny and to
break the bonds of feminine servitude that have held her captive far longer
than has Caliban.

The creation of art also offers Miranda no real opportunity for salvation
or transcendence in her time of need. On several occasions she admits that
neither writing in her journal nor painting provide her with any consolation;
they are simply reminders of the life she has been forced to abandon: "I'm
getting deperate to escape. I can't get any relief from drawing or playing records or reading. . . . I shan't go on keeping a diary when I leave here. It's
not healthy. It keeps me sane down here, gives me somebody to talk to. But
it's vain. You write what you want to hear" (*Fowles,* 212, 228).

Paul Sheldon, on the other hand, uses his art to escape the bondage that
eventually kills Miranda. Whereas Caliban recognizes that he will never
fully understand Miranda's paintings or her love of art, Annie is intrigued at
the prospect of following Paul into the creation of a new novel; in fact, she
absolutely insists upon going along. But what is initially another means of
violating Sheldon's personality is transformed into the vehicle for his
liberation.

Like Caliban, Annie is a kind of psychic vampire; she sucks out Paul's inspiration and creativity in order to fashion a self-enclosed world. Just as her
rural farmhouse, complete with its empty telephone shell and other warped
attempts at normality, mirrors her paranoid mental condition, she means to
have her favorite author create a fictional realm exactly to her specifications.
As long as the writer cooperates, Annie will exercise some restraint over her
psychopathic tendencies. She assures him, for example, that he will live long
enough to bring back Misery, Annie's favorite fictional heroine who died in
Sheldon's last romance.

While Annie's tyranny brings to the surface all of Paul's doubts about
the true quality of his art (he knows that his fame and fortune have been
purchased by writing second-rate fiction), it also issues a challenge to him to

prove once and for all that he deserves to make a living (and to continue living) through the magic of words. In summoning his authorial voice, Paul realizes for the first time that an artist possesses strength as great as that of any cage employed to restrain him: "Something in her attitude as she stood in the doorway fascinated him. It was as if she was a little frightened to come any closer—as if she thought something in him might burn her. . . . The furnace was on. Oh, not that he had written particularly well—the story was hot, but the characters as stereotyped and predictable as ever—but this time he had been able to at least generate some power; this time there was heat baking out from beneath the lines. Amused, he thought: *She felt the heat. I think she's afraid to get too close in case I might burn her*" (*M*, 137) The production of Paul's novel, *Misery's Return*, parallels his life as Annie's captive. The writer is kept alive only because Annie remains obsessed with "the power of the gotta" (*M*, 230), the need to discover what will happen next in the narrative. The writing, on the other hand, while initially Paul's only card in a deck stacked against him, becomes his conduit to survival. Although Paul never really asserts absolute control over the situation until he ends up killing Annie, he steadily gains the ability to exert leverage over her psychosis: ". . . I had a certain passive hold over her" (*M*, 230). It is, moreover, the discipline he has cultivated as a writer that enables him to restrain himself from lashing out at Annie or making any attempt to overpower her physically (thus avoiding further punishments) until he is in a position to do so successfully. In contrast to Annie's volatility, Paul's self-control keeps him focused on survival and life.

In the course of this novel Paul Sheldon matures as both a writer and a human being. In his struggle to survive the "convalescence" administered by Nurse Wilkes, Paul changes personally. He not only gains a deeper respect for the craft he had formerly taken for granted, simply viewed as a meal-ticket; he also becomes a better "reader" through the act of writing *Misery's Return*. Paul learns to "read" Annie's moods, to provide the appropriate reaction to a given situation, and her many brutal lessons in humility teach him to moderate his temper and language. If Annie is a "woman full of tornadoes waiting to happen," by the end of the novel Paul has become a "Midwest farmer observing the sky," capable of interpreting it and acting accordingly to "collect his family and herd them into the storm cellar" (*M*, 64). Thus, while Misery Chastain is initially scorned by Paul in his effort to become a "serious writer," she later helps to save his life. Like Misery herself, encased in a living suit of "the most poisonous and bad-tempered bees in all the world" (*M*, 216), Paul must avoid panic in spite of the terror he is feeling. He must likewise restrain himself—verbally, physically, and mentally —in order to avoid being stung.

While Paul is in a deadly trap and feels as though he is doomed to suffer Annie's every machination, he keeps control over himself and does not give up or make desperate mistakes. Admittedly, he is scared and aware of the exact extent of his danger, but he is always thinking and calculating. Stripped of all his vices—from cigarettes and alcohol to his own false pride—Paul fashions himself into a spartan being. When he confuses Annie with the apparent burning of *Misery's Return*, it is clear that he has taken control. The symbolic burning is revenge for Annie's earlier torching of *Fast Cars*, but this climactic event also signals Paul's emerging independence. For the first time in the narrative, he actually stands erect: "He pushed himself up and tottered erect on his right foot" (*M*, 291).

Although he will never walk normally again, having lost both a foot and a thumb to his surgical nurse, Paul emerges from his ordeal a more complete human being than when he began it. Before having met his Bourka goddess, Paul appears to have had much in common with Harry in Ernest Hemingway's short story "The Snows of Kilamanjaro." Like Harry, Paul had not been true to his craft; he had never lived up to his potential as a writer or as a human being. And while he had tried to mask his pain through alcohol, women, and material gratifications, he had always been aware of it. He had sold out his talents as an artist for the commercial success of the *Misery* series. It is certainly ironic that his redemption comes in the form of Annie Wilkes, who makes him write the best *Misery* novel of his career because this time he is able to invest his heroine with the reality of his own suffering:

"Annie was right; the story was turning out to be a good deal more gruesome than the other *Misery* books—the first chapter had not been a fluke but a harbinger. But it was also more richly plotted than any *Misery* novel since the first, and the characters were more lively. The latter three *Misery* novels had been little more than straightforward adventure tales with a fair amount of piquantly described sex thrown in to please the ladies. This book, he began to understand, was a gothic novel, and thus was more dependent on plot than on situation. The challenges were constant. It was not just a question of Can You? to begin the book—for the first time in years, it was Can You? almost every day . . . and he was finding he *could*" (*M*, 154).

When Annie brings him the old Royal typewriter, Paul's initial reaction is repulsion, primarily because he doesn't want to write another *Misery* book but also because Annie insists that he must. Nevertheless, his attention is riveted on the machine "with avid repulsed fascination" (*M*, 59) because the typewriter is a power source, and Sheldon senses this even before he has evidence of it. The typewriter not only buys him time in his life and death ordeal with Annie, but also aids him in regaining his physical strength. The machine thus functions as a tool for both his mental and physical recovery: "He had begun lifting it and setting it down whenever he was penned in the chair behind it and she was out of the room. Five lifts of six inches or so had been the best he could manage at first. Now he could do eighteen or twenty without a pause" (*M*, 148).

When her "pet writer" apparently burns the complete manuscript of *Misery's Return* before she reads its conclusion, Annie loses final control over an environment that had begun to change the afternoon she presented Paul with a typewriter. Thus, it is only slightly ironic that this same typewriter should become the weapon that brings about Annie's death when she trips over it: "She had actually died of the fractured skull she had received when she had struck the mantel, and she had struck the mantel because she had tripped. So in a way she had been killed by the very typewriter Paul had hated so much" (*M*, 307).

At the conclusion of *Misery*, Paul's misery is a recurring series of Annie Wilkes hallucinations: he sees her in the alleys of New York, in the shadows of his apartment, at the ends of dark corridors. His paranoia indicates that the mental scars of his imprisonment have not yet finished healing, even though his body has nearly fully recuperated. In his lonely suffering, Paul reconnects to the only certainty that has ever existed in his life: the stability born "through the hole in the page" in the act of writing. By commencing a new novel, he holds the Annie memories at bay. Her Norvil capsules were never as effective: "He could. He *could*. So, in gratitude and in terror, he *did*. The hole opened and Paul stared through at what was there, unaware that his fingers were picking up speed, unaware that his legs were in the same city but fifty blocks away, unaware that he was weeping as he wrote" (*M*, 310).

Without his writing, Paul Sheldon could not have survived his sentence as a prisoner in Annie Wilkes' house of horrors. There are too many occasions on which Paul's self-pity threatens to push him into the realm of madness. Annie's terrorizing has shaped his life to the point that he has become hostage to her insanity, and her warped perspective has influenced him to almost the same degree that his art has affected her: "He wondered in a dull sort of way how close he was to going insane. . . . He knew how constantly he had been terrorized, but did he know how much of his own subjective reality, once so strong he had taken it for granted, had been erased?" (*M,* 226, 239).

More than his ultimately thwarting Annie's powers of intimidation, Paul's returning to his art, to the creative process, is an affirmation of his willingness and ability to regain control over himself. The very skills required to be a real artist are also needed if one is to endure the Nietzschean abyss that King refers to in the prologue to Part I: "When you look into the abyss, the abyss also looks into you." Paul's humanity and his stubborn refusal to surrender to Annie's madness or despair keep him from sacrificing either his new book or his mind at the altar of this insane idol in a nurse's uniform. Even at the end of the novel, after having experienced the full range of Annie's psychosis, Paul is still capable of separating himself from the ultimate nihilism of her world-view. In the midst of his own nightmare, he is able to render an objective, even sympathetic response to his tormentor: "Paul thought that the occasional moments like this [Annie's infrequent acts of kindness] were the most ghastly of all, because in them he saw the woman she might have been if her upbringing had been right or the drugs squirted out all the funny little glands inside her had been less wrong. Or both" (*M,* 282).

In a journal entry written during her incarceration, Miranda recalls one of G.P.'s core tenets defining the role of an artist: "If you are a real artist, you give your whole being to your art. Anything short of that, then you are not an artist" (*Fowles,* 134). Paul Sheldon comes to comprehend the full meaning of this dictum because, unlike Miranda, he translates it into daily practice. Through his self-discipline and mental toughness, but most of all through the inspiration afforded by his writing talents, Paul Sheldon maintains his balance as he crawls along the perimeter of the abyss. Like any successful artistic endeavor, his journey shows him how to create meaning out of personal suffering, triumph out of despair. Paul's writing is the place where his only authority is found. Just as any good author holds his audience in captivity for the length of a narrative, suspended from everyday concerns in a landscape of the writer's making, Paul uses his confinement to test the full range of his artistic powers. He survives because he becomes Scheherazade.

Early in his ordeal Paul realizes that in his life the art of creating fiction dates back to his childhood. One of his deepest recollections concerns an adolescent game at which he once excelled:

"For a couple of summers his mother had sent him to day-camp at the Malden Community Center. And they had played this game . . . they had sat in a circle, and the game was like Annie's chapter-plays, and he almost always won . . . What was that game called?

He could see fifteen or twenty little boys and girls sitting in a circle in one shady corner of a playground, all of them wearing Malden Community Center tee-shirts, all listening intently as the counsellor explained how the game was played. *Can you?, the name of that game was Can You?, and it really was just like the Republic cliff-hangers, the game you played then was Can You?, Paulie, and that's the name of the game now, isn't it?"* (M, 107).

This memory forms an interesting nexus between Paul's role as a writer and King's general attitude toward adults throughout his fiction. As noted in this chapter's earlier discussion of *It,* a major task for King's adults throughout their lives is to maintain a conduit to childhood, to free the spirit of imagination relegated to that earlier state of being. The fiction writer, because he is always breaking the plane of reality—opening what Sheldon calls the "hole in the page" (M, 310)—in order to pretend, is in the advantageous position of realizing a special connection to his childhood. Thus, it is no accident that Paul Sheldon should remember the origins of the game "Can You?" at his moment of greatest crisis. In Stephen King's world adult survival is always predicated upon the survival of the child within the adult—the latter's capacity to summon forth the powers of imagination and simple faith.

In a 1983 interview first published in *Playboy,* King provided insight into the role writing occupies in his life: "Writing is necessary for my sanity. As a writer, I can externalize my fears and insecurities and night terrors on paper, which is what people pay shrinks a small fortune to do. In my case, they pay me for psychoanalyzing myself in print. And in the process, I'm able to "write myself sane," as that fine poet Anne Sexton put it. It's an old technique of therapists, you know: get the patient to write out his demons. A Freudian exorcism" (Underwood and Miller 1988, 44). Stephen King no longer writes out of financial necessity, but his rate of production over the past two decades—nearly a book a year—indicates that his writing is indeed necessary to preserving some sort of balance in his life and temperament. That he works at his art so diligently—at least half a day, seven days a week—indicates that writing for Stephen King is more than an occupation or mere enjoyment; it is a methodology for survival.

The power of language is talismanic in King's world. Many of his characters use the written word as a means for regaining control over their own lives and the lives of those who touch them. In his essay on the role of writing in King's novella *The Body,* Leonard Heldreth argues that "writing succeeds for Gordon [the protagonist] because it offers control over experience. . . . Writing permits a systematic formulation of the plan or world view and provides the means for keeping it before not only the author but all his readers."[18] Heldreth's assertions about the stabilizing influence of writing in *The Body* apply to every fictional work in King's canon in which an author makes an appearance. The one exception to this thesis is really not an exception at all: Jack Torrance in *The Shining* is a writer whose abrogation of his mind and spirit to the powers at the Overlook Hotel is paralleled in the loss of his craft. In Jack's case writer's block signifies, or is the result of, psychosis.

King's writer-protagonists make their lives their craft, but they also owe their lives to their craft. The art—the skill of writing—is real magic, and the individual man who utilizes it must also stand in awe of it. This magic remains so intoxicating that the personal identities of King's writers cannot be separated from their art. Even as Paul Sheldon anticipates working at Annie's Royal typewriter with a profound dread, once he has begun composing *Misery's Return* he can no more break the incantation than jog back to Denver.

In this sense, King inverts the clichéd romantic exultation of art as the product of madness. Instead, as the *Playboy* quotation indicates, King sees art as a means of attaining sanity and salvation: the dark chaos of the world can be managed, but only through the illumination of a mind that has labored to gain control over itself. As King reminds us in *Danse Macabre,* "fiction is the truth inside the lie, and in the tale of horror as in any other tale, the same rule applies now as when Aristophanes told his horror tale of the frogs: morality is telling the truth as your heart knows it" (*DM,* 403). The writer's illuminating magic of "telling the truth," a sort of liberation that stands in contrast to evil's oppressive lies, is the gift that emerges from the discipline of work and honest self-examination. If there is strength to be found in staring into the abyss, in confronting one's own misery, King hastens to inform us that even greater transcendence is derived from the act of writing about it.

Chapter Seven

Experiments in Genre and Form: *The Eyes of the Dragon* and *The Dark Tower* Saga

> He knew as well as we in our own world do that the road to hell is paved with good intentions—but he also knew that, for human beings, good intentions are sometimes all there are. Angels may be safe from damnation, but human beings are less fortunate things, and for them hell is always close.[1]

In 1982 Stephen King published a collection of four novellas under the title *Different Seasons*. In each of these separate narratives King moves beyond the perimeters of horror fiction to present, in the words of the lawyer-narrator of *The Breathing Method,* "tales of every sort, from the comic to the tragic to the ironic to the sentimental."[2] None of the supernatural creatures from the Gothic catalogue is present in any of the four selections. *Rita Hayworth and the Shawshank Redemption* is a comic novel of a prison escape; *Apt Pupil* is a dark study of history and its influence on the present; *The Body* is a tale of friendship, solidarity, and maturation; and *The Breathing Method* is a tale of a storytelling tradition in an exclusive men's club. There is no question that in the past two decades King has secured his reputation and fame as a result of his ability to terrify us. But as he demonstrated with the collection *Different Seasons,* he is also capable of working successfully within other categories of fiction.

The Eyes of the Dragon (1987) and *The Dark Tower* series (so far consisting of two volumes, *The Gunslinger* [1984] and *The Drawing of the Three* [1987]) represent King's excusions into the fairy tale and the western, respectively. *Eyes of the Dragon* was composed during the final stages of work on *The Talisman,* and while it does not evince the sharp contemporary sociological critique found in the larger and more complex *Talisman,* it does share one of its central locations: the Territories. And although *Eyes* is clearly indebted to the fairy-tale tradition in terms of style and cast of characters, the book is also political in nature, reflecting a dominant concern in King's canon: the manner in which individuals and whole communities are corrupted when a commitment to conscience is abandoned out of trepidation or the quest for power. In the case of *The Dark Tower*, a saga that began with the publication of the short story "The Gunslinger" in October 1978,[3] the epic qualities of *The Stand, The Talisman,* and *It* are once again in evidence as King deals in cultural archetypes and allegorical themes and characters. The fact that these aspects appear within a western milieu serves to deepen the loneliness of the gunslinger's quest.

Through the Eyes of a Medieval Fantasy

One of the pleasures of a well-constructed fantasy world in literature is that we inhabit it as we read; we sense its reality and its history. The Three Ages of Middle-Earth in Tolkien's *The Lord of the Rings* provide a famous example: the Pukul-men are crude monuments of forgotten ages, Treebeard once roamed lands now under the sea, Frodo and Sam discover the decapitated statue of an unremembered king at the crossroads in Ithilien, and so on. The historical and legendary background beautifully deepens the foreground of the narrative present and charges it with significance.

The True West and Middle-Earth and all that lies between were Tolkien's lifelong literary and mythographic preoccupation. Nothing suggests that Stephen King was nearly so involved in the creation of his kingdom of Delain in *The Eyes of the Dragon,* but he clearly gave the matter some thought. There is plenty of depth there, plenty of background fact and chronicle to give the surface of Delain and its story a rich texture. As the map of the Kingdom of Delain[4] (page 136) serves to indicate, King's sense of place in this fantasy is as much visual as it is historical.

As in most fairy tales and throughout the fantasy tradition, *The Eyes of the Dragon* features polar opposites in its story of the battle of good against evil. Peter, the good prince, who is wrongly accused of his father's murder and who has inherited his mother's highly developed moral capacities, is set in direct opposition to the magician Flagg, a recurring figure in Stephen King's gallery of villains. Flagg is associated with blackness, the absence of color; Peter is associated with white, the sum and combination of all colors.

Eyes is set entirely in the Territories, the parallel universe Jack Sawyer discovers in *The Talisman.* Given the importance of this medieval world, it is not surprising that a myriad of Shakespearean allusions and parallels resonate throughout *Eyes*. The woman who removes the royal crest from the napkins before they are taken to Peter is compared directly to the witches in *Macbeth:* "rocking and plying her needle like one of those weird sisters of

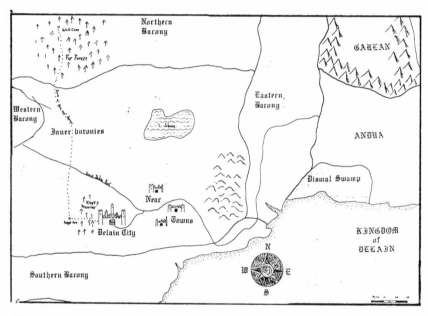

"The Kingdom of Delain"

whom you may have heard in another tale" (*Eyes*, 213). But the novel's most interesting Shakespearean resonance is found in the character development of Flagg. The wicked magician is a direct descendant from Shakespeare's lineage of villainy. He carries all the tools familiar to Iago, Edmund, and Richard III: a cunning intellect, a focused design to which he remains wholly committed, the absence of any degree of pity or remorse toward the innocent whom he has trapped, a perverse desire to see innocence punished for its own sake, a fierce will to wield power, and a total and callous disregard for the consequences his deceitful actions bring to bear upon others and the larger kingdom. Like a Shakespearean antihero, Flagg seeks to make trouble where none has been before—to wreck and destroy things just because they have been united and are flourishing. His evil is *disinterested;* he seeks power, but power is only a means to greater levels of destruction. Flagg wishes to raise taxes not because he wants to enhance his wealth or to make the king richer (that would be mere greed) but because the act is unjust in itself and will foment chaos.

The first page of the novel informs the reader that Flagg opposes "everyone in the Kingdom" in his desire to make certain that "Roland's younger son, Thomas, should be crowned King instead [of Peter]" (*Eyes*, 7). Thus we are made immediately aware of Flagg's arrogance, his disregard for the will of the people, and his willingness to use any means to enact his will. The name Flagg is highly suggestive of his personality insofar as he is a man who really possesses no civil or political allegiance to any single "flag" yet always manages to align himself at the center of human affairs: "The time before *that,* four hundred years before the time of Roland and his sons, he came as a singer named Browson, who became a close advisor to the King and Queen. Browson disappeared like smoke after drumming up a great and bloody war between Delain and Andua. . . ." (*Eyes*, 62). Flagg both lures, and is himself attracted to, leaders who are morally corrupt or vulnerable; he preys upon their insecurities. His magical skills initially promise a weighty advantage for any monarch who would choose to employ them, especially one fundamentally worried about maintaining control over his kingdom. However, when this monarch recognizes that Flagg is himself not to be trusted, it is too late; the magician has become both an integral element in the governance of the kingdom and an intimidating force to the leader himself.

Thus, King Roland, whose only regal attribute is his ability to hunt, is a perfect host for Flagg's parasitic activity. The naive are always the most susceptible to evil's sophistries, and Roland is all the more so because of his regal recalcitrance. And just as Roland is easily victimized by Flagg's machinations, his son Thomas becomes simple prey for the adroit magician. For Thomas, being Roland's second son is a constant source of personal irritation. His second-class status so warps Thomas's personality that he never fully establishes a secure identity of his own. His willingness to allow Peter to be punished for a crime Thomas knows he did not commit reflects the degree to which personal jealousy and sibling rivalry have stunted his moral capacities.

What distinguishes Peter most clearly from his brother is his ability to trust in himself. Even at the tender age of 17 Peter possesses such a highly developed sense of discipline and self-confidence that he refuses to despair over the injustice of his imprisonment. Moreover, he remains committed to righting the travesty of his father's murder. Like Hamlet in act 5 of Shakespeare's play, he is a young man in command of himself—resolved, as a result of his suffering, to punish the murderer of his father.

Peter's conception, so clearly aligned with his father's single moment of greatness in killing the dragon and with the creature's own majestic strength, defines Peter's personality. Unafraid to act decisively, Peter has no need for Flagg's counsel or deceptions. Moreover, the Prince, in contrast to his father and brother, is always shown to be capable of accepting full responsibility for each of his actions (as when he remains faithful to his pledge to place fresh poultices daily on the broken leg of a horse).

Peter is convicted of regicide, not as a result of evidence weighed against him but because of his failure to behave properly when accused. His tears of grief and shock are misinterpreted by Peyna, the prosecuting magistrate, as a sign of guilt: "Who else had been so convinced of Peter's guilt . . . and not so much by the evidence as by a young boy's shocked tears?" (*Eyes,* 253). In fact, they are a sign of sensitivity, a link to his late mother, Sasha, and the qualities that distinguish his royal lineage from that of other men. It is, moreover, his highly developed sensitivity that serves as Peter's motivation for escape. Unlike Peyna and Thomas, who simply wallow in their guilt and anguish over the changed state of Delain, Peter is unwilling to accept the injustice of fate as a final arbitrator. Armed with his mother's personal dignity and his father's commitment to the welfare of the kingdom, Peter pushes himself beyond depression and into action.

In *Eyes* the concept of seeing is very important on both literal and metaphorical levels of meaning. The narrative pivots around the murder that occurs in Roland's chamber and is communicated to Thomas through the eye of Niner, the slain dragon. Later in the novel Flagg awakens from dreams "with his left hand pressed to his left eye, as if he had been wounded there—and that eye would burn" (*Eyes,* 337). These recurring nightmares prove to be prescient, as the magician is eventually shot in the left eye by Thomas's arrow. In addition, Flagg makes use of his crystal to help him see into the future. At one point the rock is described as being "as milky as an old man's blind eye" (*Eyes,* 338). To the eyes of the magician and the dragon we must add the eye of the Needle, the only opening at the top of the stone tower that is Peter's window on the world. Late in the novel, when Dennis struggles to find the locket Peter has thrown out of his window, the former must rely upon his dead father's eyes (or intuition) to help him locate the message: "You're not SEEING anymore, boy. Stop and close your eyes for a moment. And when you open 'em look around. Really look around" (*Eyes,* 308). Even Naomi's dog, Frisky, possesses a special ability to "see" with her sense of smell in leading Ben and Naomi to the castle: "Scents are like colors to dogs . . . Some dogs have weak noses, and they read scents the way humans with poor eyes see colors'" (*Eyes,* 298). These are the literal references to eyes and seeing in this novel, and of course they are central to the narrative's unfolding. But the truest quest in this novel, however, revolves around the importance of viewing the truth: that Flagg is a liar, responsible for regicide, and that Peter is a wronged innocent. These insights occur almost individually to the citizens of Delain as each comes slowly to apprehend Peter's regal status and Flagg's role as murderer. Lastly, Thomas himself eventually acts upon what he has witnessed behind the eyes of the dragon, but only after spending the better part of the novel denying what he has seen with his own eyes (the very name of the kingdom, Delain, is an anagram for *denial*).

King's Women: A Feminist Reading of *Eyes*

In the interview I conducted with Stephen King in chapter 1, he characterized Beverly Marsh Rogan, one of the most interesting women in his canon, as an "earth mother" whose role is to bear "decent human adults." Although no one would deny the importance of this role for women, many of King's readers often object to the absence of females who are more independent. King's most successful and dynamic characters, like those of Hemingway, are male, and they usually operate (for better or worse) in a male-dominated realm. King's women generally fall into one of two opposing categories: the bitch-goddess, including Annie Wilkes, Nadine Cross (*The Stand*), Chris Hargenson (*Carrie*), and Christine; and the earth mother, including Frannie Goldsmith and Mother Abagail (*The Stand*), Sandra Stansfield (*The Breathing Method*), Liz Beaumont (*The Dark Half*), Stella Flanders, and Beverly Marsh Rogan.

Some of King's critics and readers have insisted that even King's most liberated female characters are exclusively maternal and sexual beings whose lives are completely centered on men and children.[5] I have discussed King's women characters extensively elsewhere[6] and will refrain from repeating my evaluation here. Suffice to argue that in *Eyes* King has challenged himself and the reader by attempting to create a nonsexist fairy tale. And this is no mere accomplishment, as many of the fairy tales popularized in the last century reflect the sexist biases of Western culture. King does not work from a precisely feminist orientation in *Eyes,* but he has composed a more balanced and positive perspective on gender roles.

Although the novel is centered in a patriarchal world—all of the main characters are men—Peter, the novel's hero, plays with a dollhouse. The dollhouse is a maternal signifier, linking Peter to his dead mother and her fondness for the toy when she was a girl. Furthermore, the plot revolves around a male held captive and in need of rescuing, instead of the traditional imprisoned woman found in many fairy tales. And while Peter is shown to be capable of using violence when he needs to subdue his guard, he does so because he has no other option; his attempts to reason with the man prove to Peter that violence is the only form of communication he understands. Most interestingly, Peter never attempts to escape from the tower by employing violence; rather, he uses his mother's dollhouse to weave a rope—an activity with decidedly feminine overtones.

Unfortunately, the brief portrait we see of Sasha conforms more to a gender stereotype. She is maternal and domestic, supportive and undemanding: "Roland chose Sasha because she seemed the quietest and meekest of the half dozen [women assembled as potential brides]" (*Eyes,* 10). When she desires changes within the kingdom, she doesn't debate or discuss their merits with her husband, but weeps and pleads (*Eyes,* 10). Sasha's role is clearly limited to that of loving wife and mother whose inspiration works as well when she is dead as when she was alive.

In sharp contrast to Sasha, Naomi is one of the most successfully realistic and nonsexist characters in King's entire canon. When we are introduced to her midway through the novel, she is neither wife nor mother, and her family consists of a wolf pack. Moreover, Naomi appears perfectly content in her independence. Unlike the majority of King's other female characters, Naomi is not domestic; she is more at home in the wilderness, running with her dogs. When she and Ben rush to the castle in order to rescue Peter, she does not ride on the sled while Ben runs. Instead, she matches him stride for stride, asserting, "I could go on a hundred koner from the place where you dropped dead, Ben Staad" (*Eyes,* 311). When the two sit by the fire and he pronounces that "snow's coming," she retorts, "I can read the clouds as well as you can, Ben Staad" (*Eyes,* 290). Unlike Sasha, she is unequivocal in her opinions, and perhaps her most impressive break from sex-role stereotype is that is she always treated as an equal by men.

King's strongest women have traditionally been associated almost exclusively with the family; their powers emerge from selfless devotion to their children and the men whom they support. Surely, the women in King's own life—his mother, Nellie, who was strong enough to keep the family together after her husband left her with two small children, and his wife, Tabitha, who has been married to him since 1971 and is the mother of his three children—have shaped King's opinion that a woman's most meaningful activity is to serve as the nucleus of familial life. Until his own daughter became a woman herself, King had few personal opportunities to view women in roles other than those of wife and mother. Moreover, King's bias may be the result of his own chronology and place. Like most men raised during the 1950s (an era that serves as a backdrop for so many of his novels and stories) in small working-class towns, King continues to struggle with feminist challenges to traditional sex roles.

King's positive attitude toward women in the domestic sphere notwithstanding, there are painfully few examples of independent women in his fiction. Those who do live alone, without children and/or husbands, appear particularly susceptible to the extreme perversions and psychologically unstable behavior exhibited by Annie Wilkes in *Misery*. Annie, after all, abandons her lifelong murder spree only for the duration of her brief marriage, and her divorce serves to increase the frequency and wantonness of her psychotic acts.

King wrote *Eyes* for his own daughter, Naomi, and her fictional namesake is modeled after her. Perhaps Naomi King is influencing her father to see that a woman need not focus upon men and children in order to be successful and strong. It will be interesting to follow the development of his female cast in future works. As he has indicated in several interviews (including the one for this book), when discussing black and women characters in his fiction, King is painfully aware of his limitations and remains profoundly dissatisfied with them.[7]

Other Worlds and Other Demons: *The Gunslinger*

At this writing Stephen King has published the first two volumes, *The Gunslinger* and *The Drawing of the Three*, of what he envisions as a four-volume epic saga entitled *The Dark Tower*. The interlocking short stories that constitute the first two volumes represent some of the strangest fiction King has ever written. Memory sequences blend with present action so that the two temporal planes merge together, overlaid with fantasy, violence, obsession, and ambiguity. It is the essence of a dream, Ben Indick muses, difficult to comprehend for the reader, yet somehow motivating and purposeful to the dreamer.[8]

Set in a postapocalyptic landscape that closely resembles the backdrop for *The Stand,* Roland, the last gunslinger, travels from the devil-grass of the desert to the underworld of an abandoned subway, across a terrain imbued with magical energies. The remains of gasoline pumps, highways, and railway lines attest not only to civilization's passage but also to the dwindling of mechanical power in the face of magic, the latter rising as technology wanes (Winter 1984, 73–74). Even the inanimate elements in this world pulsate with an eerie dynamism and radiance, as if infused with unseen properties on the verge of coming forth. Consequently, *The Gunslinger* contains a unique religious flavor that is approximated elsewhere in King's canon only in *The Stand.* There is a quasi-mystical quality to Roland's ambiguous quest. His fragmented memories of family and friends often intrude into his thoughts on the present, suggesting a cryptic association neither he nor the reader fully comprehends; the dark man whom he pursues provides him with more riddles on the nature of the universe and Roland's own future; and the meaning of the Tower, "a stairway, perhaps, to the Godhead itself" (*Eyes,* 209), is left unclear, although Roland stays obsessed by it. *The Dark Tower* is reminiscent of the journey of the four Free Zone representatives in their westward quest to confront Flagg; like them, Roland is a man who is journeying beyond the realm of empiricism and towards asceticism.

In the afterword to *The Gunslinger* King acknowledges that the narrative was conceived in homage to Robert Browning's poem "Childe Roland to the Dark Tower Came": "I played with the idea of trying a long romantic novel embodying the feel, if not the exact sense of the Browning poem."[9] Browning's Childe Roland has spent "a life training for the sight," and his journey to the Dark Tower is heroic if for no other reason than the knight's perseverance. Browning's Roland presses toward his goal, disregarding the physical and mental dangers that confront him. As is also the case with King's last gunslinger, Childe Roland seeks a vision he neither understands nor precisely knows where or how to pursue. But the very pursuit of an idea, a person, or a thing to its most profound level of meaning or being is an occupation Browning praises in many of his poems; such tests of perseverance strengthen the individual's spiritual resolve. Childe Roland shares with Rabbi Ben Ezra and Fra Lippo Lippi an understanding that the sufferings of this life are a vehicle for the education of the soul.

King's Roland comes to parallel Browning's heroes in each of the afore-
mentioned aspects, but his spiritual evolution is as slow and as tentative as
the quest to find the Dark Tower. The gunslinger is a man without attach-
ments; he is loved by no one, and there is no one for him to love. He lacks a
sense of community or purpose beyond the incessant hunt for the man in
black and, by extension, the Dark Tower itself. Throughout most of *The
Gunslinger* Roland is at the nadir of his spiritual development; he must
learn why "the man in black travels with [Roland's] soul in his pocket"
(*Guns*, 90) and how best to extricate it so that it may belong to Roland once
more.

Referred to as both an "interloper" and "the antichrist" (*Guns*, 59),
Roland has a capacity for violence that aligns him with the genre of the
western and its reliance upon a heroic code of male aggressiveness. In identi-
fying the dominant characteristics of the American western, David Davis includes the violent rite of passage: "Of course, most cowboy books and
movies bristle with violence. . . . These bloody escapades are necessary and
are simply explained. They provide the stage for the hero to show his heroism, and since the cowboy is the hero of the preadolescent, he must prove
himself by [preadolescent] standards."[10] The genre thus insists that the hero
possess certain training in the art of violent survival. In Tull, when the
townspeople attack the gunslinger at the urging of the dark man, it is clear
that Roland has no compunction about his use of force. His status as a western hero notwithstanding, the gunslinger initially lacks an awareness of
moral complexity and responsibility. After completely eliminating the
town's human inhabitants, we learn, Roland "ate hamburgers and drank
three beers. . . . That night he slept in the bed where he and Alice had lain.
He had no dreams" (*Guns*, 64). Furthermore, the Slow Mutants lose whatever humanity they may still retain when the gunslinger shoots indiscrimi-
nately into their midst "without allowing himself to think" (*Guns*, 179).
The gunslinger may hunt the man in black for a reason that is perhaps only
semicomprehensible to himself alone, but it is apparent that in the first four
stories of *The Gunslinger* Roland has much in common with the amoral
dark man he pursues.

The Gunslinger is a novel of ambiguities. The cryptic nature of the
book—blending fantasy, science fiction, horror, western myth, icy realism,
and romantic quests in a way unique to King's canon—so worried the
writer that he was initially reluctant to authorize a trade edition: "I believed
then and believe now that more general readers would feel both shocked
and cheated by the book's lack of resolution—it is, after all, the first section
of a much longer work" (Beahm, 198). King's self-evaluation is perceptive

enough, but the final chapter of the novel, "The Gunslinger and the Dark Man," does point the way, if not toward resolution, then at least toward the initial stages of Roland's development as a moral being. Like the cowboy in his behavior toward the American Indian, the gunslinger wants to believe in the righteousness of his westward quest, but he is sometimes bothered by the practices he must engage in during this quest: "There were such things as rape in the world. Rape and murder and unspeakable practices, and all of them were for the good, the bloody good, for the myth, for the grail, for the Tower. . . . Not for the first time the gunslinger tasted the smooth, loden taste of soul-sickness" (*Guns*, 80).

His chase after the dark man has brought the gunslinger into intimate contact with evil and its insidious ability to corrupt even the most noble intentions. The gunslinger's "soul-sickness" deepens with the guilt he must assume after Jake's sacrificial death; he does not, one should note, eat hamburgers and drink beer after the boy is killed. True to Browning's Childe Roland and the Western epic hero, the gunslinger has "descended into the underworld and ascended to the mountaintops, penetrated into himself and expanded beyond the limits of the universe" (Collings and Engebretson, 117). At the close of the first volume Roland is perhaps no closer physically to the Dark Tower than when he began his quest in the desert. On the other hand, however, he has met and confronted the dark man, who outlines several important trials that he will encounter elsewhere in the journey. And most important, Roland has opened himself to the potential for a sustaining unity that ties together the unique elements of the universe: "Suppose that all worlds, all universes, met in a single nexus, a single pylon, a Tower. A stairway, perhaps, to the Godhead itself" (*Guns*, 209). This metaphysical issue is central to the next volume of *The Dark Tower*, in which it achieves a greater level of dramatization as Roland's quest continues.

Roland Advances: *The Drawing of the Three*

In his discussion of *The Dark Tower* James Egan postulates that the saga is a mixture of two genres, the stock western and the Gothic romance: "Like the western, the gothic story may evoke an image of the lonely, isolated self pressing onward despite all obstacles, while either indulging or struggling with an internal evil. Though Roland wanders across a landscape like that of the western, the gothic elements of *The Dark Tower* suggest that he has entered a gothic universe which offers shadowy semblences of an occult order but withholds final revelation and illumination."[11] Egan elaborates on this discussion in his comparison of

The Dark Tower to Poe's "William Wilson" and Wilde's *Picture of Dorian Grey.* Poe and Wilde adapt the Gothic into highly charged moral tales; each of these writers is not only interested in presenting "the primordial power and pervasiveness of the unknown, the irrationality and unpredictability of the human psyche" (Egan, 101), but is likewise concerned with testing the relationship between Christian codes of conduct and personal egotism. The Gothic, at least as it was adapted to suit Victorian sensibilities in the nineteenth century, is more than just atmosphere and indulgence; it is also a serious means of presenting the fundamental dangers —both personal and social—that are the consequences of amoral behavior.

In *The Drawing of the Three* Eddie Dean, one of the three "prisoners" whose minds and bodies are appropriated by the gunslinger in his transworld trek from a postapocalyptic beachworld to contemporary Manhattan, offers the most trenchant evaluations of Roland's moral condition. Early in the novel Eddie pronounces an accurate condemnation of Roland that certainly defines his character throughout most of *The Gunslinger:* "There are people who need people to need them. The reason you don't understand is because you're not one of those people. You'd use me and then toss me away like a paper bag if that's what it came down to."[12] But in *The Drawing of the Three* this is neither a fair nor complete estimate of Roland's personality. If Egan is correct in his assertion that *The Dark Tower* draws upon Gothic as well as western archetypes, then the Roland who appears in this second volume has more in common with Dostoyevski's tormented protagonists than with characters of unqualified bravado, such as Vathek or Dracula.

Partly because Roland is physically vulnerable through most of this narrative (he is in a constant state of fever because of the infection in his hand after the severing of his fingers), partly because he is forced to rely on the help of the two men and woman he kidnaps to navigate in a world that is foreign to him, but most of all because of his gradual appreciation of Eddie as an individual man (and not merely a prisoner addicted to heroin and forced to serve the gunslinger's will), Roland progresses in *Drawing* toward a fuller realization of his heroic potential. He is still capable of tremendous levels of violence. Indeed, violence is his instinctual response to all conflicts. But in *Drawing,* in contrast to *The Gunslinger,* this proclivity is definitely tempered—more appropriate to the situation and to the behavior of a heroic personage.

In serving as the distraction that saves the "American" Jake from being murdered by Jack Mort, Roland displays the fullest extent of his development as a moral agent. Unwilling to allow the boy to die a second time as a result of his own selfishness and negligence, Roland relinquishes his hold on Mort long enough to permit Jake's escape. It is the first time in *The Dark Tower* that the gunslinger demonstrates a willingness to sacrifice the successful completion of his journey-quest because of its cost in human life.

The gunslinger's choice of self-sacrifice, risking the quest for the Tower itself, may be attributed in large part to the influence of his extended contact with Eddie Dean. The two men actually aid each other throughout the novel. Each possesses character traits the other desperately needs in order to become a complete human being. After sharing his mind and body with Roland, Eddie is barely recognized when he appears in front of Balazar and his henchmen. They remain justifiably afraid of him because he is no longer merely a junkie looking for a fix; a part of him has become the gunslinger. Roland's heroic stature grows ever more evident as an influence on Eddie's life, until "this hag-ridden man [comes] to behave with all the dignity of a born gunslinger despite his addiction" (*DOT,* 156). Under Roland's guidance, Eddie gains the will to break his drug dependency; his weakness is countered by Roland's self-discipline and resolve.

As Roland teaches Eddie survival skills necessary for life in the beach-world as well as in Manhattan, Eddie likewise educates Roland in virtues the latter is sorely missing: friendship and love. Moreover, Eddie's maturation, once he overcomes his drug addiction, inspires Roland's respect: "The gunslinger had smiled an oddly beautiful smile. 'I think you *have* grown up'" (*DOT,* 287). At one point in the journey Roland urges Odetta and Eddie to abandon him and go on, essentially handing down the heroic quest to a handicapped woman and a heroin addict—certainly the least likely pair capable of reaching the Tower. But as Roland discovers in this second volume, his quest is less physical than it is spiritual. In spite of the fact that he has been forced into a symbiotic relationship, Eddie's life of dedication to both the wounded gunslinger and to the schizophrenic Odetta / Detta counterbalances the self-serving life Roland has chosen. And Roland is appropriately educated by Eddie's example.

It should come as no surprise to any reader who has attentively witnessed the confluence between Eddie and Roland that the latter is no longer capable of callously destroying any impediment to his progress toward the Tower. The randomness of Jack Mort's psychopathology infuses Roland with such disgust because Mort is a reference back to Roland's own violent history of obsessive personal indulgence throughout *The Gunslinger:* "*What sort of man is this that I am supposed to use? What sort of man*—But then he thought of Jake, thought of the push which had sent Jake into this world, and he thought he heard the laughter of the man in black . . ." (*DOT,* 324). After exposure to Mort's inner being, Roland comes to appreciate more fully the value of life—even in those lives he does not respect. By the time he enters Katz's Manhattan drugstore while inside Jack Mort's body, Roland is firmly committed to the general safety of the bystanders as well as the police. The Roland who appears in *The Gunslinger* would never entertain such impulses, much less allow himself to be shaped by them: "Better to have to shoot twice from the hip, firing slugs that would do the job while travelling on an upward angle that would protect the bystanders than to perhaps kill some lady whose only crime had been picking the wrong day to shop for perfume" (*DOT,* 368).

By the conclusion of *The Drawing of the Three* the reader, if not Roland himself, recognizes that the quest for the Dark Tower is as important as the Tower itself. As Joseph Campbell argues throughout *The Hero with a Thousand Faces,* the epic journey is always an instrument for the hero's education (Campbell 1949, 82–101). Indeed, Roland's development in this novel demonstrates that his quest alone has provided the gunslinger with as many insights into himself and the human condition as he hopes to gain upon reaching the Tower itself.

In Balazar's office, the delicate latticework of Balazar's card tower appears to 'Cimi as an act of defiance against the existential forces that always seem to dwarf humankind in our powerlessness: "it reached almost three quarters of the way from the top of the desk to the ceiling, a lacy construct of jacks and deuces and kings and tens and Big Akers, a red and black configuration of paper diamonds standing in defiance of a world spinning through a universe of incoherent motions and forces; a tower that seemed to 'Cimi's amazed eyes to be a ringing denial of all the unfair paradoxes of life. If he had known how, he would have said: *I looked at what he built, and to me it explained the stars*" (*DOT,* 118). The card tower, a symbol of Roland's very quest, reflects the human ability to triumph over the uncertainties of fate and unfavorable odds. Its very construction suggests at least the range of possibilities available to us despite the randomness of a hostile universe. Roland and Eddie build a few card towers of their own in *Drawing.* They learn that it is possible to find order in defiance of ruin, to impose meaning and purpose over their environment, and to recognize that a metaphysical transformation must precede any other kind. Their behavior in *Drawing* signals a break with the enervated decadence of the two worlds they inhabit (Egan, 104). Their courage, radical individualism, evolving moral commitment to others, and willingness to confront infinity renew our faith in "life and good will and simple imagination—just one more pipeline to the infinite" (*DM,* 409).

In the typical western, as James Folsom points out, "the professional gunfighter sells his skill . . . to someone else for wages." But another option exists: the gunfighter can "remain unattached to any party, true to some kind of vision of moral justice."[13] In *The Drawing of the Three* Roland provides a modifier to this latter option. Recalling the examples of Jack Sawyer, the Losers, and Eddie himself, Roland learns that a "vision of moral justice" becomes an alternative only as the "need for other people" (*DOT,* 170) is acknowledged and embraced.

Chapter Eight
Toward a Third Decade: Points of Reflection and Departure

> At its best [horror] literature is a visionary literature, with its feet in blood and its eyes on transformation; a literature not blinded by the conventions of "acceptable" subject matter, a little in love with death, and all the more honest for that; a literature that looks, and looks again, and never flinches.[1]

King's Contribution to American Fiction

I do not believe it is possible to explain fully either Stephen King's phenomenal influence on contemporary fiction and popular culture over the past two decades or the sheer volume of money his novels and films have earned in that time. Certainly, any attempt to assess King's contribution to the field of contemporary American fiction must account for those elements that distinguish his work from the artistically sloppy productions of other writers in the horror genre. King's canon must be evaluated as somehow superior—in terms of themes, subtexts, character development, and narrative experimentation—to the myriad grotesque paperbacks that appear at the supermarket checkout counter one week and disappear the next. And any evaluative judgment of King's work, while necessarily subjective, should not be influenced by King's enormous popular appeal. The horror genre, like the subliterature of its eighteenth-century Gothic forefather, has always attracted an audience that is not often an accurate barometer of artistic quality (witness, for example, the longevity of the *Friday the 13th* saga). Unlike the less adept practitioners of contemporary horror, King has created memorable and vivid literary sketches—as he does so deftly throughout Book II of *The Tommyknockers* and in the penultimate chapter ("Lot IV") of *'Salem's Lot*—of a Maine community, a domestic environment, or a unique personality. There are few writers, living or dead, who in a single paragraph can so fully embody a human being that the reader wishes to learn more about that fictional character, even if it requires an investment of the time it takes to read a thousand-page novel (as is frequently the case in King).

No literature, not even the literature of supernatural terror, can be understood as discrete from the culture out of which it arises. At the heart of King's fictional universe is a profound awareness of the most emotional and deep-seated American anxieties. Behind the supernatural veneer of wolfmen and spiders, which remains one of the great popular attractions of his fiction, his world mirrors our own. On a subconscious (or perhaps hyperconscious) level, many of the loyal fans who read King's works for his delicious terrors are also drawn to them because of his explorations of social and personal conflicts. Not only is Stephen King working within the American Gothic tradition—a tradition firmly linking him, as we have seen, to mainstream American authors such as Hawthorne, Twain, and Faulkner—but he is also embellishing that tradition, developing it further, by placing its themes and situations in a contemporary social context.

King's stories are richly evocative; they often speak to us of unresolved tensions that are both endemic to our time and particular to an individual's identity formation. Like the inherent suggestiveness of dream archetypes, King's fiction delves into the realm of the collective and personal unconscious—a landscape that may be explored artistically only in the world of the fantastic, remaining essentially inaccessible in realistic prose (as D. H. Lawrence once said of one of Poe's classic horror tales, "It is lurid and melodramatic, but it is true."[2]). A novel such as *The Shining,* for example, is disturbing not because of its obviously Gothic trappings—ghost women as dancing partners, hedge animals that move—but because it forces the reader into a reidentification with archetypal childhood phobias about parental discord, devouring mother and father figures, separation and abandonment, and child abuse. These are highly relevant concerns to contemporary American men and women. When left unresolved, as psychotherapists are wont to tell us, they remain motivating forces in an individual's psyche long after the transition to adulthood has been completed. King's characters carry tremendous internal scars; their psychological baggage is heavy. Each of his novels and many of the stories features at least one escapist individual who suffers from some type of substance abuse. Liquor, cocaine, heroin, Valium, Norvil, and perverted sexuality are the drugs that numb the consciousnesses of so many King characters; their abuse suggests all the symptoms of social decay and all the modes of self-destruction that flourish, largely tolerated, in our society.

The distinctly American qualities present in King's fiction—from the physical size of his novels, to their geographical scope, to their grappling with the eternal philosophical battle between good and evil—have been noted by several scholars but never fully or convincingly pursued. The importance of reading King as an American writer cannot be overemphasized. The core concerns in King's literary world are reminiscent of those that dominate nineteenth-and twentieth-century American literature. As Robert Kiely reminds us:

"Mr. King has not only read his Melville but also his Whitman and Dos Passos. Like his predecessors, Mr. King is aware that there is a menace as well as promise in the immensity of the United States. What appears modern (or postmodern) in Mr. King is that both the menace and the promise have been tainted by a cheap tedium, a repetition of bravado and monotony of violence. [King's fiction] is not about a still raw, untried, half-hidden America, but a nation exposed over and over to itself, as in an enormous mirror, part trite situation comedy, part science fiction, part cop show. . . . In many ways [his books] are for the 1990's, when America is beginning to see itself less and less in the tall image of the Lincoln or even the robust one of Johnny Appleseed and more and more as a dazed behemoth with padded shoulders."[3]

King's fiction centers on various American rites of passage, especially this nation's coming of age in an era of recognizably diminished expectations and resources. As in the works of Melville and Dos Passos (Whitman's voice is only a lost echo in King's work), the epic dimensions of King's novels are ironically eroded by the consistency of their themes: America on the verge of destroying itself internally (morally) and externally (financially and environmentally). In King's view of contemporary society, the American dream is no longer viable or accessible; we are left with only the stubborn perpetuation of its myth, the shadow of the form it once took. Only from this sobering perspective is a reader fully capable of experiencing the true torment of a Jack Torrance, a Jack Sawyer, or a Jim Gardener.

A Critique of the American Dream

The social subtext of a novel such as *The Shining* is a subtle critique of the American dream and its promise of a system of reward commensurate with individual sacrifice and level of commitment to a given goal. Following generations of American idealists, Jack Torrance embarks on his westward journey in search of a fresh beginning that will bring him wealth and fame as a writer. The Overlook Hotel fans his hopes with just the right amount of inspiration, provided by its own history, which is conveniently disclosed in a scrapbook located in the boiler room. And that history, as Jack indicates to Al Shockley, "forms an index of the whole post–World War II American character" (*Shin*, 187). The hotel's ensemble of corpses and freaks deludes Jack into believing that he, like post–World War II America, is on the road to a new and better life. But instead of realizing the American dream, Jack Torrance experiences a terrifying parody of it—sacrificing his family, his autonomy, and his soul in a futile effort to ingratiate himself with the ghostly hierarchy that governs the Overlook. In return, he is manipulated and betrayed by the American dream's corruption, graphically manifested in the history of the hotel. As King himself reminds us in the interview that begins this book, "whatever is going on in the Overlook . . . is connected to a kind of capitalism run mad. It is the American dream run amok. You can rise in the hotel hierarchy, you just have to be willing to tread on enough dead bodies. The hotel's whole history is evidence of this."

In a recent article tracing the historical shift in the journey motif as it appears in American cinema, Caryn James argues that the recurring metaphor of the voyage across America mirrors our culture's most resilient hopes and, conversely, its worst realities:

"Films like *The Wizard of Oz* (1939) and Preston Sturges's *Sullivan's Travels* (1941) defined the standard pattern for road movies: whether the hero was a scarecrow or a rich film director bumming cross-country during the Depression, characters traveled through danger and disillusionment to healthy self-knowledge and back to safety at home. They followed an optimistic course as old as the American West and as deeply entrenched in our culture as Whitman's "Song of the Open Road."

But today's best road movies are bizarre, comic, one-way journeys to the dark side of self and society. In *Wild at Heart* (1990) and Jonathan Demme's *Something Wild* (1988) . . . the road is a bleak and grimy landscape where hapless, unimaginative heroes seek out small grains of luck or love. These roads are fraught with dangers more real than flying monkeys; botched robberies, prison cells and even death are surprisingly common."[4]

As Douglas Winter reminds us throughout *The Art of Darkness*, the journey is one of the most characteristically American features unifying King's canon. Spiritually akin to the contemporary "road" films James cites in her essay, particularly *Wild at Heart* and *Easy Rider*, King's works deliver a scathing critique of American society. Even when his protagonists manage to survive their journeys and gain self-knowledge as a result, that knowledge is born of tragic experience. The interstate highways that crisscross the pages of King's novels contain lurid dangers that make his characters' worst nightmares come true. These hard concrete roads symbolize the hardhearted uniformity found in the American towns they connect. In King's hands, Walt Whitman's open road of limitless possibility stops at the front door of the Overlook Hotel, where America's historical dream is transformed into its decadent nightmare. King forces his readers to examine issues about themselves and their society that they might prefer to deny or ignore. The truth of his fiction makes us uncomfortable—but as I have argued throughout this book, what makes us most uncomfortable has less to do with the supernatural than with the everyday.

Ursula Le Guin has commented on the particularly American cultural aversion to fantasy and horror, which she connects to "our Puritanism, our work ethic, our profit-mindedness, and even our sexual mores." Americans are taught "to repress their imagination, to reject it as something childish or effeminate, unprofitable, and probably sinful."⁵ Yet all around us our cocoons of self-denial and ordered purposefulness show signs of stress and cracking: subway riders are pushed onto the tracks by strangers, young men are assaulted and killed for entering the "wrong" neighborhood, women are raped in toilet stalls and in Central Park, infants are left by their parents in garbage dumpsters. Some people find escape from the imminent reality of such horrors by denying their existence, engaging in a continuous suspension of disbelief. But others, Stephen King among them, prefer to see the reality flushed out into the open. The very act of watching our collective and personal fears reworked into a narrative affords us some sense of control over our experience. Even in an era in which God has been pronounced dead and secular authority no longer rings true, we yearn to seek some meaning in tragedy.

The sociopolitical critique that is an omnipresent element in King's canon can be traced almost directly to his undergraduate years at the University of Maine, Orono. The Vietnam War protests and campus politics transformed King from a conservative supporter of Nixon in 1968 to a noisy radical who led marches against the war and in support of left-wing organizations and causes. In 1969 King began writing a weekly column for the school newspaper entitled "King's Garbage Truck," "because you never know what you're going to find in a garbage truck." What scholars stand to glean from these early editorials is a sense of King's nascent political discontent. In his final column, printed just prior to his graduation in 1970, King rendered the following personal inventory:

"Political views: Extremely radical, largely due to the fact that nobody seems to listen to you unless you threaten to shut them down, turn them off or make some kind of trouble.

Favorite color: Blue, although during the last four years, after the death of Robert Kennedy, Martin Luther King, Fred Hampton, four young men and women at Kent State, two black students at Jackson College, 114 people at My Lai, the entrance of the United States into Cambodia and Laos—after all these things, black, in the form of arm bands seems more in vogue.

Future prospects: Hazy, although nuclear annihilation or environmental strangulation seem to be distinct possibilities."[6]

Few scholars and readers sufficiently appreciate the extent to which King's fiction remains influenced by the same political orientation he expressed in this self-description over 20 years ago. Its rhetorical tone may now appear less strident, as these issues are presented in more subtle contexts, but the essential blend of social activism and indignation that informs this final piece of undergraduate prose is a distinct feature of King's subsequent work. It is possible to argue that unlike so many young Americans who were radicalized by the sixties only to be corrupted by the seventies and eighties, King has held to the political consciousness he developed as an undergraduate.

Child abuse; familial tensions, particularly in the form of unresponsive and openly antagonistic parents; the genetic predisposition to alcoholism, and its consequences for the individuals and families who are its victims; the absolute fear and rejection of technological advances that are beyond our means of comprehension, much less our ability to control; religious zealotry and its link to societal oppression; the general inability of social institutions to maintain their viability in the face of changing values and needs—these are the dominant issues at the heart of Stephen King's first two decades of writing. Not surprisingly, they constitute the unresolved agenda that American society faces as it approaches the millenium.

The degree to which King's fictional dramatization of personal and cultural endangerment reflects contemporary American life is perhaps most comprehensively delineated by sociologist Christopher Lasch, who argues in both *Haven in a Heartless World* (1977) and *The Culture of Narcissism* (1978) that the loss of traditional ethical principles and institutions of authority have produced a culture of profoundly alienated sociopaths. Lasch's two books, appearing in the same years in which King published *The Shining* and *The Stand,* respectively, supply the statistical and theoretical basis for properly understanding the sociopolitical backdrop of Stephen King's fiction. King and Lasch differ little in their attitudes except when it comes to popular literature; Lasch is highly critical of the work of writers such as King. The irony inherent in Lasch's attack on popular fiction, at least in the case of King, is that King uses horror fiction to offer his readers essentially the same social critique put forth by Lasch. Echoing a dominant concern of Lasch and many other contemporary social scientists, King's work highlights the ways in which American society undermines the morality necessary for love of self and love for others. Both Lasch and King depict a government and political system that remain unsupportive of individuals who strive to sustain moral life in the community, in the workplace, or within the intimacy of familial relationships. External social pressures and the wholesale failure of social institutions have so eroded the integrity of American citizens that we are forever on the brink of psychic fragmentation.[7]

Looking Back to See Forward

King's second decade of work, while related to the first in the ways just described, distinguishes itself by the self-reflective attention it pays to the role of protagonist-writers who are struggling to adjust to their own sudden fame. As King indicated in the chapter 1 interview, conducted in 1989, "What I have written about writers and writing in the last five years or so has been a real effort on my part to understand what I am doing, what it means, what it is doing to me, what it is doing for me. Some of it has been out of an effort to try and understand the ramifications of being a so-called famous person, or celebrity. What does it mean when somebody who is a novelist is invited to appear on 'Hollywood Squares'? I am trying to understand these things."

This biographical commentary can be seen fictionally encoded in the separation that is maintained between King's first-decade character-authors Jack Torrance and Ben Mears, who are still struggling to secure reputations as writers, and Paul Sheldon, Bill Denbrough, and Thad Beaumont, who possess the popular acclaim and financial abundance King has experienced during his second decade. The novels from the second decade tend to reflect a literary self-absorption that is a direct result of King's evolving stature as a writer. King's enormous success occurred abruptly; perhaps, if *Misery* and *The Dark Half* are accurate barometers of King's personal life, this success may have been too enormous and too abrupt. In less than two decades King has emerged from the obscure status of an unpublished novelist working two jobs (high-school English teacher and summer laborer in a Bangor laundry) and become an American icon. Like their creator, Sheldon and

Beaumont find themselves suddenly liberated from the task of making a living, but now they must confront other occupational hazards—such as how to maintain their artistic integrity in the face of public expectations. In the second decade this has become an omnipresent concern for Stephen King, personally as well as fictionally. But has this self-consciousness served King well? More important, will the issue of adjusting to fame in America continue to haunt King's fiction in his third decade as an author?

King's strengths as a writer in his first decade of publication are perhaps best exemplified in *The Shining* and *Pet Sematary*, two novels that were grandly composed and executed. In the second decade King's greatest accomplishments have been *It* and *Misery*. *The Shining* and *It* have much in common insofar as both are novels with tremendous historical scope and moral vision; King's epic vision is never stronger than in the social, historical, and mythological matrix at the epicenter of these two books. *Pet Sematary* and *Misery*, on the other hand, show evidence of King's ability to produce highly circumscribed, tightly wrought fictions with none of the epic tendency toward narrative and thematic expansiveness. If *The Shining* and *It* are best likened to cinematography because of their epic embrace of ethics and history, *Pet Sematary* and *Misery* may be compared to classic Greek tragic dramas played upon a small stage in front of a theater audience.[8]

King's less satisfying work through the years—*Christine, Firestarter, The Tommyknockers, The Dark Half*—somehow manages to miss either the epic and mythic scope of *It* and *The Stand* or the circumscription of *Misery*. Harlan Ellison has suggested that King's tendency to overwrite is a possible explanation for the failure of such novels: "Stephen King is neither Marcel Proust nor is he Salman Rushdie, to take the current icon. King is one of the most accomplished storytellers the twentieth century has produced. As a consequence, his strengths are in the storytelling area, and his weaknesses are in more specific areas. For instance, I can't think of any King novels with the possible exception of maybe *It* or the two *Dark Tower* books, that could not have been told just as well as a novella. This is to me the main flaw in Stephen's work" (Beahm, 147).

I would concur with Ellison's assessment; all of King's canon might be strengthened by the tightening of a prose style that too often suffers from the "loss of control of, and perhaps interest in, material after the midpoint" of a particular narrative.[9] Another novelist might be dismissed because of such stylistic failings, but in King's case they seem to come with the territory. When a writer is working on as many narratological and thematic levels of discourse and meaning as King does in such texts as *It* and *The Stand*, a certain "loss of control" is almost inevitable. If King's books suffer as a result of his loquaciousness, it is as a result of his trying to accomplish too much within a single text. His narratives often seem overworked and overloaded, as though King, like Faulkner before him, were stretching the very perimeters of narrative and genre.

Joseph Reino concludes his study of King's first decade of publication with the following plaudit: "One must acknowledge that [King's] range of literary skills in psychology, character, comedy, Gothic symbology, and natural-sounding dialogue is easily one of the most stunning in twentieth-century American fiction" (Reino, 139). This summation touches on both the achievement and the curse of King's first two decades as a writer. It underscores King's achievement by enumerating the strongest elements of his fiction, which like all great literature inspires in the reader a passion to keep reading. The curse, as I have already noted, is that King often seeks to employ all of those elements in a single text, sometimes producing the effect of having "piled just about everything he could think of into a book and too much of each thing as well."[10]

This chapter attempts to underscore the main thesis of this book: King must be viewed as a serious social critic whose work reflects some of the core concerns treated throughout the American literary tradition. Yet how few of his fans and professional reviewers are willing or capable of considering him in such terms. Maria Scrivani, for example, in a recent review of the second edition of *The Stand,* focuses her analysis on the weakest and least important aspect of King's writing: "Why be subtle if you can hit someone over the head with a baseball bat to make your point? King seems to delight in new ways to describe vomiting and defecation, and with a superflu epidemic raging, the gross-out possibilities are endless. . . . As his fans can attest, King has no match in layering on the horrific hyperbole."[11] Scrivani's emphasis is not unusual; it is the norm. For the past two decades Stephen King's fiction has largely been misinterpreted by both the popular press and academicians. As Scrivani illustrates, King is seldom appreciated as a writer capable of creating complex characters who live in complicated times. His fiction is frequently reduced to its basic plot line, with special attention given only to the new supernatural horrors presented. The problem, of course, is that this bias always overlooks the real horrors in King's novels because these are neither new nor supernatural. This reductive tendency is especially disquieting in King's case because, as Andrew Klavan has acknowledged grudgingly, not only do "King's works have a subtext, but that subtext is all they have."[12]

In two decades of reading Stephen King's fiction I have discovered that most Americans are unequivocal in their response to his work: they either belittle his art or consume it passionately. Curiously, critics who dismiss King often do so precisely because his work is thus consumed. There remains an unfortunate, but nonetheless persistent, distrust in this culture of any living writer who accrues too much money and fame through his books. Only dead artists who have endured an appropriate amount of suffering and neglect during their lifetimes are justified in having large popular audiences.

It has been my experience that academicians and censorious religious fundamentalists who disparage King's fiction do so out of an uninformed emotional response. The intellectuals view him as a threat to literacy, while the fundamentalists believe him to be a threat to decency.[13] It is always amusing to note the similarities in the arguments of both camps. Sectarian fundamentalists mount onslaughts against freedom for the arts, and they are joined by political progressives and cultural elitists who are threatened by artistic expression that they deem reactionary or anti-intellectual.[14] Both camps condemn King—usually before they have bothered to read him— for the restrictiveness of his vision and intention. As Clive Barker notes, this response is similar to, but no less valid than, that leveled at erotic literature: that the desire to scare, like the desire to arouse, is a fundamentally shallow one (Barker, 4).

The millions of high-school and college students who choose to purchase and read King's works are excited about a written text. For many of them, King's novels represent their first exposure to literature as something other than a painful experience. What educators need to reconsider is the value inherent in such a response. Reading Stephen King is a clear alternative to video games and television, especially as the written word comes to occupy an ever more marginal position in our increasingly nonliterate world. If students are embracing his work with such alacrity, is it not conceivable that they might also turn to other writers for similar reasons? High-school and college English department curricula should include Stephen King's fiction, not only because it is a rich and trenchant body of work but also because any reader or writer, especially a young one, ought to be encouraged to pursue whatever literature he or she finds inspirational. The distinctions maintained between high art and popular art have done little more than placate the insecurities of America's intellectual elite. At their worst such rigid demarcations have helped to alienate generations of students from the joy of reading and writing about literature at all.

Throughout his iconoclastic career Leslie Fiedler has argued, often as a lone voice in the academy, for the importance of reading popular literature seriously. He maintains that all cultural productions, high or low, are worthy of examination because all texts equally reveal the social meanings of our world. According to Fiedler, literary scholars and teachers "must not only confront the popular arts, but deal with them, and the high arts too, in a style consonant with a sensibility altered by the former. . . . Some writers, particularly in America, have even begun to suspect that the very distinction between 'serious books' and 'best sellers' upon which conception of the 'art novel' depends was an error from the start."[15] As King's career heads into its third decade, there is no doubt that he has earned the title "America's storyteller" as the most popular writer this country has ever produced. Literary critics, English teachers, and school boards must now address seriously Fiedler's call for the creation of a new kind of criticism, one that will result in a more broadly based canon and curriculum. Toward this end they will need to assess the importance of two decades of Stephen King's fiction in light of its contribution to the larger body of American literature. This volume, along with the kindred efforts of Douglas Winter, Joseph Reino, and Michael Collings, is intended to aid that enterprise.

Notes and References

Preface

1. Tony Magistrale, "Native Sons: Regionalism in the Work of Nathaniel Hawthorne and Stephen King," *Journal of the Fantastic in the Arts* 2 (1989): 761–88.

Chapter One

1. Tabitha Spruce King, born in 1949, is also a successful novelist who has lived most of her life in Maine. She and her husband are the parents of three children.

2. Charles Beaumont (1929–67) was an American scriptwriter and short-story author. Many of his works were either adapted into, or written especially for, episodes of Rod Serling's television series "The Twilight Zone." It is most likely that King first encountered Beaumont's work during the 1960s, when that program aired weekly.

3. "The Crate," the only tale in *Creepshow* (1982) not written specifically for the film.

4. Tony Magistrale, "Hawthorne's Woods Revisited: Stephen King's *Pet Sematary*," *Nathaniel Hawthorne Review* 14 (1988), 9–13. This essay examines the importance of place, both geographical and moral, in King's 1982 novel, and its relationship to Hawthorne's use of forests as settings in several short stories and *The Scarlet Letter*. For a more elaborate and specific comparison of King and Hawthorne as regional writers, see the last section of chapter 2 of this book.

5. See "Banned Books and Other Concerns: The Virginia Beach Lecture," in *The Stephen King Companion,* ed. George Beahm (Kansas City, Mo.: Andrews & McMeel, 1989), 51–61. Beahm hereafter cited in text.

6. "Head Down," *The New Yorker,* 16 April 1990, 68–111.

Chapter Two

1. *Danse Macabre* (New York: Berkley, 1981), 385; hereafter cited in text as *DM*.

2. Tim Underwood and Chuck Miller, eds., *Bare Bones: Conversations on Terror with Stephen King* (New York: McGraw-Hill, 1988), 53; hereafter cited in text.

3. Emily Dickinson, poem 390, in *The Complete Poems of Emily Dickinson,* ed. Thomas H. Johnson (Boston: Little, Brown & Co., 1960), 186.

4. See Tim Underwood's essay, "The Skull Beneath the Skin," in *Kingdom*

of Fear: The World of Stephen King, ed. Tim Underwood and Chuck Miller (New York: New American Library, 1986). The author argues that "There's not much concern with beauty in any of King's works, it doesn't seem to inspire him. . . . Before kids can grow up and control their own lives, their youth is ruined. This apparently for King is part and parcel of the human condition. He offers no solutions or alternatives to this sad situation, just a few laughs along the way" (261, 258; hereafter cited in text.

    5. Robin Wood, "Return of the Repressed," *Film Comment* 14 (July/August 1978), 28; hereafter cited in text.

    6. Bernard G. Gallagher, "Reading Between the Lines: Stephen King and Allegory," in *The Gothic World of Stephen King: Landscape of Nightmares,* ed. Gary Hoppenstand and Ray B. Browne (Bowling Green, Ohio: Bowling Green State University Popular Press, 1987), 40.

    7. Tony Magistrale, *Landscape of Fear: Stephen King's American Gothic* (Bowling Green, Ohio: Bowling Green State University Popular Press, 1988), focuses upon King as a critical sociologist of contemporary American life who relies upon a social and political subtext in the creation of horror; I will not delve into such concerns here. The reader is referred to chapters 2 and 5 of that book for treatment of these subtextual elements of King's work. (hereafter cited in text.)

    8. Michael Sadleir, *The Northanger Novels: A Footnote to Jane Austen,* English Association Pamphlet no. 68 (November 1927), 7.

    9. Theodore Ziolkowski, *Disenchanted Images: A Literary Iconology* (Princeton, N.J.: Princeton University Press, 1977), 84.

    10. Frederick S. Frank, "Proto-Gothicism: The Infernal Iconography of Walpole's *Castle of Otranto," Orbis Litterarum* 41 (1986), 199–212; hereafter cited in text.

    11. The association between *Dracula* and the liberation of the libido is, of course, not original to King. *Danse* certainly identifies one of the more important elements in Stoker's text, but King's analysis is neither highly explicit in its detailing nor conscious of what other critics have already contributed.

    Dracula scholars have elaborated on the connection between vampire literature and sexuality for many years, but two of the finest studies of *Dracula* as sexual text have appeared since the publication of *Danse:* James B. Twitchell's *Dreadful Pleasures: An Anatomy of Modern Horror* (New York: Oxford University Press, 1985) and Terry Heller's *The Delights of Terror: An Aesthetics of the Tale of Terror* (Urbana: Illinois University Press, 1987).

    12. Bruno Bettelheim, *The Uses of Enchantment: The Meaning and Importance of Fairy Tales* (New York: Vintage, 1977), 25; hereafter cited in text.

    13. Maria Tatar, *The Hard Facts of Grimm's Fairy Tales* (Princeton, N.J.: Princeton University Press, 1987), 10.

    14. See Ronald T. Curran, "Complex, Archetype, and Primal Fear: King's Use of Fairy Tales in *The Shining,"* in *The Dark Descent: Essays Defining Stephen*

King's Horrorscape, ed. Tony Magistrale (Westport, Conn.: Greenwood), forthcoming, 1992.

15. See Carl Belz, "The Terror of the Surreal" in *Focus on the Horror Film,* ed. Roy Huss and T. J. Ross (Englewood Cliffs, N.J.: Prentice-Hall, 1972), 144–48; hereafter cited in text. Belz argues in the opposite direction of influence, insofar as his analysis concerns the manner in which commercial film—particularly Hitchcock's *The Birds*—has been shaped by surrealism. Horror films "demonstrate, without being formally Surrealistic, that the legacy of this style continues to bear artistic fruit" (145).

16. Carl Jung, *The Archetypes and the Collective Unconscious,* trans. R. F. C. Hull (Princeton, N.J.: Princeton University Press, 1969), 6; hereafter cited in text.

17. Chelsea Quinn Yarbro, "Cinderella's Revenge—Twists on Fairy Tale and Mythic Themes in the Work of Stephen King," in *Fear Itself: The Horror Fiction of Stephen King,* ed. Tim Underwood and Chuck Miller (New York: New American Library, 1982), 62; hereafter cited in text.

18. Ben Indick, "King and the Literary Tradition of Horror and the Supernatural" in *Fear Itself,* 175.

19. In an interview I conducted with Stephen King on 6 November 1986 at the University of Maine, Orono, I asked him to comment specifically on the Hawthornean echoes in *Pet Sematary.* He informed me that "the place to begin making serious connections is with his best short story, 'Young Goodman Brown.'" At other points in our conversation King made reference to "Ethan Brand," "The Birthmark," and *The House of the Seven Gables.* My overall impression from this interview was that King is clearly aware of Hawthorne's presence and that Hawthorne is part of a literary tradition with which King strongly identifies. Indeed, while referring to his own development as a horror writer in *Danse,* King essentially acknowledges Hawthorne's legacy: "After awhile it began to seem to me that what I was doing was playing an interesting—to me, at least—game of literary racquetball: . . . while my ball existed in the twentieth century, my wall was very much a product of the nineteenth" (*DM,* 25).

20. Frederick S. Frank, "The Gothic Romance," in *Horror Literature: A Historical Survey and Critical Guide to the Best of Horror,* ed. Marshall Tymn (New York: R. R. Bowker, 1981), 14.

21. Hyatt Waggoner, *The Presence of Hawthorne* (Baton Rouge: Louisiana State University Press, 1979), 45; hereafter cited in text.

22. Burton Hatlen, "Beyond the Kittery Bridge: Stephen King's Maine," in *Fear Itself,* 48; hereafter cited in text.

23. *Pet Sematary* (New York: Doubleday, 1983), 114; hereafter cited in text as *PS.*

24. Reginald Cook, "The Forest of Young Goodman Brown's Night: A Reading of Hawthorne's 'Young Goodman Brown,'" *New England Quarterly* 43 (1970), 478.

25. Nathaniel Hawthorne, "Fancy's Show Box," in *Selected Tales and Sketches* (New York: Viking Penguin, 1987), 284; hereafter cited in text.
26. *The Tommyknockers* (New York: G. P. Putnam's Sons, 1987), 33; hereafter cited in text as *Tom*.
27. Alfred Kazin, *An American Progression* (New York: Vintage, 1984), 88.
28. Stephen King, *It* (New York: Viking, 1986), 159; hereafter cited in text as *It*.

Chapter Three

1. *Roadwork*, in *The Bachman Books* (New York: New American Library, 1985), 411; hereafter cited in text as *RW*.
2. Joseph Reino's Twayne volume, *Stephen King: The First Decade, Carrie to Pet Sematary* (Boston: G. K. Hall & Co., 1988), virtually ignores the Bachman series, referring to them on only one occasion. One can understand Reino's decision to exclude them from the scope of his analysis, however, since the novels do extend beyond his book's purview and create a chronological bridge into King's second decade of work. Similar rationalizations, on the other hand, are not so easily provided for other critics grappling with King's canon. No essayist in the collection *The Gothic World of Stephen King: Landscape of Nightmares*, for example, treats any of the Bachman fiction; the collection *Kingdom of Fear: The World of Stephen King* features Stephen Brown's essay "The Life and Death of Richard Bachman: Stephen King's Doppelganger," which is more a biographical history of the novels' origins than a serious exegesis; the first edition of Douglas Winter's excellent study *The Art of Darkness* (New York: New American Library, 1984) excludes any treatment of these texts (although his 1986 edition features a brief sketch of the Bachman books in an appendix); Don D'Ammassa's essay, "Three by Bachman," in the collection of essays *Discovering Stephen King*, ed. Darrell Schweitzer (Mercer Island, Wash.: Starmont House, 1985), provides little more than plot summations of *The Long Walk, The Running Man,* and *Thinner;* and even my own scholarly work on King to date is bereft of much more than a passing citation to *Thinner*. In the realm of King scholarship, Bachman's novels remain nearly as anonymous as Richard Bachman himself. When these texts do command attention, it is only in terms of King's biography; the novels themselves are virtually ignored.

To date, the only real effort toward interpretive criticism of the Bachman canon is Michael Collings's *Stephen King as Richard Bachman* (Mercer Island, Wash.: Starmont House, 1985). The book is weakest when Collings distracts the reader by drawing elaborate parallels between the Bachman novels and other literary works and genres. His chapter on *The Running Man* is the most blatant example of this; Collings devotes scant attention to the novel itself and instead essentially prepares an introduction to the science-fiction genre. His attempt at delineating metatextual parallels, particularly those that connect the Bachman novels to King's other fiction, would have been more successful if he had devoted an entire chapter exclusively to that enterprise. My critical laments notwithstanding, *Stephen King as*

Richard Bachman remains the best of the six or seven books Collings has written on King for Starmont House. His analysis is extremely thorough, from the individual plot details, to central issues developed in each book, to biographical and publishing data. But what is perhaps most valuable in Collings' work are his examinations of core elements that reappear throughout the texts, essentially unifying the Bachman canon. Collings is particularly adept at tracing King's uses of cancer (both as a disease and as a metaphor for social disintegration) and of the failure or misuse of sexuality in these novels. My own analysis of the Bachman novels owes a debt to his pioneering efforts. (All abovementioned critical texts hereafter cited in text).

3. "Why I Was Bachman," introduction to *The Bachman Books,* ix.

4. Daniel C. Hallin, "We Keep America on Top of the World," in *Watching Television,* ed. Todd Gitlin (New York: Pantheon, 1986), 9–41; hereafter cited in text.

5. *Rage,* in *The Bachman Books,* 15; hereafter cited in text as *R.*

6. *The Long Walk,* in *The Bachman Books,* 147; hereafter cited in text as *LW.*

7. I cannot overemphasize Hemingway's impact on the Bachman novels. In *The Art of Darkness* (236–37), Douglas Winter documents Hemingway's influence on King, dating back to the latter's undergraduate classes in American literature at the University of Maine. Since *Rage* and *The Long Walk* were conceived at about the same time that King was introduced to, and so impressed by, Hemingway's prose, it is not surprising that the earliest of the Bachman books should bear important similarities to Hemingway's. George Dawes, King's protagonist in *Roadwork,* even claims literal kinship to Nick Adams (a "cousin from Michigan") when he seeks information about the use of firearms early in the novel (*RW,* 335).

Not only is King-Bachman interested in probing the sporting arena that so fascinated Hemingway, he also reflects the existential despair that dominates Hemingway's work. The sense of the individual alone and at odds with an environment that is actively opposed to his survival is a central theme for both King and Hemingway. As is the case throughout Hemingway's canon, the basic philosophical premises from which all of Bachman's characters proceed are that man is lost in this world, that society will strip dignity and independence from the individual if he follows its rules and rituals, and that ultimately human beings must pick their way from moment to moment to create whatever meaning is available in life.

8. Susan Sontag, *Illness as Metaphor* (New York: Vintage, 1978).

9. For more information on *Blade Runner* as a critique of technology and its influence on the future, see Peter Ruppert, "*Blade Runner:* The Utopian Dialectics of Science Fiction Films," *Cineaste* 17 (1989), 8–13.

10. *The Running Man,* in *The Bachman Books,* 567; hereafter cited in text as *RM.*

11. *Thinner* (New York: New American Library, 1984), 307; hereafter cited in text as *Thin.*

12. King interview in *Faces of Fear: Encounters with the Creators of Modern Horror,* ed. Douglas Winter (New York: Berkley, 1985), 253.

13. In an interview with *WB* (Walden Books) 1[November / December 1989], 7) prior to the publication of *The Dark Half,* King acknowledged that Richard Bachman is the darker, more violent side of Stephen King, just as Stark is the dark half of Thad Beaumont: "The thought that finally drove me to start writing was the idea: Suppose Bachman wasn't dead? Suppose Bachman collaborated on a book with me? And so, originally, *The Dark Half* was submitted as a collaboration by Stephen King and Richard Bachman. But Viking didn't like the idea. They thought it was confusing and that people would think it was a collaboration like *The Talisman.*"

14. *The Dark Half* (New York: Viking, 1989), 27; hereafter cited in text as *DH.*

15. Christopher Lehmann-Haupt, "From Stephen King, A Writer's Demon," review of *The Dark Half, New York Times,* 23 October 1989, C20.

16. Edward Bullough, "'Psychical Distance' as a Factor in Art and an Aesthetic Principle," in *Critical Theory since Plato,* ed. Hazard Adams (New York: Harcourt Brace Jovanovich, 1971), 758.

17. Quoted in Stephen P. Brown, "The Life and Death of Richard Bachman," in *Kingdom of Fear,* 118.

Chapter Four

1. Peter Straub, "Meeting Stevie," in *Fear Itself,* 9.

2. King and Peter Straub, *The Talisman* (New York: Viking, 1984), 3; hereafter cited in text as *Tal.*

3. *The Talisman* is further linked to *Huckleberry Finn* and, by extension, to the tradition of American literature by its reliance upon a union between a young, naive white male and the dark stranger whose roots are pagan and primitive. Many such relationships are represented in nineteenth-century American fiction, from Cooper's Natty Bumppo and Chingachgook to Queequeg and Ishmael in *Moby-Dick.* King is profoundly aware of American literature's tendency toward such an intercultural mix, having frequently acknowledged the influence of Leslie Fiedler's *Love and Death in the American Novel* on his own fiction (see interview in chapter 1). King once remarked that "*The Talisman* plays a little bit, in an impish way, with these Leslie Fiedler conclusions about light and dark in America, 'Come back to the raft, Huck honey,' the homosexual thing . . ." (Beahm, 287).

4. Mark Twain, *Adventures of Huckleberry Finn* (Berkeley: University of California Press, 1884; reprint, 1985), 271.

5. Leo Marx, *The Machine in the Garden: Technology and the Pastoral Ideal* (New York: Oxford University Press, 1964), 339.

6. Douglas Winter, "Stephen King, Peter Straub, and the Quest for *The Talisman,*" *Twilight Zone Magazine,* January / February 1985, 68.

7. Elizabeth Kolbert, "The Drink of Millions," *New York Times Magazine,* 4 March 1990, 33.

8. Jessie Weston, *From Ritual to Romance* (New York: Macmillan, 1951), 90. James George Frazer's *The Golden Bough* (New York: Macmillan, 1922; reprint, 1950) cites numerous examples of the elaborate connections made by primitive peoples around the world between the pestilence of crops and water and the dominion of evil (638–50). But perhaps the most persuasive evidence of *The Talisman*'s relationship to the tradition of mythic archetypes is the manner in which it conforms to Joseph Campbell's formulation of the mythological adventure. The novel's narrative structure and the evolution of Sawyer's quest adhere perfectly to what Campbell has named the "nuclear unit of the monomyth," or, more simply stated, the hero's rite of passage: "A hero ventures forth from the world of common day into a region of supernatural wonder: fabulous forces are there encountered and a decisive victory is won: the hero comes back from this mysterious adventure with the power to bestow boons on his fellow man" (Campbell, *Hero with a Thousand Faces* [New York: Meridian, 1949; reprint, 1956), 30; hereafter cited in text).

9. The Blasted Lands are a fantastic vision easily referenced in Ovid, Bosch, or Dante. Even the trees themselves, mutated versions of tortured Treebeards brought to life in a futuristic version of Tolkien, embody the spirit of the dying landscape itself: "As long as Jack was not looking directly at the trees, he saw their tortured faces in perfect detail, the open O of the mouth, the staring eyes and drooping nose, the long, agonized wrinkles running down the cheeks. They were cursing, pleading, howling at him—their unheard voices hung in the air like smoke. Jack groaned. Like all the Blasted Lands, these trees had been poisoned" (*Tal,* 467).

10. Twain, *Huckleberry Finn,* 155.

11. Joseph Grixti, *Terrors of Uncertainty: The Cultural Contexts of Horror Fiction* (London: Routledge, 1989), 5; hereafter cited in text.

12. Barry Commoner, "Nuclear Pollution: The Myth of Omnipotence," in *Politics and Environment,* ed. Walt Anderson (Pacific Palisades, Calif.: Goodyear Publishing Company, 1970), 76.

13. I am indebted to Ed Casebeer for sharing his ideas with me on the role of King's communal psyche and its oppositional elements. His paper "The Communal Psyche in '*Salem's Lot,*'" which I heard at the International Conference for the Fantastic in the Arts, Ft. Lauderdale, Florida, 24 March 1990, was most instructive and inspiring.

Chapter Five

1. *The Mist,* in *Skeleton Crew* (New York: G. P. Putnam's Sons, 1985), 101. All references to selections from *Skeleton Crew* hereafter cited in text as *SC.*

2. Michael Collings and David Engebretson, *The Shorter Works of Stephen King* (Mercer Island, Wash.: Starmont House, 1985), 130; hereafter cited in text.

3. For an insightful glance into King's relationship to Bangor's Little

League, the reader should consult King's essay "Head Down" (*New Yorker,* 16 April 1990, 68–111). The commission King received from *The New Yorker* upon publication of this essay was donated to purchase new uniforms for all the baseball teams in Bangor's Little League system. Aside from being an expansive treatise on King's great love (and thorough knowledge) of baseball, the article also reveals a good deal about the author's fascination with adolescent American boyhood and the solidarity among atheletes playing in team competition.

4. Quoted in Jeff Connor, *Stephen King Goes to Hollywood* (New York: New American Library, 1987), 82.

Chapter Six

1. Just after the publication of the novel, King acknowledged in an interview, "As far as I'm concerned *It* is my final exam" (Underwood and Miller 1988, 176). He has also called the novel "the summation of everything I have learned and done in my whole life to this point" (Winter 1984, 184).

2. In *Pet Sematary,* Jud Crandall articulates this point in his recognition that he has crossed a barrier of his own in introducing Louis Creed to the Micmac burial ground: "It has a power . . . and I think that power goes through phases, same as the moon. It's been full of power before and I'm ascared it's coming around to full again. I'm ascared it used me to get at you through your son. . . . The place might have *made* Gage die because I introduced you to the power of the place" (*PS,* 275). Similarly, in *The Shining* one of several reasons the Overlook Hotel is able to exert its dark influence over Jack Torrance is that the hotel convinces Jack that he has a "responsibility to [the hotel's] history" (*The Shining* [New York: New American Library, 1978], 159; hereafter cited in text as *Shin*), and the scrapbook becomes the visible means by which Jack uncovers that history. But most of all, Jack views the scrapbook in personal terms, as the key to achieving the wealth, power, and fame that have so far eluded him.

3. Lloyd Rose, "The Triumph of the Nerds," review of *It, Atlantic* 258 (September 1986), 103.

4. It is significant that Beverly's "personal encounter" with It should occur upon her return to Derry as an adult woman. She is the only one of the group to whom this happens. Since Beverly's vision is so clearly linked to paternal conflicts she has yet to resolve, she is set apart from the other members of the Losers' Club, and the appearance of It in the form of the witch-father suggests that her father complex shapes her adult life.

5. King's awareness of Wendigo lore is omnipresent in *Pet Sematary.* Perhaps the best source for tracing the legend is the edited collection of essays entitled *Windigo: An Anthology of Fact and Fantastic Fiction,* edited by John Robert Colombo (Saskatoon, Saskatchewan: Western Producer Prairie Books, 1982). The reader should also consult *Windigo Psychosis: A Study of a Relationship between Belief and Behavior among the Indians of Northeastern Canada,* edited by Verne F. Ray (Seattle: American Ethnological Society, 1960). Among some of the more likely

parallels that connect the Wendigo myth to King's novel is the belief that once the spirit of the Wendigo has tasted human blood, its appetite turns insatiable and it wanders the woods in search of another meal. Many of the legends claim that the spirit of the Wendigo has the potential to appear in the dreams of human men and women. Once visited, the dreamer must, like Louis Creed after Pascow's nocturnal warning, choose to reject the temptations of the Wendigo's power; otherwise the victim will become the Wendigo's willing protégé (Colombo, 128). In Indian folklore the Wendigo is sometimes described as a creature in human form, either a man or woman, that stands 20 to 30 feet tall. The Wendigo is "so powerful that when it marches along it can brush aside the great pine tree as an ordinary man does the grass of the prairies" (Colombo, 32). Late in *Pet Sematary* King's evidence of the Wendigo's passing reflects his knowledge of the Indian superstition: "The tree was broken off—splintered off . . . and on the other side was a monstrous indentation out of which he had to scramble and climb, and although the juniper and low pump-laurel bushes had been stamped right to the earth, [Louis] would not let himself believe it was a footprint" (*PS,* 364–65). Finally, it is worth noting that King may have actually named Louis Creed after the Cree Indians of Saskatchewan, a woodland tribe who believed in the Wendigo spirit (Colombo, 29).

6. Julian Tondriau and Roland Villeneuve, *Devils and Demons: A Dictionary of Demonology* (New York: Pyramid Communications, 1968), 21.

7. Leonard G. Heldreth, "Rising Like Old Corpses: Stephen King and the Horrors of Time-Past," *Journal of the Fantastic in the Arts* 2 (Spring 1989), 5–13. Heldreth neglects to mention other instances in King's fiction in which the past is certainly no curse and actually an aid to survival. In *Misery,* for example, Paul Sheldon (as I discuss at great length later in this chapter) is saved by his acquired skill as a writer. He acknowledges this truth in the admission that "*Art consists of the persistence of memory*" (*Misery* [New York: Viking, 1987], 219; hereafter cited in text as *M*).

8. Burton Hatlen, "Good and Evil in Stephen King's *The Shining*" in *The Shining Reader,* ed. Tony Magistrale (Mercer Island, Wash.: Starmont House, 1991), 85.

9. Joseph Campbell, *The Power of Myth* (New York: Doubleday, 1988), 215.

10. Fredric Jameson, "Postmodernism, or The Cultural Logic of Late Capitalism," *New Left Review* 164 (1984), 53–92.

11. M. M. Bakhtin, *Problems of Dostoevski's Poetics,* trans. R. W. Rostel (New York: Ardis, 1929; reprint, 1979), 24.

12. M. M. Bakhtin, *The Dialogical Imagination,* ed. Michael Holquist, trans. Caryl Emerson and Michael Holquist (Austin: University of Texas Press, 1981), 250.

13. Jeanne Campbell Reesman, "Riddle Games: Stephen King's Metafictive Dialogue," in *The Dark Descent*.

14. *New York Times Book Review,* 11 June 1989, 32.

15. In his lecture of 6 November 1986 as the Lloyd H. Elliott lecturer at the University of Maine, Orono, King described his novel in these terms: "Like William Carlos Williams' *Paterson*, which I cite on several occasions in the novel, *It* is an epic poem of the city as organism." The epic elements in this novel extend well beyond the allusions to *Paterson*. As in many epic poems, *It* is set in a past that is imagined as greater than the present. While the action is simple and focused on a single deed, the task presented is amplified to the point of cosmic significance. Gods (e.g., the Turtle) often participate in the story, helping the heroes, and there is also the requisite trip to the underworld (the sewers of Derry) so often occasioned in the epic tradition.

16. Section 3, "Paul," begins with a quote from *The Collector*, and earlier in the novel Paul wonders dourly if Annie possesses a copy of "Fowles's first novel on her shelves" (*M*, 151). Aside from these two explicit references, it is interesting that Caliban's misanthropic aunt is named Anne, and that before winning the lottery Caliban was once employed in a government agency called the Annexe.

17. John Fowles, *The Collector* (New York: Dell, 1963), 9, 53; hereafter cited in text.

18. Leonard Heldreth, "Viewing *The Body:* King's Portrait of the Artist as Survivor," in *The Gothic World of Stephen King*, 72–73.

Chapter Seven

1. *The Eyes of the Dragon* (New York: New American Library, 1987), 271; hereafter cited in text as *Eyes*.

2. *The Breathing Method*, in *Different Seasons* (New York: Viking, 1982), 471; hereafter cited in text as *DS*.

3. "The Gunslinger," *Magazine of Fantasy and Science Fiction*, October 1978.

4. I am indebted to Professor Michael Stanton for discussions he shared with me on the fantasy tradition and its connection to *Eyes*. The map of Delain is the work of one of his former students, Chris Jasparro of Cumberland, Rhode Island, who graduated from the University of Vermont in 1988. It is published here for the first time.

5. See Jackie Eller, "Wendy Torrance, One of King's Women: A Typology of King's Female Characters," in *The Shining Reader*, ed. Tony Magistrale (Mercer Island, Wash.: Starmont House, 1990), 11–22; and Mary Pharr, "Partners in the *Danse:* Women in Stephen King's Fiction," in *The Dark Descent*.

6. See chapter 7, "Giving Birth to Salvation: The Mystery of Motherhood," in my book *The Moral Voyages of Stephen King* (Mercer Island, Wash.: Starmont House, 1989), 93–105.

7. In his 1983 interview with *Playboy* magazine, for example, King was asked to respond to critic Chelsea Quinn Yarbro's comment that "it is disheartening when a writer with so much talent and strength of vision is not able to develop a believable woman character between the ages of 17 and 60." King concurred with her

ı, acknowledging that "it is probably the most justifiable of all the criti-
ied at me." Later in his response, however, he added that he "recognizes the
but can't yet rectify it" (Underwood and Miller 1988, 47), which suggests
hasn't yet given up trying.

3. Ben P. Indick, "Stephen King as an Epic Writer," in *Discovering Modern*
ed. Darrell Schweitzer (Mercer Island, Wash.: Starmont House, 1985), 63.

9. Stephen King, *The Dark Tower: The Gunslinger* (West Kingston, R.I.:
Donald M. Grant, 1982), 221; hereafter cited in text as *Guns*.

10. David B. Davis, "Ten-Gallon Hero," in *The Western: A Collection of Critical Essays,* ed. James K. Folsom (Englewood Cliffs, N.J.: Prentice Hall, 1979),
28–29.

11. James Egan, "*The Dark Tower:* Stephen King's Gothic Western" in *The
Gothic World of Stephen King,* 101; hereafter cited in text.

12. Stephen King, *The Dark Tower II: The Drawing of the Three* (New York:
New American Library, 1987), 170; hereafter cited in text as *DOT.*

13. James K. Folsom, *The American Western Novel* (New Haven, Conn.:
College and University Press, 1966), 125–38.

Chapter Eight

1. Clive Barker, introduction to *Night Visions: Hardshell,* ed. Clive Barker
(New York: Berkley, 1988), 4; hereafter cited in text.

2. D. H. Lawrence, *Studies in Classic American Literature* (New York:
Penguin, 1923; reprint, 1977), 85.

3. Robert Kiely, "Armageddon, Complete and Uncut," review of *The
Stand, New York Times Book Review,* 13 May 1990, 3.

4. Caryn James, "Today's Yellow-Brick Road Leads Straight to Hell," *New
York Times,* 19 August 1990, sec. 2, p. 1.

5. Ursula K. Le Guin, "Why Are Americans Afraid of Dragons?" in *The
Language of the Night: Essays on Fantasy and Science Fiction,* ed. Susan Wood
(New York: G. P. Putnam's Sons, 1979), 39, 41–2.

6. See Sanford Phippen, "The Student King," *Maine 70* (Fall 1989), 18–
24. Also see Tyson Blue, *The Unseen King* (Mercer Island, Wash.: Starmont House,
1990).

7. For parallel illustrations of King's dramatic fiction—*The Dead Zone* and
Cujo in particular—and Lasch's social perspective, see Bernard J. Gallagher,
"Breaking Up Isn't Hard to Do: Stephen King, Christopher Lasch, and Psychic
Fragmentation," *Journal of American Culture* 10 (Winter 1987), 59–67. Also see
Kenneth S. Wagner's introduction to my book *Landscape of Fear.*

8. It is interesting, in light of this comparative discussion of King novels,
that the writer originally intended to model *The Shining* after a five-act Shakespearean tragic drama. As King recognized the larger possibilities of its narrative scope in
the tale's unfolding, however, he abandoned the dramatic adaptation. (See Stephen

King, "On *The Shining* and Other Perpetrations," *Whispers* 17/18 [August 1982], 11–16.)

9. Annie Gottlieb, "Something Lurks in Ludlow," review of *Pet Sematary, New York Times Book Review,* 6 November 1983, 15.

10. Walter Wager, review of *It, New York Times Book Review* 24 August 1986, 9.

11. Maria Scrivani, "Only Horror Fans Will Stand for This King," review of *The Stand, Buffalo News,* 12 August 1990, G-10.

12. Andrew Klavan, "The Pleasure of the Subtext: Stephen King's Id-Life Crisis," *Village Voice,* 3 March 1987, 46.

13. For a listing of libraries and their rationales for the banning of King texts, see Beahm, 49–51. The most frequently cited reasons for censorship appear to be King's "vulgar language," "explicit sex scenes," and a tendency toward "graphic acts of violence." One is forced to wonder how many librarians, school-board members, and parents have decided likewise to ban the Bible and Shakespeare's plays for identical violations.

14. George Steiner, in *Real Presences* (Chicago: Chicago University Press, 1989), insists that "There is a politics in the marketing of the 'classical' as there is a counterpolitics in the bartering of the subversive and the anarchic" (184).

15. Leslie A. Fiedler, *What Was Literature?* (New York: Simon and Schuster, 1982), 115, 64.

Selected Bibliography

PRIMARY WORKS

Novels

Carrie. Garden City, N.Y.: Doubleday, 1974; New York: New American Library, 1975.

Christine. West Kingston, R.I.: Donald M. Grant, 1983; New York: Viking, 1983; New York: New American Library, 1984.

Cujo. New York: The Mysterious Press, 1981; New York: Viking, 1981; New York: New American Library, 1982.

Cycle of the Werewolf. Westland, Mich.: Land of Enchantment, 1983; New York: New American Library, 1984.

The Dark Half. New York: Viking, 1989; New York: New American Library, 1990.

The Dark Tower: The Gunslinger. West Kingston, R.I.: Donald M. Grant, 1984; New York: New American Library, 1988.

The Dark Tower II: The Drawing of the Three. New York: New American Library, 1987.

The Dark Tower III: The Wastelands. New York: New American Library, 1991.

The Dead Zone. New York: Viking, 1979; New York: New American Library, 1980.

The Eyes of the Dragon. New York: Viking, 1987; New York: New American Library, 1987.

Firestarter. Huntington Woods, Mich.: Phantasia Press, 1980; New York: Viking, 1980; New York: New American Library, 1981.

It. New York: Viking, 1986; New York: New American Library, 1987.

[Richard Bachman, pseud.] *The Long Walk.* New York: New American Library, 1979.

Misery. New York: Viking, 1987; New York: New American Library, 1987.

Needful Things. New York: Viking, 1991.

Pet Sematary. Garden City, N.Y.: Doubleday, 1983; New York: New American Library, 1984.

[Richard Bachman, pseud.] *Rage.* New York: New American Library, 1977.

———— *Roadwork.* New York: New American Library, 1981.

———— *The Running Man.* New York: New American Library, 1982.

'Salem's Lot. Garden City, N.Y.: Doubleday, 1975; New York: New American Library, 1978.

The Shining. New York: Doubleday, 1977; New York: New American Library, 1978.

The Stand. Garden City, N.Y.: Doubleday, 1978; New York: New American Library, 1979; 2d ed., rev. and unexpurg., New York: Doubleday, 1990.

[With Peter Straub.] *The Talisman.* West Kingston, R.I.: Donald M. Grant, 1984; New York: Viking and G. P. Putnam's Sons, 1984; New York: Berkley, 1985.

[Richard Bachman, pseud.] *Thinner.* New York: New American Library, 1984.

The Tommyknockers. New York: G. P. Putnam's Sons, 1987; New York: New American Library, 1988.

Collections

The Bachman Books: Four Early Novels. New York: New American Library, 1985.

Creepshow. New York: New American Library, 1982.

Different Seasons. New York: Viking, 1982; New York: New American Library, 1983.

Four Past Midnight. New York: Viking, 1990.

Night Shift. Garden City, N.Y.: Doubleday, 1978; New York: New American Library, 1983.

Skeleton Crew. New York: G. P. Putnam's Sons, 1985; New York: New American Library, 1986.

Nonfiction

Danse Macabre. New York: Everest House, 1981; New York: Berkley, 1982.

Nightmares in the Sky: Gargoyles and Grotesques. New York: Viking, 1988.

SECONDARY WORKS

Interviews

Underwood, Tim, and Chuck Miller, eds. *Bare Bones: Conversations on Terror with Stephen King.* New York: McGraw-Hill, 1988. Contains the major interviews conducted with King from March 1979 to May 1985, assembled from publications ranging from daily U.S. newspapers to periodicals such as *Playboy, Rolling Stone, Yankee,* and *English Journal.*

"Interview: Stephen King." *Gallery* (January 1986).

"Stephen King." *Andy Warhol's Interview* (February 1986).

Winter, Douglas, ed. "Stephen King." In *The Faces of Fear: Encounters with the Creators of Modern Horror.* New York: Berkley, 1985.

"Stephen King." *WB* (Waldenbooks) (November / December 1989).

"Talking Terror with Stephen King." *Twilight Zone Magazine* (February 1986).

Books

Beahm, George, ed. *The Stephen King Companion.* Kansas City, Mo.: Andrews & McMeel, 1989. An assortment of essays and anecdotes—from the trenchant to the mundane—covering various aspects of King's biography, writing, and critical reception. Details not always accurate.

Blue, Tyson. *The Unseen King.* Mercer Island, Wash.: Starmont House, 1989. Particularly valuable for its emphasis on texts usually overlooked by King scholars—uncollected short stories, poetry, screenplays, and especially King's early writing as an undergraduate columnist for the newspaper of the University of Maine, Orono.

Browne, Ray, and Gary Hoppenstand, eds. *The Gothic World of Stephen King: Landscape of Nightmares.* Bowling Green, Ohio: Bowling Green State University Popular Press, 1987. Wide-ranging collection of criticism on King's major work, with particular emphasis on *Pet Sematary.*

Collings, Michael R. *The Films of Stephen King.* Mercer Island, Wash.: Starmont House, 1986. Good resource for critical appraisals of film adaptations of King's novels.

_____ *Infinite Explorations: Art and Artifice in Stephen King's It, Misery, and The Tommyknockers.* Mercer Island, Wash.: Starmont House (in progress).

_____ *The Many Facets of Stephen King.* Mercer Island, Wash.: Starmont House, 1985. Discussion of Stephen King's career as writer and popular-culture phenomenon.

_____ *The Stephen King Concordance.* Mercer Island, Wash.: Starmont House, 1985.

_____ *Stephen King as Richard Bachman.* Mercer Island, Wash.: Starmont House, 1985. Perhaps the most critically focused of Collings' many volumes on King. Major examination of the themes and publication data on the novels King has written under the Bachman pseudonym.

_____ *The Stephen King Phenomenon.* Mercer Island, Wash.: Starmont House, 1986. Evaluation of King's influence on contemporary culture, particularly the American literary and film industries.

Collings, Michael R., and David A. Engebretson. *The Shorter Works of Stephen King.* Mercer Island, Wash.: Starmont House, 1985. Primarily plot summaries of King's short stories and the novellas found in *Different Seasons.*

Connor, Jeff. *Stephen King Goes to Hollywood.* New York: New American Library, 1987. Examination of film adaptations of King's work. Good source of information on production aspects (e.g., casting of actors, interpretation of written text on film, creation of special effects).

Docherty, Brian, ed. *American Horror Fiction: From Brockden Brown to Stephen King* (New York: St. Martin's, 1990). Overview of the horror tradition in American fiction and King's place therein.

Herron, Don, ed. *Reign of Fear: Fiction and Film of Stephen King.* Los Angeles:

Underwood-Miller, 1988. Collection of critical essays on Stephen King's fiction and films. Uneven in interpretive quality.

Horsting, Jessie. *Stephen King at the Movies.* New York: Starlog / New American Library, 1986. More valuable for still shots than for scholarly insights. Includes movies up to and including *Stand By Me* (1986).

Magistrale, Tony, ed. *The Dark Descent: Essays Defining Stephen King's Horrorscape.* Westport, Conn.: Greenwood, forthcoming 1992. A collection of critical essays covering King's major work from *Carrie* to *Misery.*

———— *Landscape of Fear: Stephen King's American Gothic.* Bowling Green, Ohio: Bowling Green State University Popular Press, 1988. King's work placed in the context of nineteenth-century American literature and viewed as a critique of contemporary American institutions and values.

———— *The Moral Voyages of Stephen King.* Mercer Island, Wash.: Starmont House, 1989. Treatment of some of the most important recurring elements in King's fiction, with particular emphasis on defining his moral polarities of good and evil.

————, ed. *The Shining Reader.* Mercer Island, Wash.: Starmont House, 1990. A collection of critical essays on various aspects of the novel and of Stanley Kubrick's film adaptation.

Murphy, Tim. *The Darkest Night: A Student's Guide to Stephen King.* Mercer Island, Wash.: Starmont House (in progress).

Reino, Joseph. *Stephen King, The First Decade: From Carrie to Pet Sematary.* Boston: Twayne, 1988. Surveys the major work of King's first decade of writing. Very good on *Different Seasons;* less convincing when speculating on symbolic meanings of names and when trying to link King to classical western literary tradition.

Schweitzer, Darrell, ed. *Discovering Stephen King.* Mercer Island, Wash.: Starmont House, 1985. One of the first collections of critical essays on King's early work. Quality very uneven.

Spignesi, Stephen J. *The Shape Under the Sheet: The Complete Stephen King Encyclopedia.* Bangor, Maine: Philthrum Press 1991.

Terrell, Carroll F. *Stephen King: Man and Artist.* Orono, Maine: Northern Lights Publishing Company, 1990. Religious dimensions of King's work.

Underwood, Tim, and Chuck Miller, eds. *Fear Itself: The Horror Fiction of Stephen King.* San Francisco, Calif.: Underwood-Miller, 1982. Examines a broad range of King's fiction, from his short stories to his major novels, up to and including *Cujo.*

———— *Kingdom of Fear: The World of Stephen King.* New York: New American Library, 1986. Seventeen original essays and introductions about King and his novels and stories. Offers several chapters of solid scholarship, but most of the contributions are neither intellectually rigorous nor well written.

Van Hise, James. *Enterprise Incidents Presents Stephen King.* Tampa: New Media, 1984.

Winter, Douglas E. *The Reader's Guide to Stephen King.* Mercer Island, Wash.: Starmont House, 1982. One of the first biographies and critical introductions to King and his initial decade of published writing. Embellished, updated, and expanded in *The Art of Darkness.* Important not only for its intelligent critical commentary but also for its interviews with King.

_____ *The Stephen King Bibliography.* West Kingston, R.I.: Donald M. Grant (in progress).

_____ *Stephen King: The Art of Darkness.* New York: New American Library, 1984. See *The Reader's Guide to Stephen King.*

Zagorski, Edward J. *Teacher's Manual: The Novels of Stephen King.* New York: New American Library, 1981 (pamphlet). Pedagogical approaches to exploring the works of Stephen King in the high-school classroom.

Articles

Adams, Michael. "*Danse Macabre.*" In *Magill's Literary Annual 1982,* vol. 1, edited by Frank N. Magill. Englewood Cliffs, N.J.: Salem Press, 1982.

Alexander, Alex E. "Stephen King's *Carrie*—A Universal Fairy Tale." *Journal of Popular Culture* (Fall 1969).

Allen, Mel. "The Man Who Writes Nightmares." *Yankee Magazine* (March 1979).

Ashley, Mike. "Stephen King." In *Who's Who in Horror and Fantasy Fiction.* New York: Taplinger, 1977.

Babington, Bruce. "Twice a Victim: Carrie Meets the BFI" [British Film Institute]. *Screen* 23 (September / October 1982).

Bleiler, Richard. "Stephen King." In *Supernatural Writers: Fantasy and Horror,* edited by Richard Bleiler and Everett Franklin. New York: Scribners, 1985.

Bradley, Marion Zimmer. "Fandom: Its Value to the Professional." In *Inside Outer Space,* edited by Sharton Jarvis. New York: Ungar, 1985.

Breque, Jean-Daniel. "Stephen King: L' Horreur Moderne." *Revue Litteraire Mensuelle* 707 (March 1988).

Bromell, Henry. "The Dimming of Stanley Kubrick." *Atlantic* (August 1980).

Brown, Royal S. "Dressed to Kill: Myth and Fantasy in the Horror Suspense Genre." *Film / Psychology Review* 4 (Summer / Fall 1980).

Bunnell, Charlene. "The Gothic: A Literary Genre's Transition to Film." In *Planks of Reason: Essays on the Horror Film,* edited by Garry Keith. Metuchen, N.J.: Scarecrow, 1984.

Caldwell, Larry W., and Samuel J. Umland. "'Come and Play with Us': The Play Metaphor in Kubrick's *The Shining.*" *Literature / Film Quarterly* 14 (1986).

Cheever, Leonard. "Apocalypse and the Popular Imagination: Stephen King's *The Stand.*" *Artes Liberales* 8 (Fall 1981).

Cook, David A. "American Horror: *The Shining.*" *Literature / Film Quarterly* 12 (1984).

Egan, James. "Antidetection: Gothic and Detective Conventions in the Fiction of Stephen King." *Clues* 5 (Spring / Summer 1984).

———— "Apocalypticism in the Fiction of Stephen King." *Extrapolation* 25 (Fall 1984).

———— "A Single Powerful Spectacle: Stephen King's Gothic Melodrama." *Extrapolation* 27 (Spring 1986).

———— "Technohorror: The Dystopian Vision of Stephen King." *Extrapolation* 29 (Fall 1988).

Ehlers, Leigh A. "*Carrie:* Book and Film." *Literature Film Quarterly* 9 (Spring 1981). (First published in *Ideas of Order in Literature and Film,* edited by Peter Ruppert. Tallahassee: University of Florida Press, 1980.)

Ferguson, Mary. "*The Stand.*" In *Survey of Modern Fantasy Literature,* edited by Frank N. Magill. Englewood Cliffs, N.J.: Salem Press, 1983.

———— "'Strawberry Spring': Stephen King's Gothic Universe." *Footsteps* 5 (April 1985).

Fiedler, Leslie. "Fantasy as Commodity, Pornography, Camp and Myth." *Fantasy Review* (June 1984). Paper presented at the International Conference on the Fantastic in the Arts, March 1984.

Gallagher, Bernard J. "Breaking Up Isn't Hard to Do: Stephen King, Christopher Lasch, and Psychic Fragmentation." *Journal of American Culture* 10 (Winter 1987).

Gareffa, Peter M. "Stephen King." *Contemporary Authors,* new rev. ser., 1.

Geduld, Harry M. "Mazes and Murders." *The Humanist* (September / October 1980).

Gibbs, Kenneth. "Stephen King and the Tradition of American Gothic." *Gothic* 1 (1986).

Graham, Allison. "'The Fallen Wonder of the World': Brian De Palma's Horror Films." In *American Horrors: Essays on the Modern American Horror Film,* edited by Gregory A. Waller. Chicago: University of Illinois Press, 1987.

Grant, Charles L., David Morrell, Alan Ryan, and Douglas E. Winter. "Different Writers on *Different Seasons.*" *Fantasy Newsletter* (February 1983). First published in *Shadowings,* edited by Douglas E. Winter. Mercer Island, Wash.: Starmont House, 1983.

Greenspun, Roger. "*Carrie,* and Sally and Leatherface Among the Film Buffs." *Film Comment* 13 (January / February 1977).

Handling, Piers, ed. *The Shape of Rage: The Films of David Cronenberg.* Toronto: Toronto General Publishing, 1983.

Hatlen, Burton. "The Destruction and Re-Creation of the Human Community in Stephen King's *The Stand.*" *Footsteps* 5 (April 1982). Paper presented at the International Conference on the Fantastic in the Arts, March 1984.

———— "The Mad Dog and Maine." In *Shadowings,* edited by Douglas E. Winter. Mercer Island, Wash.: Starmont House, 1983.

_____ "*'Salem's Lot* Critiques American Civilization." *Maine Campus* (December 1975).

_____ "Steve King's Third Novel Shines On." *Maine Campus* (April 1977).

Heldreth, Leonard G. "Rising Like Old Corpses: Stephen King and the Horrors of Time-Past." *Journal of the Fantastic in the Arts* 2 (Spring 1989).

Hicks, James E. "Stephen King's Creation of Horror in *'Salem's Lot:* A Prolegomenon Towards a New Hermeneutic of the Gothic Novel." In *Consumable Goods: Papers from the North East Popular Culture Association Meeting, 1986,* edited by David K. Vaughan. Orono: University of Maine National Poetry Foundation, 1987.

Hoile, Christopher. "The Uncanny and the Fairy Tale in Kubrick's *The Shining.*" *Literature / Film Quarterly* 2 (1984).

Indick, Ben P. "Stephen King as an Epic Writer." In *Discovering Modern Horror Fiction,* vol. 1, edited by Darrell Schweitzer. Mercer Island, Wash.: Starmont House, 1985.

Jameson, Richard T. "Kubrick's Shining." *Film Comment* (July / August 1980).

Kauffman, Stanley. "The Dulling." *New Republic,* 14 June 1980.

Keeler, Greg. "*The Shining:* Ted Kramer Has a Nightmare." *Journal of Popular Film and Television* (Winter 1981).

Kendrick, Walter. "Stephen King Gets Eminent." *Village Voice,* 29 April 1981.

Kennedy, Harlan. "Kubrick Goes Gothic." *American Film* (June 1980).

Kilbourne, Dan. "*Christine.*" In *Magill's Cinema Annual 1984,* edited by Frank N. Magill. Englewood Cliffs, N.J.: Salem Press, 1984.

Kimberling, Ronald C. *Kenneth Burke's Dramatism and Popular Arts.* Bowling Green, Ohio: Bowling Green State University Popular Press, 1982.

King, Tabitha. "Living with the Bogey Man." In *Murderess, Ink,* edited by Dilys Winn. New York: Bell, 1979.

Klavan, Andrew. "The Pleasure of the Subtext: Stephen King's Id-Life Crisis." *Village Voice,* 3 March 1987.

Lidston, Robert. "*Dracula* and *Salem's Lot:* Why the Monsters Won't Die." *West Virginia University Philological Papers* 28 (1982).

Lorenz, Janet. "*Carrie.*" In *Magill's Survey of Cinema,* vol. 1, edited by Frank N. Magill. Englewood Cliffs, N.J.: Salem Press, 1981.

Luciano, Dale. "*Danse Macabre:* Stephen King Surveys the Field of Horror." *The Comics Journal* 72 (May 1982).

_____ "E. C. Horror Stories Mistranslated into Film." *The Comics Journal* 79 (January 1983).

Macklin, F. Anthony. "Understanding Kubrick: *The Shining.*" *Journal of Popular Television and Film* (Summer 1981).

Magill, Frank N., ed. *Survey of Modern Fantasy Literature.* Englewood Cliffs, N.J.: Salem Press, 1983.

Magistrale, Tony. "Art Versus Madness in Stephen King's *Misery.*" In *The Celebration of the Fantastic: Selected Papers from the Tenth Anniversary Interna-*

tional Conference on the Fantastic in the Arts, edited by Donald E. Morse, Marshall B. Tymn, and Csilla Bertha. Westport, Conn.: Greenwood, forthcoming 1992.

———. "'Barriers Not Meant to Be Broken': Where the Horror Springs in Stephen King." In *Consumable Goods: Papers From the North East Popular Culture Association Meeting, 1986,* edited by David K. Vaughan. Orono: University of Maine National Poetry Foundation, 1987.

———. "Crumbling Castles of Sand: The Social Landscape of Stephen King's Gothic Vision." *Journal of Popular Literature* 1 (Fall / Winter 1985).

———. "Hawthorne's Woods Revisited: Stephen King's *Pet Sematary.*" *Nathaniel Hawthorne Review* 14 (Spring 1988).

———. "Inherited Haunts: Stephen King's Terrible Children." *Extrapolation* 27 (Spring 1985).

———. "Native Sons: Regionalism in the Work of Nathaniel Hawthorne and Stephen King." *Journal of the Fantastic in the Arts* 2 (Spring 1989).

———. "Stephen King's Vietnam Allegory: An Interpretation of 'Children of the Corn.'" *Footsteps* 5 (April 1985). First published in *Cuyahoga Review* (Spring / Summer 1984.) Paper presented at the International Conference on the Fantastic in the Arts, March 1984.

Malpezzi, Frances M., and William M. Clements. "*The Shining.*" In *Magill's Survey of Cinema,* vol. 5, edited by Frank N. Magill. Englewood Cliffs, N.J.: Salem Press, 1981.

Meyer, Richard E. "Stephen King." In *Beacham's Popular Fiction in America,* vol 2, edited by Walton Beacham. Washington, D.C.: Beacham, 1986.

Moore, Darrell. *The Best, Worst, and Most Unusual Horror Films.* Skokie, Il.: Publications International, 1983.

Moritz, Charles. "Stephen King." *Contemporary Biography Yearbook 1981.* New York: H. H. Wilson, 1981.

———. "*Different Seasons.*" In *Magill's Literary Annual 1983,* vol. 1, edited by Frank N. Magill. Englewood Cliffs, N.J.: Salem Press, 1980.

Morrison, Michael A. "Author Studies: Stephen King." In *Horror Literature: A Reader's Guide,* edited by Neil Barron. New York: Garland, 1990.

———. "*Pet Sematary:* Opposing Views." *Fantasy Review* 64 (January 1984).

Murphy, Patrick D. "The Realities of Unreal Worlds: King's *The Dead Zone,* Schmidt's *Kensho,* and Lem's *Solaris.*" In *Spectrum of the Fantastic: Selected Essays from the Sixth International Conference on the Fantastic in the Arts,* edited by Donald Palumbo. Westport, Conn.: Greenwood, 1988.

Neilson, Keith. "Contemporary Horror Fiction, 1950–88." In *Horror Literature: A Reader's Guide,* edited by Neil Barron. New York: Garland, 1990.

———. "*The Dead Zone.*" In *Magill's Literary Annual 1980,* vol. 1, edited by Frank N. Magill. Englewood Cliffs, N.J.: Salem Press, 1980.

———. "*Different Seasons.*" In *Magill's Literary Annual 1983,* vol. 1, edited by Frank N. Magill. Englewood Cliffs, N.J.: Salem Press, 1983.

Nelson, Thomas A. "Remembrance of Things Forgotten: *The Shining.*" In *Kubrick: Inside the Artist's Maze.* Bloomington: Indiana University Press, 1982.

Norris, Darrell A. "Evolving Landscapes of Horror: Recent Themes in American Fiction." In *Consumable Goods: Papers from the North East Popular Culture Association Meeting, 1986,* edited by David K. Vaughan. Orono: University of Maine National Poetry Foundation, 1987.

Patrouch, Joseph F., Jr. "Stephen King in Context." In *Patterns of the Fantastic,* edited by Donald M. Hassler. Mercer Island, Wash.: Starmont House, 1983.

Pearce, Howard D. "*The Shining* as *Lichtung:* Kubrick's Film, Heidegger's Clearing." In *Forms of the Fantastic: Selected Essays from the Third International Conference on the Fantastic in Literature and Film.* Westport, Conn.: Greenwood, 1986.

Phippen, Sanford. "Stephen King's Appeal to Youth." *Maine Life* (December 1980).

———. "The Student King." *Maine* 70 (Fall 1989).

Price, Robert M. "Fundamentalists in the Fiction of Stephen King." *Studies in Weird Fiction* 5 (Spring 1989).

Radburn, Barry. "Stephen King and John Carpenter: Cruisin' with *Christine.*" *Footsteps* 5 (April 1985).

Rudin, S. "The Urban Gothic, from Transylvania to the South Bronx." *Extrapolation* 25 (1984).

Schaefer, S. "The Director is King." *Film Comment* 22 (1986).

Schiff, Stuart David. "The Glorious Past, Erratic Present, and Questionable Future of the Specialty Presses." In *Inside Outer Space,* edited by Sharon Jarvis. New York: Ungar, 1985.

Schweitzer, Darrell. Introduction to *Discovering Modern Horror Fiction,* vol. 1, edited by Darrell Schweitzer. Mercer Island, Wash.: Starmont House, 1985.

Senf, Carol A. "Stephen King: A Modern Interpretation of the Frankenstein Myth." *Science Fiction: A Review of Speculative Literature* 8 (1986).

———. "Donna Trenton, Stephen King's Modern American Heroine." In *Heroines of Popular Culture,* edited by Pat Browne. Bowling Green, Ohio: Bowling Green State University Popular Press, 1987.

Snyder, Stephen. "Family Life and Leisure Culture in *The Shining.*" *Film Criticism* 6 (Fall 1982).

"Stephen King." *Contemporary Literary Criticism,* vol. 12, edited by Dedria Bryfonski and Garard Senick. Detroit, Mich.: Gale Research, 1980.

"Stephen King." *Current Biography Yearbook, 1981,* edited by Charles Moritz. New York: H. W. Wilson, 1981.

Stewart, Robert. "The Rest of King." *Starship: The Magazine About Science Fiction* 18 (Spring 1981).

Tuchman, Michael. "From Niagara-on-the-Lake, Ontario." *Film Comment* 19 (May–June 1983).

Westerbeck, Collin. "The Waning of Stanley Kubrick." *Commonweal*, 1 August 1980.

Wilson, William. "Riding the Crest of the Horror Craze." *New York Times Magazine*, 11 May 1980.

Winter, Douglas E. "The Art of Darkness." In *Shadowings*, edited by Douglas E. Winter. Mercer Island, Wash.: Starmont House, 1983.

————— "I Want My Cake! Thoughts on *Creepshow* and E. C. Comics." In *Shadowings*, edited by Douglas E. Winter. Mercer Island, Wash.: Starmont House, 1983.

Wood, Robin. "Cat and Dog: Lewis Teague's Stephen King Novels." *Action* 2 (Fall 1985).

————— "King Meets Cronenberg." *Canadian Forum* (January 1984).

Index

The Author

Tony Magistrale was born and raised in Buffalo, New York. He received his B.A. from Allegheny College in Meadville, Pennsylvania, where he majored in English. As a Mellon Fellow at the University of Pittsburgh, he earned both M.A. and Ph.D. degrees, writing a dissertation on Flannery O'Connor and William Faulkner. After completing his graduate training, he won a Fulbright postdoctoral fellowship to the Università Statale di Milano, Italy. Dr. Magistrale is currently an associate professor of English at the University of Vermont, where he directs the freshman composition program and teaches courses in American literature. He is the author of a writing textbook, *Writer's Guide: Psychology* (D. C. Heath), and two earlier books on Stephen King, *Landscape of Fear: Stephen King's American Gothic* (Bowling Green State University Popular Press) and *The Moral Voyages of Stephen King* (Starmont House). Professor Magistrale and his wife, Jennifer, are parents to two sons and reside in South Burlington, Vermont.

The Editor

Warren French (Ph.D., University of Texas, Austin) retired from Indiana University in 1986 and is now an honorary professor associated with the Board of American Studies at the University College of Swansea, Wales. In 1985 Ohio University awarded him a doctor of humane letters. He has contributed volumes to Twayne's United States Authors Series on Jack Kerouac, Frank Norris, John Steinbeck, and J. D. Salinger. His most recent publication for Twayne is *The San Francisco Poetry Renaissance, 1955–1960.*